Robert Naylor

THE LIFE AND TIMES OF A YORKSHIRE TENOR

Robert Naylor

THE LIFE AND TIMES OF A YORKSHIRE TENOR

BOB NAYLOR

First published in the United Kingdom in 2010 by
Bank House Books
PO Box 3,
NEW ROMNEY
TN29 9WJ UK

www.bankhousebooks.com

British Library Cataloguing in Publication Data
A catalogue record for this book is available from the British Library

ISBN 9781904408659
Printed and bound in Great Britain by
CPI Antony Rowe, Chippenham and Eastbourne

Typesetting and origination by Bank House Books

To Sophie, Georgina and Olivia

CONTENTS

List of Illustrations   ix

Foreword by John Briggs   xiii

Introduction and Acknowledgements   xv

Chapter One: Early Years 1899–1922   1

Chapter Two: The London Years 1922–1931   19

Chapter Three: The West End Stage and the
      Recording Studio   41

Chapter Four: The Land of Smiles   59

Chapter Five: The Variety Circuit 1931–1934   71

Chapter Six: Summer Shows and the Big Screen   101

Chapter Seven: The War Years 1939–1945   135

Chapter Eight: Later Years 1946–1968   145

Footnotes   159

Discography   169

Filmography   185

Bibliography   187

Index   191

LIST OF ILLUSTRATIONS

1. Map of Luddenden, Halifax, *c.* 1900. (Calderdale Library)
2. Robert helping his uncle at Shepherd House Farm, *c.* 1912. (*Halifax Courier*)
3. Robert in *Cupid & the Ogre, c.* 1920. (Author's collection)
4. Herbert Teale, Robert's first music teacher. (Author's collection)
5. Fred Sutcliffe. (Author's collection)
6. Walter Widdop. (Author's collection)
7. Naylor family portrait, *c.* 1916. (Author's collection)
8. Plymouth Festival certificate awarded to Robert, 1918. (Author's collection)
9. Plymouth Festival silver medal awarded to Robert, 1918. (Author's collection)
10. Scottish Engineering Choral Festival medal, 1919. (Author's collection)
11. Glasgow Choral Festival medal, 1919. (Author's collection)
12. Cecilia Farrar, aged about eighteen. (Author's collection)
13. Poster for *The Yeomen of the Guard*, Todmorden, 1921. (Author's collection)
14. Robert in *The Yeomen of the Guard*, 1921. (Author's collection)
15. Cecilia in *The Yeomen of the Guard*, 1921. (Author's collection)

16. Montana, Robert's home from 1921 until his marriage. (Bob Naylor)
17. Robert, *c.* 1922. (Author's collection)
18. Cecilia, *c.* 1922. (Author's collection)
19. Robert and Cecilia's wedding portrait, September 1922. (Author's collection)
20. A report of Robert and Cecila's wedding. (Author's collection)
21. A portrait of Robert, early 1920s. (Author's collection)
22. Cecilia, 1925. (Author's collection)
23. The Queens Hall, London. (Author's collection)
24. Landon Ronald, Principal of the Guildhall School of Music. (Author's collection)
25. Alfred and Catherine Howard Prize awarded to Robert, 1928. (Author's collection)
26. Guildhall School of Music students' concert programme, 1928. (Author's collection)
27. Red Roofs, Wembley Park: Robert and Cecila's home. (Author's collection)
28. Robert and Cecilia at Red Roofs, early 1930s. (Author's collection)
29. Robert in Verdi's *Rigoletto,* 1928. (Author's collection)
30. Robert at Red Roofs, early 1930s. (Author's collection)
31. Robert and Cecilia at Red Roofs, mid-1930s. (Author's collection)
32. The programme for *The House That Jack Built,* Adelphi Theatre, 1929. (Author's collection)
33. Robert in *The Three Musketeers,* Drury Lane, 1930. (Author's collection)
34. Robert in a signed publicity photograph. (Author's collection)
35. Piccadilly Records. (Maurice Robson)
36. Robert and Cecilia enjoying the trappings of success. (Author's collection)
37. Parlophone Records. (Maurice Robson)
38. The Theatre Royal, Drury Lane. (Author's collection)
39. Edith Day, Robert's stage partner 1931–2. (Author's collection)
40. *The Land of Smiles* programme. (Maurice Robson)
41. *The Land of Smiles* cast list. (Maurice Robson)
42. Richard Tauber. (Author's collection)
43. Robert in *The Land of Smiles* (Author's collection)

44. Telegram sent to Robert by Richard Tauber. (Author's collection)
45. Pen and ink vignette from *Punch* magazine, 1931. (*Punch* magazine)
46. Advertisement for Parlophone Records, 1931. (*Gramophone* magazine)
47. Advertisement for Chappell music publishers, 1932. (*Gramophone* magazine)
48. Robert in a studio portrait, *c.* 1932. (Author's collection)
49. Olive Groves, who recorded with Robert in 1931. (Author's collection)
50. Robert and Cecilia with their son Michael. (Author's collection)
51. Annie Croft, with whom Robert toured in 1932. (Author's collection)
52. Robert in a studio portrait, *c.* 1932. (Author's collection)
53. *Daily Mail* Mystery Record. (John Watson)
54. *Daily Mail* Mystery Record: solution. (John Watson)
55. Josie Fearon, with whom Robert worked in 1933. (Author's collection)
56. Imperial Broadcast label. (Maurice Robson)
57. Robert and Cecilia at home. (Author's collection)
58. Robert performing for Pathetone, 1934. (British Pathé/ITN)
59. Sylvia Cecil, with whom Robert recorded, 1934. (D'Oyly Carte Opera Company)
60. Robert performing for Pathetone, 1934. (British Pathé/ITN)
61. A Rex record. (Maurice Robson)
62. Anona Winn, with whom Robert recorded, 1934. (Author's collection)
63. *Abdul the Damned*: a Gallagher cigarette card. (Author's collection)
64. *Abdul the Damned*: a Gallagher cigarette card. (Author's collection)
65. Robert in a studio photograph, *c.* 1936. (Author's collection)
66. Rose Perfect, with whom Robert starred, 1936. (Author's collection)
67. Robert in a studio photograph, *c.* 1936. (Author's collection)
68. Robert, Sylvia Cecil and the cast of *Gaiety Whirl*, Ayr, 1937. (University of Glasgow Library collection)
69. Robert performing for Pathetone, 1934. (British Pathé/ITN)

70. Poster for *On With The Show*, 1936. (Author's collection)
71. Programme for *On With The Show*, 1936. (Author's collection)
72. Tessie O'Shea, who starred with Robert, 1938. (Author's collection)
73. Sheet music for 'Tears In My Heart'. (Author's collection)
74. Sheet music for 'When Granny Wore Her Crinoline'. (Author's collection)
75. Press release, 1938. (*Gramophone* magazine)
76. Advertisement: Offers Invited, 1938. (*Gramophone* magazine)
77. Robert, 1938. (Author's collection)
78. Naylor family grave, Luddenden cemetery. (Bob Naylor)
79. Peggy Desmond, who worked with Robert in 1938. (Author's collection)
80. Programme for a concert in Elland, 1940. (Author's collection)
81. Robert at a dinner party, *c.* 1941. (Greaves photographers)
82. Concert at the New Victoria, Bradford. (*Telegraph & Argus*, Bradford)
83. *The Good Old Days*, featuring the Robert Naylor Valentine Girls, 1956. (*Radio Times*)
84. Jean Hindmarsh, one of the Valentine Girls. (D'Oyly Carte Opera Company)
85. Robert's business card. (Harrogate Operatic Society)
86. Robert, *c.* 1960. (Author's collection)
87. Robert and Dorothy, *c.* 1960. (Author's collection)
88. Robert, *c.* 1966. (Author's collection)
89. Label of Metropole test pressing, 1926. (Maurice Robson)
90. Parlophone test pressing, 1932. (Maurice Robson)
91. Piccadilly Records advertisement, 1931. (*Gramophone* magazine)
92. Parlophone Farewell Party, 1933. (Author's collection)
93. Rex Records advertisement, 1933. (*Gramophone* magazine)
94. Rex records advertisement featuring Robert Naylor. (*Gramophone* magazine)
95. Eclipse record by 'Derek Powell', 1934. (Bob Naylor)
96. Robert and Cecilia in costume. (Author's collection)

FOREWORD

In my early teens I went to hear a performance of Mendelssohn's *Elijah* at the Zion Methodist Chapel in Bingley. Until that day my musical appreciation had been entirely of piano music, but when the tenor soloist stood up and started singing his first aria, 'If With All Your Hearts', the whole world tipped upside down and my life changed for ever. At that moment I fell in love with the operatic tenor voice – a love that still burns bright, and has grown over the years.

The tenor soloist on that occasion was Robert Darnborough, and some forty or so years later we are good friends. Over the years we have given many performances together, including a number of the songs sung by Robert Naylor mentioned in this book. Robert Darnborough had been a student of Naylor's and he often reminisced about him, so that although we never met I feel I knew him. It is wonderful to be able to read so much more about him in this marvellous book, and to learn all about the man they called 'the English Tauber' and the era in which he lived.

John Briggs, MBE, DLitt

INTRODUCTION AND ACKNOWLEDGEMENTS

At 8.15pm on Monday 11 May 1931 the audience at Theatre Royal, Drury Lane, had taken their seats for the third performance of *The Land of Smiles,* a romantic operetta written by Franz Lehár (1870-1948). The show had been originally produced in Vienna in 1923 and this was its first London outing. Lavishly staged, the operetta had been devised largely as a showcase for its star, the Austrian tenor Richard Tauber.

But on this particular evening, just before the curtain rose, the theatre's acting manager Sidney Webb announced that Mr Tauber would not be appearing; his part, that of Sou Chong, would be played by Mr Robert Naylor. There were mutterings of disappointment at this news, for many in the audience had come especially to hear the famous Richard Tauber in his London début. However, their disappointment was to be short lived, for Robert Naylor took over the part in magisterial style, completely winning the hearts and minds of the audience with his fine voice and acting talent. When the show concluded there was a tremendous outpouring of cheers and applause. He took encore after encore, singing the show's big number 'You Are My Heart's Delight' six times. It was his finest hour, and his performance that evening and in the weeks ahead earned him the title of 'The English Tauber'.

It was while at school in Bradford during the late '50s that I first became aware of Robert Naylor. I see now, but didn't then, that by an odd coincidence there was also in my class a boy named John McCormack. The teacher would often tease John and me in front of the other pupils about her having two famous singers in her class. At the time I must admit to feeling awkward and largely unimpressed by this fact – for, needless to say, I hadn't heard of either of them. In those days singers to me were Elvis Presley, Buddy Holly and, my own particular favourites, the Everly Brothers. Nevertheless the knowledge about my namesake, a well-known singer from the past, must have registered in my mind – although I would not recall this information until many years later.

As I grew up I became familiar with the name of the Irish tenor John McCormack, who was of course world famous, but I never heard anything more about Robert Naylor. Not, that is, until one day in the summer of 1993, some thirty-five years after leaving school, when a friend passed on to me, with great amusement, a 78rpm record he had found in a junk shop. It was on the Parlophone label, and under the song titles it said 'Robert Naylor – Tenor'. On seeing this I was transported back to the classroom; my memory of the singer's name came flooding back. I laughed it off, telling my friend he wasn't the first person to pull my leg about this. However, I was grateful for the record and instantly intrigued by it. So I shared my name with a professional singer after all, but who was he?

A short while afterwards, in the central library in Bradford, I looked up Robert Naylor in a music encyclopaedia, and to my surprise I found he wasn't listed. I turned to various other reference books, but I could find no trace of his name. However well known he had once been, he appeared to have been completely forgotten. It was many months before I had my first breakthrough, when I found an entry in a 1937 edition of *Who's Who in Music*: it read 'Robert Naylor, tenor, born 1899, Luddenden Foot, nr Halifax'.

I confess I was delighted with this information, but not perhaps entirely surprised by it. After all, I knew my family name was common to the region, particularly so around Calderdale, where there is at least one Naylor Lane to be found. What I felt was a curious mixture of emotions – an urge to discover more about this forgotten singer, and a sense of injustice that his name and achievements should be so readily ignored by today's writers.

Having played the 78rpm record a few times, in one way I understood why this should be. The two songs were called 'I Still Love

Mary' and 'Three Little Words', and they expressed the sentiments of an age now gone. I had to admit that these light and inoffensive ballads had no place in today's cynical society, but I felt this was hardly reason to ignore Robert's achievements. After all, many of his contemporaries are to be found listed in any one of a dozen music books – performers such as Jack Hulbert, Cicely Courtneidge, Richard Tauber, Al Bowlly and Leslie Hutchinson. True, these artistes had been bigger stars than Robert in their day; but, as I was slowly to discover, his star had also shone very brightly, at least for a time – a time in which he was reputedly the highest paid tenor in the country.

Robert Naylor passed away many years ago, and as far as I know he was never properly interviewed during his life. From my research I suspect that this is something he would have shunned. My impression of the man is that he was somewhat self-effacing and entirely modest about his achievements. As a result, considerable details about his professional career are unrecorded and are likely to be lost forever. Here, however, is an attempt to piece together what information I have been able to establish about Robert's life and times – a journey that starts and ends in Yorkshire. It begins in 1899, in the Calder Valley among the steep hillsides and non-conformist chapels where Robert grew up. It ends in the spa town of Harrogate, where in the winter of 1968 he died in relative obscurity – the way he appeared to want it.

Many local people will remember Robert Naylor; some may still own a few scratched copies of Robert's gramophone recordings. This short biography will be of special interest to them, but I hope, too, that others may be curious to read about this local lad who, some eighty years ago, left the industrial heartland of West Yorkshire to go to London and became a singing star.

I want here to take a leaf out of Mike Carey's book[1] and pay tribute to all the composers and lyric writers, musicians, arrangers and recording engineers who contributed something to Robert's career. I have a soft and sentimental regard for all those 'turns' who shared variety bills with Robert Naylor up and down the country. They, too, are part of a long-vanished era. I have sought to include as many of their names as possible, no matter how obscure, in the hope that to someone, somewhere, they may bring a glimmer of recognition or a fond memory, and in the belief that their efforts should not pass unrecognised.

This book couldn't have been written without the help I received from Maurice Robson MBKSTS, gramophone record historian, who made available to the author his collection of photographs, press cuttings, and gramophone recordings. My grateful thanks also to John Watson for his expert advice on the record industry of the 1930s, the late Arthur Badrock for his work on the discography of Robert's recordings, Daniel O'Hara for his overall advice and support, in particular for his knowledge about the Parlophone Company and 78rpm recording technicalities, Betty Feavers (Robert Naylor's niece), the Rev. John Naylor (Robert's stepson) and Peter Mason (nephew of Robert's first wife), for providing useful family details and photographs. I am grateful to Jean Collen for sharing her expert knowledge of vocal music and singing techniques.

My thanks also for the help I received from Anna Fineman, Theatre Collection Officer, University of Bristol Theatre Collection; Amanda Nash, Marketing Manager, Gaiety Theatre, Ayr; Elaine C. Lee, General Secretary, Mrs Sunderland Music Festival, Huddersfield; Elliott Rooney, ITN – British Pathé; Rose Taylor, Librarian, Crossley Heath School, Halifax; Linda Graham, Special Collections, Mitchell Library, Glasgow; Rachel Dyson, Alumni Relations Manager, Guildhall School of Music & Drama; Jeff Walden, BBC Written Archive, Caversham Park, Reading; Howard Dobbs, London Metropolitan Archives.

I am grateful for helpful information provided by the staff of Bradford Local and Family History Library, Halifax Local Studies Library, Harrogate Library, Huddersfield Local Studies Library, the Local and Family History Centre at Blackpool Library, Plymouth Local and Naval Studies Library, the West Yorkshire Archive Service and the British Library, Boston Spa, Wetherby.

I would also like to acknowledge the following individuals who responded to my cries for help along the way: Peggy Roberts, Brian Rust, Malcolm Naylor, Pauline Wood, Robert Darnborough, David Taylor, Alan Williams, Peter Cliffe, Anne Tetlaw, Alan Brown and Len Barnett. Special thanks to Hilda and Paul King for their help in initial proof-reading, making valuable editorial suggestions and for their unstinting encouragement and support.

I am particularly grateful to Ann Parry for her conscientious and sterling work in preparing the index.

CHAPTER ONE
Early Years 1899–1922

Set high in the Pennines amid the steep hills of the Calder Valley is Halifax, one of the many West Riding towns that grew up reflecting the early days of the wool trade. At the turn of the century the skyline was a forest of belching mill chimneys, and soot and grime filled the atmosphere. It was this town that inspired Blake's vision of 'dark satanic mills'. Running northwards from the town is an area of unsurpassed rolling moorland and steep-sided hills. The valley is a link with Burnley and other Lancashire towns. After the road came the canal and the Yorkshire to Lancashire railway line, all following the course of the Calder river along the valley bottom. Villages sprang up along the route, and communities were established, each with their own identity: the village of Friendly, with its brass band, Mytholmroyd, Hebden Bridge, Eastwood and Luddenden Foot.

It was at Well Field House, 11 Lane Side, Luddenden Foot, that Robert Naylor was born on 15 April 1899. His parents were Robert Sutcliffe Naylor and Sarah Elizabeth Naylor (née Clayton). He was one of two children, his brother James being two years older. Robert was usually referred to by those who knew him as Bobbie (sometimes Robbie) and in later years he always signed himself 'Bobbie' for friends and family. However, as he used the name Robert professionally I shall refer to him by this name throughout for the sake of clarity.

The boys' father, Robert senior, worked as a solicitor's

1

managing clerk in Halifax, a respectable profession then and now, and this gave the family a stable income and a foothold on the social ladder. His wife Sarah had worked before her marriage as a corsetière at J.H. Waddington, dressmaker and drapers, Rawson Street, Halifax. The two brothers were of very different temperaments, as siblings often are. James was quietly mannered, reserved, and modest. He followed his father into the legal profession after he left school, first working for, then owning, the solicitors W. Boocock & Sons in Halifax. Robert, by contrast, was always the extrovert one, full of confidence, cheerful and outgoing by nature. By the time he reached adulthood he stood 5ft 7in tall, with brown hair, blue eyes and a fresh complexion.

The village of Luddenden stands on the sides of the valley of the Luddenden Beck. The name means Ludd valley, or valley of the loud stream. Originally the settlement grew up in the valley bottom called Luddenden Foot, but later homes were built higher up the hillside. The closely packed huddle of stone buildings, some built as weavers' cottages, and the narrow twisting streets are typical of many other Pennine villages. The fast flowing waters of Luddenden Beck have been taken advantage of since the earliest days, initially by corn mills but later, following the industrial revolution, by textile mills.

The Naylor family's background was rooted in the local area. Robert's great-grandfather, Jonathan Naylor (1781–1852), had farmed some 7 acres at Shepherd House Farm just up the road from Luddenden in Warley; it is situated on the hillside overlooking the valley. Robert's father had been born at the farm. The chief interest in the house today lies in the fact that previously it was the home of Thomas Lister, the clockmaker, who was born there in 1745. Lister's long-case clocks were much in demand for the smiling moon engraved on his dials. It was Lister who constructed the clock and chimes in the tower of Halifax parish church and he also kept St Paul's Cathedral clock regulated and in repair.[2] Robert's aunt, Martha Naylor, married Samuel Wilkins in 1911, and the couple continued to farm at Shepherd House Farm. There is a photograph taken in about 1912 that shows Robert leading a horse while helping his uncle with the haymaking.[3]

The young Robert and his brother James attended Luddenden

Foot Council School. The school was built in 1894 by the local School Board and stands on the main Burnley Road, which passes through the centre of the village. Its stolid appearance is like that of the many other Victorian elementary school buildings still to be found throughout the area. Robert started there in 1902 when he was three and half years of age. Both he and James were bright boys and left at the age of twelve to go to Heath Grammar School in Halifax. This was a prestigious fee-paying school, founded in 1585 by Dr John Favour, later to become Vicar of Halifax. His brother, Henry Favour, gave 2 acres of land in Skircoat Green, Halifax, for the building of the school, and at his own expense obtained the school charter from Elizabeth I of England. The school was originally called the Free Grammar School of Queen Elizabeth.

Robert was admitted to Heath Grammar School on 12 September 1911. During his time there he was a pupil of William Bunting Crump (1868–1950). Crump, with his wire-rimmed spectacles, was a keen botanist who edited the monthly magazine called the *Halifax Naturalist.* He was also a pioneer in the study of ecology and came to know every inch of the ancient parish of Halifax.[4] At the school he taught science, during Robert's time as a pupil under the headship of William Edwards, headmaster from 1908 to 1916.

In the Objects of Heath School it was stated that 'each boy, according to his position in the School, receives accurate training in Writing, English Grammar and Composition; in General Geography; in the Political and Literary History of England and its Constitution and Literature; in the Facts contained in the Old and New Testaments; in the Prayer-book and Catechism of the Church of England; and in Arithmetic, Geometry, and Algebra. If intended for a University, he learns everything requisite for obtaining the highest position in Classics or Mathematics. Every boy however must, in accordance with the Statutes, learn Latin, and his position in the School is chiefly determined by the progress which he makes in it: and, when promoted to the Second Class, he must commence Greek.'[5]

Although privileged to have a superior education, Robert doesn't appear to have been especially academic, and although he reached Grade V little is known about his studies. He had, however, begun to take a lively interest in singing and both he and his elder brother joined the choir at Luddenden Foot United Methodist Chapel. This plain and functional building stood alongside the main road in the village, and was demolished in 1961 when property on Burnley Road was cleared.

A boy's voice typically changes pitch between the ages of eleven and fourteen. As the larynx gets bigger and the vocal cords lengthen and thicken, so the male voice gets deeper. Cavities in the sinuses, the nose and the back of the throat grow bigger, creating space that gives the voice more room to resonate. Once Robert entered his teenage years and his voice had broken, he discovered he had a good tenor singing voice.

A tenor is the highest male vocal range, normally extending from approximately one octave below middle C to one octave above middle C. Although vocal range is the primary characteristic that defines a tenor, it is not the only one. A tenor voice is ultimately classified by several vocal traits – range, tone quality and lift or transition points ('*passaggio*') within the singer's range. It is generally recognised that the average transitional area of the tenor begins with a lift around middle C or C# and ends with a lift at F or F# above.[6]

It remains a mystery just why music is so inherent in the people, the towns and the valleys that make up the West Riding. The sheer number of bands, orchestras and choirs that has developed in the region is nothing short of remarkable. It is said this upsurge sprang out of the industrial revolution, when people descended on the towns and helped to create an environment where bands and choirs flourished.

One of the important features of music-making in Victorian Britain was the rise of choral societies. In the West Riding towns the large number of nonconformist chapels, with their mixed choirs, provided a pool of singers. Halifax Choral Society, the oldest choral society in Britain, was formed in 1817 by William Priestley (1779–1861), a local wool clothier and eminent musician. The choir was given a permanent home when on 8 February 1901 the new 1,512-seater Victoria Hall was opened. Throughout its existence the choir has played an important role in the social, musical and cultural life of Halifax, never more so than during the many civic and national celebrations that typified Vitorian England. Many other choral societies were formed in this period; for example, Huddersfield

Choral Society was established in 1836 and Bradford Choral Society in 1856.[7]

It is this musically rich background of choirs, operatic groups and choral societies that influenced Robert's formative years. Everyone who had a voice, it seems, sang. The community from which he sprang, in addition to the aforementioned choirs, also gave rise to a number of male solo singers who were to experience varying degrees of fame.

One was Herbert Teal (1881–1969) born at 5 Copley Hall Row, Copley, Halifax. He trained as an engineer with J.F. Smith of Halifax, but was always interested in music. He was a chorister at Copley church and became principal tenor at All Saints' Church on Dudwell Lane, Halifax. In 1910 he competed in the Blackpool Festival, one of the biggest in the north, and won the solo tenor class. The following year he was back to win both solo and dramatic tenor sections. He sang 'Your Tiny Hand Is Frozen' from *La Bohème* and pieces by Brahms and Mendelssohn. His early training was with Arthur Hinchcliffe, the Halifax music teacher, who gave lessons from his home at 222 Saville Park Road; he also studied in London. Herbert practised for hundreds of hours, and would go on to Greetland Moor above Halifax to sing because he found the fresh air was good for his lungs. He was offered engagements to perform all over the country, including at the Royal Albert Hall, and he appeared in the Promenade concerts under Sir Henry Wood, held at that time in the Queen's Hall, London. In the early 1920s, when an offer came to join Sir Thomas Beecham's British National Opera Company, Herbert turned it down.

In 1912 Herbert Teal made his first gramophone recordings for Beka (or more correctly Beka-Grand) a label established in Germany at the start of the twentieth century. They started exporting to Britain in 1905, and in 1913 British pressings first appeared. He also cut some sides for Beltona, produced for the Murdoch Trading company of 59–61 Clerkenwell Road, London, EC1. However, most of Herbert's recordings were made for HMV, where he recorded twenty-one two-sided discs over a five year period. His final four recordings were made for Parlophone.[8]

Another successful singer was Fred Sutcliffe (1895–1971), a bass-baritone who came from Sowerby Bridge. He took lessons in Halifax from Herbert Teal for many years and then found success in music festivals at Blackpool, Manchester, Buxton and in north Derbyshire. He went on to sing at dinners and concerts. One evening in the 1920s the aforementioned British National Opera Company was appearing at Halifax's Theatre Royal. The manager of the company was in bed with flu at the White Swan Hotel, where that particular night Fred was performing. When he heard Fred singing he sent for him to audition, and then offered him the chance of joining the company. However, like Herbert before him, Fred turned down the offer. Fred recalled, 'He asked me to join the company straight away, but I had two young sons and a steady job so I decided against it. I am glad I did, because it was only a few years later that the company closed.'[9] Instead of turning professional, Fred joined Sowerby Bridge West End Opera Company, Sowerby Bridge and District Madrigal Society, and Halifax Choral Society. In the early 1920s Fred went with Herbert to a Beltona recording session in London and was asked to record six songs himself, which were released on three 78rpm records. Fred also made about two dozen radio broadcasts for the BBC from their studios in Manchester, Leeds and Cardiff.[10]

The most famous Calder Valley singer, however, was Walter Widdop, who became one of the great operatic British tenors in the years between the wars. He was born on 19 April 1892, in a cottage in Sparkhouse Lane, Norland Moor, just above Halifax. He was the youngest of four children born to John Henry Widdop, a stone quarryman, and his wife Charlotte. His three elder siblings – Fred, Mary Louisa and Harold – all worked in the textile trade. In 1901 the family was living in a four room house at 27 Upper Wall Ing, Norland. Walter left school at fourteen and headed for work in the mill, first at Sowerby Bridge and then at Washer Lane dye works in Halifax. The Wainhouse Tower, one of the area's most famous local landmarks, was originally built to carry smoke from the dye works out of the valley, but was never used. Walter was eventually to take the advice of friends, who had heard his fine voice, and undergo professional voice training under the watchful eye of Halifax singing teacher Arthur Hinchliffe. He began to enter competitions and fulfilled many professional engagements, including stints with the Halifax Chamber Choir. Widdop's big chance came in 1923 when he accepted an invitation to join the British National Opera Company. A down payment of £400 was a condition of membership and this was provided by Widdop's former employers, the Bradford Dyers Association. This must have been one of the earliest examples of commercial sponsorship.[11] He made his début as Radames in Verdi's *Aida* in 1923 at a British National Opera concert in Leeds. The following year he made his London début playing Siegfried in a performance of Wagner's opera at Covent Garden. From then on he never looked back, and played in major operatic productions throughout the world, also recording extensively for HMV. His last engagement in London was in 1949, when he sang 'Lohengrin's Farewell' under Sir Adrian Boult at the Royal Albert Hall. He collapsed in his dressing room immediately after the performance and died the following day, 6 September, at his Hampstead home.[12]

Robert's teenage years covered a momentous time in British history. On 28 June 1914 the assassination took place of Archduke Franz Ferdinand of Austria, an event which triggered the First World War. Britain declared war on 4 August, and immediately mobilised the British Expeditionary Force. The declaration of war caused tremendous excitement throughout the country, resulting in magnificent displays of patriotism everywhere. That same month Lord Kitchener was appointed Secretary of State for War and began a massive recruitment campaign to expand Britain's army. His appeal produced an overwhelming response from men of all classes. In the Halifax area many enlisted at the Duke of Wellington's (West Riding) Regiment based at Wellesley Barracks on Gibbet Street. By 1915 major battles had already taken place at Ypres and elsewhere along the Western Front, with an appalling loss of life on both sides.

Although the battlefields were in Europe, Zeppelin air raids became a regular feature of life for hundreds of people living in London and in towns along the East coast, which brought the war closer to home. If that were not enough, just before 8.00am on 14 December 1914 the Germans attacked the undefended seaside resort of Scarborough. The bombardment lasted over half an hour and killed seventeen civilians, including eight women and four children. Further north, Hartlepool was much harder hit. Morale slumped, and for the first time the British Empire seemed vulnerable. The attack on the East coast outraged Britain and was seized upon by the War Office in their recruitment campaign.

Posters appeared displaying an image of Britannia complete with Corinthian helmet and sword, bearing the caption 'Remember Scarborough! Enlist Now'.

Robert left Heath Grammar School on 29 July 1915. Having no leaning towards the legal profession he started work as a wool sorter at J. & J. Baldwin and Partners Ltd, Clarke Bridge Mills, Halifax – a huge edifice that was one of the town's monuments of industrial architecture.[13] Wool sorters identified the correct quality of fleece for a specific cloth, essential to ensure top quality fabrics. Badly soiled parts were discarded, and then the fleece was sorted by sight, touch and experience into wool of various qualities: it was a highly skilled job. The company was founded in 1785 by James and John Baldwin, worsted and woollen yarn manufacturers. In 1920 they merged with John Paton, Son & Company of Alloa, Scotland, to form Patons & Baldwins. They produced mainly yarns for commercial knitting machines, but diversified into producing wool for home knitters. The Patons beehive trademark continues in use on knitting wool to this day.

When Robert was not working he spent his leisure time concentrating on developing his singing. He had started to take music seriously, and sought out guidance and advice on furthering his talent. He was about fifteen years of age when he began to take lessons from Herbert Teal in Copley, which he continued for the next four years. However, both Robert's textile career and emerging musical plans were interrupted by the escalation of the war.

In 1916 Robert's elder brother, James, was granted a commission in the Royal Horse Artillery. Within the army hierarchy the regiment stands very high in order of precedence, and James's commission illustrates the Naylor family's social connections and influence. A family portrait taken at this time shows James in officer uniform, seated with his proud parents. Robert, by contrast, appears to have been a reluctant warrior – but conscription had started in 1916, and towards the end of 1917 he was called up and enlisted in the Royal Naval Air Service. He reported for duty in London on 22 January 1918, and two days later found himself stationed at Tregantle Fort in Plymouth. This nineteenth-century fortification overlooks Whitsand Bay and had been used as a military barracks since 1900. At the time of the First World War it was a shore establishment of the Royal Navy.

The Royal Naval Air Service was the air arm of the Royal Navy until 1 April 1918, when it merged with the British Army's Royal Flying Corps to form a new service, the first of its kind in the world – the Royal Air Force. So although Robert joined the RNAS, by the time he was demobbed he was in the RAF. The main role of the RNAS was fleet reconnaissance, patrolling coasts for enemy ships and submarines, attacking enemy coastal territory and defending Britain from enemy air-raids. Tregantle Fort operated dirigible airships on anti-submarine duties.

Robert's service record gives his rank as Aircraftsman 2nd Class. His ability was listed as 'satisfactory' and his character as 'very good'. Whatever military demands were placed on the young recruit, in November 1918 Robert still found time to enter the Plymouth Competitive Music Festival. Most of the competition's events took place at Plymouth Guildhall. This magnificent building, 150ft long and 70ft high with seating for 2,600 people, was a testament to Victorian architecture. The seating was separated from the aisles by arcades of seven arches with polished grey granite pillars. A large orchestral platform dominated the west end, with a series of ante-rooms to its rear; an ornate gallery was to be found at the eastern end.

At the Guildhall, Robert succeeded in winning the silver and gold medals in the tenor solo class. The two test pieces Robert performed were the serenade 'I Hear A Thrush At Eve', words by Nelle Richmond Eberhart and music by Charles Wakefield Cadman, and 'Best Of All', written in about 1900 by Frank F.L. Moir. The adjudicator was Henry Walford Davies, later Sir Henry Walford Davies and Master of the Kings Music from 1934 to 1941. Davies noted of Robert's performance: 'He has the voice and the temper; he must now listen and look every time he sings and love his audience as himself.' He further remarked, 'A good vigorous voice with a fine *sostenuto*[14] and a power of fluency. Excellent singer, fine vigour, but,' he warned the young performer, 'don't jerk your arms.'[15]

A word here about music festivals might be helpful. These weren't the same as the events we refer to as music festivals today, being the equivalent of competitive festivals for music, drama and so on. In 1921 the British Federation of Musical Competition Festivals was formed for 'the advancement of music, elocution, drama and dancing by means of Competition Festivals'.[16] In the years before the Second World War the federation registered as many as 235 affiliated festivals. Many were primarily organised by voluntary effort as competitions for musical amateurs. They often covered a range of activities such as folk-dancing, children's percussive bands, orchestras, dramatic and solo singing and choral contests, etc. They awarded prizes, often trophies and medals, to winners in various classes of the competitions being held. Keen amateurs used them to gain exposure and first-class assessment of their potential. In the inter-war years these festivals were hugely popular, both with competitors and audiences.

Once the war was over Robert, being a 'hostilities rating', was given an early release from the forces. By late 1918 he had returned home to Halifax and resumed working at Patons & Baldwins, where he rose to become the manager in the wool-sorting department. However, his time in the mill was to be brief as he concentrated more and more on his singing. For a while he adopted the stage name Dennis Ludd, Ludd being taken from Luddenden, his home village.

As well as a choir, Luddenden Foot United Methodist Chapel had an amateur operatic group, which Robert also joined. Such groups were not unusual in the area at the time. Much depended on the influence and attitude of local ministers, but there was a growing trend among churches, and particularly among non-conformist ones, which had a strong sense of local independence, to broaden the Church's role in society by using entertainment as evangelism.[17] A photograph survives of the Luddenden Foot Methodist Church Amateur Operatic Group just after the First World War. They were performing *Cupid and the Ogre,* a largely forgotten operetta published in 1912 with music by Chastey William George Hector and a libretto by Stanley C. West. The small cast is assembled on the stage for the photograph, and Robert can be seen seated on the floor at the front wearing a soldier's uniform.

Around this time Robert began to study under Paul Le Vallon, a professor of singing who had a studio at 134 Deansgate, Manchester.[18] By road from Robert's home in Calderdale, this entailed a 60 mile round trip. It is likely that he made the journey by train from Luddenden Foot railway station, where the Lancashire to Yorkshire Railway Trans-Pennine line linked the Calder Valley with

Manchester Victoria. The railway, always affectionately known as the 'Lanky', was built to connect the major Lancashire cotton towns in the west with the major Yorkshire woollen towns in the east. Although the line took the easiest route across the Pennines, following the deeply incised valleys around Hebden Bridge and Todmorden, it still required the cutting of a number of lengthy tunnels to get through the Pennines.

In 1919 Robert entered the Mrs Sunderland Music Festival in Huddersfield. Mrs Susan Sunderland was a famous soprano, born in Brighouse in 1819. She was a founder member of the Huddersfield Choral Society. After she sang at the opening of Leeds Town Hall in 1858 in front of Queen Victoria, she was invited to sing at a Royal Command Performance at Buckingham Palace the same year. The Queen is said to have remarked, 'I may be the Queen of England, but you are the Queen of Song.' Thereafter Mrs Sunderland was known as the Yorkshire Queen of Song. In 1888 she and her husband Henry celebrated their golden wedding anniversary with a special concert. With the money raised from this, a committee of distinguished local men decided to inaugurate a vocal solo competition, to be held annually in Huddersfield, in tribute to the famous Yorkshire soprano. As a result of their efforts the first Mrs Sunderland Music Festival was held in April 1889. Since then the festival has expanded vastly and, except for 1940, has been held annually.

In 1919 the tenor solo competition took place over two days. As an entrant, Robert would have been informed of the test pieces before the event. These were the recitative 'O Loss Of Sight' and the air 'Total Eclipse' from Handel's opera *Samson*. Anxious to do his best, Robert went to see his old teacher Herbert Teal, who had sung the opera many times, to ask Teal to teach him the pieces. In an interview many years later Teal told the story of Robert's unexpected visit. No doubt put out by the fact that Robert had not been to see him lately, Teal said, 'What have you come to see me for? Can't that fancy professor you've been going to see teach it to you then?' Mrs Teal told the interviewer that 'Young Bobby Naylor sat in that chair and cried with shame.'[19]

The preliminary test was held on Friday 7 February 1919 at Huddersfield Technical College, where the test pieces were performed. Robert scored 80 marks out of a possible 100. This put him into the competition final, which took place the following day at 6.00pm in the Town Hall. The test piece for the final was 'There Is A Garden' (a Mrs Sunderland composition prize piece from 1918), composed by Allan Biggs. Robert scored 75 marks out of 100, beating his rival Jesse Kilburn from Rothwell into second place. His first prize won him 3 guineas and a silver medal.

It was the usual practice at such festivals for winners to receive silver medals. Historically many commendations and honours were awarded with a silver medal: this included the first (modern) Olympic Games in 1896, where the winners' medals were silver. The custom of gold-silver-bronze for the first three places only dates from the 1904 Games. Over the years this system has been copied by so many sporting events and competitions that we have now come to associate a silver medal with second place.

The Mrs Sunderland Music Festival was one of the many local competitive music festivals operating at the time, but (as we have seen with Plymouth) Robert entered festivals much farther afield if the opportunity presented itself. Two such opportunities arose in the spring of 1919.

Robert had two friends who were members of the Glasgow Orpheus Choir. This choir had been founded by Sir Hugh Roberton in 1906. This gentleman was held in such high regard by his singers that when he resigned in 1952, shortly before his death, the choir disbanded as a mark of respect. While visiting his friends, Robert won a silver medal at the Scottish Engineering & Munitions Workers Benevolent Association Choral Festival, held on Saturday 5 April. Later the same month Robert entered the 9th Annual Festival of the Glasgow Musical (Competition) Festival, held at St Andrew's Hall between Saturday 26 April and Saturday 3 May. On 2 May five tenors competed for the final adjudication in the Tenor Solos General Class. The outright winner was W. Hamilton from Glasgow, who was a member of the Orpheus Choir. Robert came second, winning for himself the bronze medal.[20]

As a result of these successes, Robert started to undertake local concert appearances. An early example took place on Sunday 12 October 1919 in a Grand Concert held at Co-operative Hall, Hebden Bridge, with the Hebden Bridge Prize Band. Robert appeared with Miss W.O. Braithwaite, a soprano from Elland, and Miss Audrey Townsend, a contralto from Keighley. They were accompanied on the piano by Mr Percy Blackburn. The band performed pieces selected by their conductor, Mr H. Parker.

On Thursday 30 September 1920 Robert performed at an evening of social entertainment organised by the Mytholmroyd KRRC and CLB Cadets. (The 16th (Service) battalion of The Kings Royal Rifle Corps was raised in 1914 from former and serving members of the Church Lads Brigade. It was known throughout the war as 'The Churchman's Battalion'.) The event was held in the Drill Hall, Dale View, Mytholmroyd. Despite what sounds like a drab and cheerless setting, it turned out to be a memorable occasion for Robert, for he shared the bill with a young, petite soprano called Cecilia Farrar, who was to become his wife.

Robert and Cecilia were mutually attracted, and began courting. Cecilia's correct name was Elizabeth Alice Farrar and she was two years older than Robert, having been born in the spring of 1897 at 794 Burnley Road, Cornholme, a village about 2½ miles north-west of Todmorden. The village originally lay in Lancashire, but is now right on the edge of the Calderdale district of West Yorkshire. It was a self-contained community where everyone knew each other and from which people seldom travelled far. When Cecilia was a child her family moved house to live at 1 Cornholme Terrace, which was situated alongside the main Burnley Road that winds its way through the Cliviger Valley towards Lancashire.

Cecilia's parents, Walter and Hannah Farrar (née Crabtree), both worked in the local cotton mills. For many years they worked for Wilson Brothers Bobbin Company Ltd, at Cornholme Mills in Todmorden. As the name suggests, the company made wooden bobbins for the textile industry. It was once the largest bobbin manufacturer in the world, exporting its products to all parts of the world; it was large enough to have its own fire brigade. The mill closed in about 1930 when the business moved to new premises at Garston, Liverpool, in the 1890s. The Todmorden buildings were reused but finally demolished; a housing estate now stands on the site.

Cecilia's father was a notable amateur violinist, and he taught her the instrument. As a girl, however, Cecilia displayed more aptitude for singing than playing, and graduated as a soprano with the Cornholme United Methodist Church Choir. The history of Cornholme Mount Zion Chapel, as it was called, is closely linked with that of the Wilson family, which ran Cornholme Mills. The church was built in 1884 mainly through the efforts of Mrs Alice Wilson and her followers. Consequently the church had a captive congregation in the Wilson company workers; indeed, they may have been inhibited from attending church elsewhere for fear of been frowned upon by their employer. The church closed in 1968 and the building is now derelict, but the burial ground can still be seen.

When Cecilia first left school she worked as a weaver at Joshua Smith's Frostholme Mills, Cornholme, where it was said her powerful singing could be heard above the noise of the looms. Her first music teacher was Frances Collinge, under whom she studied for three or four years. She continued her studies under Kingsley Lark and later like Robert, under Paul le Vallon in Manchester. She began performing in music festivals, and after meeting with success at the Ilkley and Wharfedale festivals[21] she launched out as a professional soprano vocalist on the concert platform at the age of sixteen. In 1914 she entered the choral contests held at Belle Vue Gardens, Manchester, and came first in the solo soprano competition. The following year she came second, losing out to Miss Hettie Crabtree from Hebden Bridge. Cecilia became a vocalist of some fame, often appearing in London on the stage of the Queen's Hall, and her services were in great demand in the provinces. She was also a member of the Aeolian Concert Party, a local organisation that was formed just before the First World War and gave concerts in Todmorden and other towns.

Handel's oratorio *The Messiah*, composed in 1741, is perhaps the most popular choral work ever written. By the middle of the nineteenth century people in the West Riding had adopted the work as the cornerstone of their Christmas festivities. It is performed in the area annually by choral societies both large and small; perhaps most famously by the Huddersfield Choral Society, which has presented it every season since 1836. On Sunday 19 December 1920 a performance of *The Messiah* was given by Birchcliffe Chapel Choir in Hebden Bridge, the choir augmented to about sixty voices for the occasion. Robert Naylor (prize winner) was the tenor soloist. The other soloists were: soprano, Miss E. Crowther (prize winner) from West Vale; contralto, Miss A. Shuttleworth from Todmorden; bass, Mr J.W. Greenwood (prize

winner) from Hebden Bridge. The organist was Mr Frank
Greenwood Mus. Bac. FRCO, ARCM from Rochdale.

In January 1921 Robert appeared in the annual production
of the Todmorden Amateur Operatic Society. Todmorden is a
market town lying on the historic county boundary between
Yorkshire and Lancashire. It now lies entirely within Yorkshire,
administered by the Metropolitan Borough of Calderdale; in
1921 it was a municipal borough. The show in 1921 was Gilbert
and Sullivan's *The Yeomen of the Guard*. With music by Arthur
Sullivan and libretto by W.S. Gilbert, the show had premiered at
the Savoy Theatre on 3 October 1888. The society's show was
presented at the Todmorden Hippodrome for six nights, 17–22
January. The town's Hippodrome Theatre, an impressive plain red-
brick building in Halifax Road, had been built in 1908. It was
designed to seat 1,500 patrons, and in 1911 it was converted with
facilities for showing moving pictures.

The Todmorden Amateur Operatic Society had been founded
in 1917 and *The Yeoman of the Guard* was their inaugural
production that year. For this 1921 revival of the show the part of
Colonel Fairfax (under sentence of death) was played by Robert. It
is interesting how, right from the outset of his stage career, his fine
voice and acting ability were noticeable. The reporter from the local
paper observed that, 'As Colonel Fairfax, Mr Robert Naylor made a
striking figure, vocally as well as physically. His big, robust tenor
voice was well suited to the part, and he did not hesitate to make
good use of it. His acting was free and apparently easeful, and he
carried through his various changes of personality and character
without undue violence. In all his solos he was heard to good
advantage, and earned his share of applause and encores.'[22] Playing
the part of Elsie Maynard (a strolling singer) was Miss Cecilia Farrar,
by now Robert's fiancée, who 'was in fine voice and gave great
pleasure'.[23]

The Hippodrome Theatre in Todmorden was a popular venue
for Sunday Evenings for the People concerts, which were organised
by the National Sunday League and usually starred a local brass
band plus regional artists. The National Sunday League had been
formed in 1855 to campaign for 'The opening of Museums, Art
Galleries and libraries on Sunday afternoons, maintaining the
"Sunday Evenings for the People", Sunday Excursions, Sunday

Bands in the Parks and generally to promote intellectual and Elevating Recreation on that Day'.[24] In fact the relaxation of the draconian laws preventing entertainment on Sunday didn't occur fully until the 1960s.

One such Hippodrome concert in 1921 featured Miss Cecilia Farrar (soprano), Miss Addyce Shuttleworth (contralto) and Charles Thomas (tenor), Todmorden Old Brass Band and violinist Stewart Dennett. The accompanist was Ronald Cunliffe, founder of the local boys' choir, which won national fame in 1925 when it presented Rimsky-Korsakov's *Golden Cockerel.* Out of the cast of thirty-six, thirty-four of the boys were less than fifteen years old.

As already indicated, Cecilia was in great demand during these years. She sang at numerous concerts in the local area – at Walsden Wesleyan Church, in February 1918; the Co-operative Hall, Todmorden, in October 1920; York Street Wesleyan Church, in September 1920; Todmorden Town Hall in March 1919; and the Hippodrome Theatre, Todmorden, in November 1920 – among many others.

In 1921 the Naylor family moved from Lane Side to live at Montana, Burnley Road, Luddenden Foot. The house is one of four substantial stone properties built in 1909 and is perched high on a bank, with a steep path leading to the front door. That same year a war memorial was erected nearby to commemorate the sixty-one soldiers from the village who had lost their lives in the First World War, which had ended three years earlier. Robert's mother would remain here until her death thirty-five years later.

The following year, at 2.00pm on Tuesday 26 September, Robert and Cecilia were married at Mount Zion United Methodist Church, Cornholme, where as a girl Cecilia had sung in the choir. At the time of their marriage she was twenty-five years old and Robert was twenty-three. News of their wedding was reported in a number of local papers, the *Yorkshire Observer* carrying a large picture of Robert and Cecilia under the caption 'West Riding Vocalists Married': 'The bridegroom Mr Robert Naylor is a tenor vocalist, who has risen to much eminence as a concert artist, and like his bride, has frequently fulfilled engagements in the highest circles. Both are very accomplished vocalists.'

A large assembly of friends and well-wishers watched the wedding ceremony, which was performed by the resident minister, the Rev. W.W. Wilkinson. For the occasion Robert wore a morning suit – tailcoat, waistcoat and striped trousers complete with spats. Cecilia was given away by her father and was dressed in white charmeuse, with an embroidered veil and coronet of pearls and orange blossom. Robert's brother James acted as best man. The reception was held at Mount Zion Sunday School adjacent to the chapel, after which Robert and Cecilia departed for their honeymoon. The bride travelled in a blue Moroccan costume with a short beaver coat, a gift from her new husband. The staff of the wool sorting department of Patons & Baldwins, where Robert had been manager, presented the couple with an oak timepiece.

The couple went for their honeymoon to St Anne's-on-Sea. Located just south of Blackpool, this peaceful, genteel town could not be more different from its brash neighbour. Although it boasts a Victorian pier, a bandstand and promenade gardens, St Anne's, both then and now, provides a haven for retirement and is dominated by the prosperous Victorian and Edwardian villas along Clifton Drive. The town's sandy beach is flanked by dunes.

Newly married, and full of the confidence of youth and the new optimism that was to be found in those post-war years, Robert and Cecilia decided to take up residence in London in order to pursue jointly their careers as professional vocalists. After their honeymoon they left for the capital, with a full book of engagements. Initially they went to live at Brook House, Sneath Avenue, Golders Green. For the young couple a new chapter was beginning, and one that would bring Robert the recognition and acclaim his talent deserved.

CHAPTER TWO
The London Years 1922–1931

By the 1920s social life in Britain was changing fast. A whole generation of young people who had responded to Kipling's call to arms had been made old by the futility of war. Millions had lost their lives. Young women who had acted as nurses had witnessed at first-hand the consequences of battle, and had seen horrific injuries and mental suffering. All this served to create the mood that life was short and meant to be enjoyed. Society too was becoming more democratic and less deferential than before. By the end of the war the old order with its inherent inequality, and imbalance of wealth and power, was no longer acceptable in the eyes of the general population, which began to challenge the injustice of the class system.

To a young couple arriving from the West Riding, London in the 1920s must have seemed a very exciting place. The years of war led to a reaction, when many people were determined to have as much fun as possible. As prices fell, people had more money to spend on enjoying themselves, and entertainment was marketed to fill the need. For many the 'Roaring Twenties' was a time of fun, parties, prosperity and jazz music. New dances and music were all the rage, including the Charleston and the Black Bottom. The period after the war saw great changes in the social habits of the young. It was an era filled with celebrities and glamour. Famous personalities set fashion examples, such as short skirts and bobbed hair for women and Oxford bag trousers for men. The capital began to feel more modern and less traditional. The West End became alive as entrepreneurs opened nightclubs and cocktail bars – cocktails being the latest craze, considered degenerate by the older generation who mostly retained their pre-war values. The antics of the young set were reported in the press in distaste. 'There is a section of the community . . . whose life seems to consist of cocktails and sherry parties, cabarets and midnight revelries . . . These are decadent "bright young things",' railed the *Morning Post* as late as 1936.

'Wireless' was the technological marvel of the decade. The BBC had been formed in 1922 and its first official broadcast was the evening news presented by Arthur Burrows on 14 November that year. It was transmitted by station 2LO whose studios were in Marconi House, Strand, London. 2LO was a reference to the number on the broadcasting licence issued by the Post Office. To begin with programmes were broadcast for just an hour a day. Listeners were often kept waiting while a piano was shifted, and people in the studio were sometimes heard saying things that should have never been broadcast. But listeners didn't bother about such things: it was a miracle that anything was heard at all.[25] As the listening public grew, and at the time only a few thousand people in the capital held radio licences, the 2LO transmitter was moved to the roof of the Selfridges building on London's Oxford Street in order to extend the station's range. Shortly after 2LO's initial broadcast the Postmaster General's Office was inundated with applications from manufacturers of wireless equipment wanting licences to broadcast. The government's response was to request that the companies form a single consortium. An agreement was eventually reached, with the largest concerns led by Marconi: the consortium was called the British Broadcasting Company. By the end of 1924 a further ten medium wave stations had been opened in Birmingham, Manchester, Newcastle, Cardiff, Glasgow, Aberdeen, Bournemouth, Sheffield, Plymouth and Belfast. Each of these broadcast locally produced programmes. As we shall see, many of Robert's early radio broadcasts were made for these regional stations.

By 1923 Robert and Cecilia had moved from their original accommodation and were living at 19 Boundary Road, on the west side of St John's Wood, London. On 21 February 1923 Cecilia was a principal vocalist when the Carlisle Choral Society gave its second concert of the season. She performed Coleridge-Taylor's *Hiawatha's Wedding Feast* and the *Death of Minnehaha*. In June Robert made his London début, at the Chelsea Palace Theatre, which was at 232-42 Kings Road, Chelsea. Built in 1903, with a capacity of 2,524, the theatre closed in 1957 and briefly became a studio for Granada Television before being demolished. Robert had the leading role in *Faust,* an opera in five acts by the French composer Charles Gounod, which was performed by a vacation company of the Old Vic under Lilian Baylis.

The redoubtable Lilian Mary Baylis (1847-1937) was an English theatrical producer, who managed the Old Vic and Sadler's Wells theatres. Her iron will and tempestuous nature seldom endeared her to others, but Robert stayed happily with the Old Vic for the next seven years, until 1930, appearing in over twenty leading roles.

In opera voice types are commonly categorised by tessitura (texture), vocal weight and timbre, and the roles they sing are chosen according to where the voice has the finest timbre and easiest volume. Robert Naylor is perhaps best described as a lyric tenor – a graceful voice that is strong but not heavy. His later recordings reveal him to have been musical, with a good technique and clear diction, a typically English tenor without the baritonal qualities in the lower range that affect some other singers. As a vocalist he is comparable to tenors of his day such as Richard Tauber, John McCormack and Webster Booth, who all had lighter voices than the Italian tenors.

The same year Robert took part in an afternoon Ballad Concert at the Royal Albert Hall, where he sang 'The Faery Song' from *The Immortal Hour* by the English composer Rutland Boughton. This opera was playing to packed houses in London that year. Boughton, a music teacher at the Birmingham and Midland Institute, adapted his own libretto from the works of the Scottish poet Fiona MacLeod, whose real name was William Sharp. At the concert Robert also sang a boisterous Maori song called '*Waiata*

Poi adapted by the Australian composer Alfred Francis Hill, a song recorded and made famous by fellow countryman Peter Dawson.

Ballad concerts were a system whereby publishers paid a royalty to well-known singers to promote their songs by including them in concerts. The aim was to increase sales of sheet music to amateurs for home performance, a very substantial market at the time. The name first appears in the 1870s. Publishing houses such as Boosey & Co. and Chappell & Co. were among those who organised such events. Both the songs Robert performed on this particular afternoon were published by Chappells, who ran their ballad concerts until 1926.

More unusually, Robert also undertook this year to appear as a guest performer in a school production. The school was Brandon Board School, Market Hill, Brandon, Suffolk. The headmaster at Brandon was a Walter Percy Coe, who, in addition to his educational activities, was a skilled violinist and a member of the Norwich Philharmonic Society; he also played in the orchestra of the Bury St Edmunds and Thetford Operatic Societies. As a result he strongly encouraged music at Brandon School and formed a choral society there. In 1923 the operetta *Merrie England* was presented, with Robert taking the lead part of Sir Walter Raleigh. The engaging score evokes the colourful Tudor period, combining pomp and ceremony with ballads and romantic arias. How Robert came to be involved in this school project is not known, though it is likely that he had met Walter Percy Coe at some point and had been asked to offer his services.

Merrie England was composed in 1902 by Edward German. Born Edward German Jones in Whitchurch, Shropshire, in 1862, after Sullivan he was probably the most popular English composer of light music in the period before 1914. He was knighted in 1928 for his services to music, and was made an Honorary Freeman of the Worshipful Company of Musicians in 1936. German was a leading light in the Performing Rights Society, fighting for composers' rights to fair compensation for the performance of their works. Sadly, like so many musicians we will encounter in this narrative, his fame dwindled after his death in 1936, and German is barely remembered today.

The Rhondda Music Festival was held on Christmas Day and Boxing Day 1923, in Treorchy, South Wales. The soloists were

Robert and Cecilia, Frederick Taylor and the contralto Miss Muriel Brunskill, a member of the British Opera Company. A choir of three hundred and an orchestra conducted by Mr J.T. Jones performed Mendelssohn's *St Paul*, Parry's *Job* and Verdi's *Requiem*.

On Wednesday 30 January 1924 Robert made the first of his regular radio broadcasts for the BBC, now operating from its studio at Savoy Hill, this one with the Wireless Orchestra. The number he performed was 'Phyllis Has Such Charming Graces' (1899), an old English folk melody arranged by Lane Wilson. Henry James Lane Wilson was born in Gloucester in 1871 and died in London on 8 January 1915. He was a man of many talents, a composer, organist and baritone singer who studied composition at the Royal Academy of Music in London. He turned out a great many ballads and songs, including the song cycles *Dorothy's Wedding Day* and *Flora's Holiday*. He is best remembered for his skilful and and elegant arrangements of many old English melodies such as 'A Dewy Morn', 'When Dull Care', and 'The Slightest Swain', published by Chappells in the 1890s.

On Saturday afternoon 2 February 1924 the Central London Choral and Orchestral Society gave a concert at Central Hall, Westminster. The soloists were Robert, Cecilia and Miss Mabel Aitken. The main work performed was Mendelssohn's *Hymn of Praise*, which was followed by (in a remarkable programme by today's standards) the concert version of Edward German's *A Princess of Kensington* – a 1903 comic opera with a story by Basil Hood and set in Kensington Gardens. It may have been suggested partly by *A Midsummer Night's Dream*, its theme being a game of cross-purposes played by certain mortal lovers as a consequence of Puck's practical jokes. Another likely source is the poem 'Kensington Gardens' by Thomas Tickell.

Robert next performed on radio on Sunday 30 March 1924 during an organ recital from the National Institute for the Blind at 224 Great Portland Street, London. Again he was partnered by his wife Cecilia. He sang 'My Arms! Against This Gorgias Will I Rise' and 'Sound An Alarm' from Handel's *Judas Maccabaeus*. In a lighter vein there were '*Vale*' (Farewell) by Kennedy Russell with words by Burgh d'Arcy, and 'Give Me Youth and A Day', music by Frederick Drummond and words by Edward Teschemacher. Robert was joined by Cecilia for the delightful duet between Mimi and Rudolfo from the ever popular *La Bohème* by Puccini. The programme also included L.A. Marsh (organ), Nancy Phillips (violin) and H. Lyttler (flute).

On Sunday 11 May 1924 Robert broadcast from the Piccadilly Hotel in London with De Groot and the Piccadilly Orchestra. David De Groot (1880–1933) usually known simply as De Groot, was a violinist. Dutch by birth, he was for much of his life a naturalised British subject. He directed the Piccadilly Hotel Orchestra between 1909 and 1928 as well as larger orchestras from time to time, often from the leader's chair. A photograph of the ensemble in the early 1920s suggests that it comprised ten players: piano, four violins, viola, two cellos and two double basses. De Groot was a regular artist on the radio, and it is said that income from the orchestra's residency at the Piccadilly Grill Room and their 160 recordings for labels such as HMV enabled him to purchase a Stradivarius violin.

Interspersed with Robert's many London performances were occasional out of town engagements, for example the weekly Sunday evening concerts at the Winter Gardens, New Brighton, which attracted large audiences. In those days New Brighton was a thriving coastal resort on the Wirral, with an historic promenade loved by generations of holidaymakers. On 21 August 1924 the Winter Gardens played host to Robert, Cecilia and Foster Richardson (bass), accompanied by Dorothy Hogben on piano.

A further Sunday concert was aired on 26 October. Robert was heard with Cecilia and the Wireless Orchestra, under Dan Godfrey Jnr. Their selection included 'Lovely Maid In The Moonlight' from *La Bohème* (Puccini) and 'Come To Arcadia' from *Merrie England.*

Robert and Cecilia continued their partnership the following year with a broadcast on Saturday 10 January, when they were accompanied by the Wireless Military Band, once again conducted by Dan Godfrey Jnr. His father Sir Dan Godfrey, had founded the Bournemouth Municipal Orchestra; he was one of the country's principal orchestral conductors until 1934, four years before his death. Robert performed 'For You Alone' (Geehl), 'Passing By' (Purcell) and, with Cecilia, 'The Voyagers' (Sanderson) and 'Seven O'Clock In The Morning' from *The Princess of Kensington* by Edward German. Also performing on the broadcast were the pianist and sometime composer Alba Rizzi and the entertainers

Mabel Fitzgerald and J. Duncanson.

Robert and Cecilia were next heard on the wireless on Sunday 5 July 1925, in a programme entitled *Suites and Duets*. Their varied selections included 'Dear Love Of Mine' from the opera *Nadeshda* by Arthur Goring Thomas, 'It Was A Lover And His Lass' (Shakespeare's words; music by Richard Walthew), 'O, Lovely Night' (Landon Ronald), and the 'Love Duet' from Act 1 of Puccini's *Madam Butterfly*. Also on the programme were piano duets performed by C. Weber and Maud Dixon, and violin duets from A. Sherman and Una Chevington.

The Promenade concerts are now as much a part of the British summer as Wimbledon or the Boat Race. They were originally held at the Queen's Hall, built in 1885 and situated in Langham Place in central London. The hall had seventeen entrances from three different streets and could seat more than 2,500 people. Robert Newman, the hall's manager, organised the first Promenade Concert season in August 1895, employing Henry Wood to conduct. The concerts became an annual event, and were soon established as a great British tradition.

Robert made two guest appearances at the 'Proms'. The first was on 20 August 1925, when he performed '*E Lucevan Le Stelle*' from Puccini's *Tosca*; the *Times* reviewer noted that he had 'exactly the right kind of light tenor'.

Robert appeared in a second concert on 8 September, this time with the Scottish soprano Isobel Baillie. First billed as Bella Baillie, she changed her name at the suggestion of the conductor Hamilton Harty, who felt that Bella Baillie sounded too much like the name of a music hall performer. Robert performed 'Ballade In A Minor' by the Afro-British composer Samuel Coleridge-Taylor and 'In Native Worth And Honour Clad' from Joseph Haydn's oratorio *The Creation,* first heard in 1798.

These concert appearances must have felt like a career breakthrough for Robert, for the Promenade concerts were held in high regard. Henry Wood had an enormous influence on musical life in Britain: he introduced the public to a vast repertoire of music and was particularly keen to promote and encourage British composers such as Frederick Delius and Ralph Vaughan Williams. When he died in 1944 the concerts became known as the Henry Wood Promenade Concerts. On the night of 10 May

1941 Queen's Hall was completely destroyed in the London Blitz – and the BBC Proms now take place each year in the Royal Albert Hall.

In the autumn of 1925 Robert and Cecilia were heard together in a spate of regional radio broadcasts from Aberdeen, Manchester, Newcastle, Belfast and Cardiff. The songs they performed included 'Yearning' (Eric Coates), 'Love Went A-Riding' (Frank Bridge), 'Sound An Alarm!' (Handel), 'The Gentle Maiden' (a traditional Irish air), 'Lovely Maid In The Moonlight' from *La Bohème* (Puccini), 'I Hear A Thrush At Eve' (Cadman and Eberhart), 'The Minstrel Boy' (Thomas Moore) and 'In A Little Old Garden' (Hewitt).

These radio selections give an indication of Robert's repertoire during these years – a mixture of oratorio, opera, sentimental ballads and parlour songs. These songs are very much a reflection of the content of radio programming schedules before the Second World War. Hymns and sentimental songs were extremely popular with the public, who liked music that made them shed a tear. Thus songs looked back to the days of yore, many of them expressing a yearning for the old village pump, the old family clock, the old spinning wheel, and the old garden – 'old' being an essential ingredient of conservative popular songs.[26]

The following year, on Friday 8 January, Robert and Cecilia recorded a two hour programme with the pianist Jessie Furze, broadcast from Daventry with the Radio Quartet. Daventry was an early BBC transmitter broadcasting on Long Wave from the heart of England. The BBC had built the station in 1925 on Borough Hill just outside the town. From 1932 the BBC Empire Service – now the World Service – was broadcast from there: the radio announcement 'Daventry calling' made the Northamptonshire town famous across the globe – although it was never anything more than a name on the dial, as it broadcast material produced elsewhere. By 1926 there were two million licence holders in Britain. The wireless had become important in promoting music that the BBC considered 'suitable'; its output did not reflect the increasing Americanisation of popular music. The BBC saw its role very much as that of custodian of public taste. The Victorian idea that if good music was presented to the masses they would eventually eschew the inferior was still very much in the air.[27]

As already noted, not all the Naylors' work was in the capital. On Saturday 17 April 1926 they took part in a 'Borough Recital and Concert' at the Town Hall, Middlesbrough. Since its earliest days the Town Hall has been the home of entertainment in the town, and many famous names have appeared there, including Harry Lauder, Gracie Fields, Johann Strauss and Richard Tauber. This particular evening Cecilia was described as 'the distinguished soprano' and Robert as 'the famous new English tenor'. Cecilia's songs included Eva Dell Acqua's '*La Villanelle*' and Edward German's 'Song From Tom Jones'. Among Robert Naylor's contributions were William Sharp (also known as Fiona MacLeod) and Rutland Boughton's 'The Faery Song' and Eric Coates's 'Yearning'. The two duetted on Edward Teschemacher and Wilfred Sanderson's 'The Voyagers', which had first been heard in 1912.[28]

During the week of 12 July Robert performed at the West End Cinema in Birmingham. The building had been opened the previous year on Suffolk Street, and also contained a ballroom and a restaurant. He was heard in another broadcast from the Daventry transmitter on Friday 23 July, this time with the Radio Quartet, the contralto Hope Jackson and the cellist Adelina Leon.

On 31 December 1926 the British Broadcasting Company became the British Broadcasting Corporation and gained control of the airwaves under the terms of a royal charter. Sir John Reith, the company's general manager, had been in favour of the company being taken into public ownership. It is worth bearing in mind that in these early years of radio the BBC was still a small organisation that catered for a minority of the public. In 1927, for instance, it employed a total of 773 people. Indeed, it was not until the Second World War that it fully achieved what had always been its aim, that of informing, inspiring – and diverting – a whole community.[29]

Nonetheless, by the mid-1920s radio had grown from a minority interest into a popular obsession. People talked about 'radio fever', demand outstripped supply and everyone wanted the new entertainment in their homes. The radio trade at this time was largely in components and home-construction kits; even cigarette manufacturers issued cards detailing how to build your own set. The magazine *Practical Wireless* was founded in 1932. It wasn't until the 1930s that mains-powered sets in bakelite cabinets, manufactured by companies such as Philco, Phillips and Bush, began to appear in the shops.

Around this time Robert and Cecilia became members of the Concert Artistes Association, which was based at 20 Cranbourn Street, London WC2. The organisation was founded in 1897 in order to safeguard artistes' interests in every possible way, encourage talent, foster public interest in entertainments, provide opportunities for artistes to perform and to meet those who were likely to be helpful to them in their profession, and promote good-fellowship and co-operation among members. Members met regularly throughout the winter season at social events and dinners.

Most importantly, the CAA annually supplied to interested parties lists of members who were available for after-dinner entertainment, luncheon clubs, smoking concerts and Masonic lodge functions. Over the next few years Robert and Cecilia undertook numerous bookings of this kind. The artiste's fee for a single engagement in the 1920s was around the 1 guinea mark. As an aside, it is interesting to note this odd snobbery: fees were always paid in guineas. Popular artistes booked through agents, particularly those attached to department stores like Harrods, sometimes commanded higher fees, especially for private house work. By the 1930s the fees had gone up to 1½ or even 2 guineas.[30]

The CAA changed its name in the 1980s and is now known as the Club for Acts and Actors, thus expanding its membership to encompass the whole theatrical profession. Now based at 20 Bedford Street, London WC2, it continues to represent the interests of, and provide assistance to, members of the stage profession.

On 8 January 1927 Robert appeared at a weekend concert held on Hastings pier, East Sussex. The pier opened in 1872, had two pavilions and during this period provided much entertainment. It was noted by a reviewer at the concert from *The Stage* that 'Robert Naylor is a fine dramatic tenor with a voice of unusual purity of tone.'[31] It would appear that the organisers were impressed enough to invite him back for a further concert on 19 January 1927. This time the programme was a selection of works by Coleridge-Taylor. The Municipal Orchestra performed under the direction of Basil Cameron, with the assistance of the Hastings and St Leonard's Madrigal Society. 'Robert Naylor, a cultured tenor, sang "Onaway

Awake" with fine effect.'[32] 'Onaway! Awake, Beloved!' is an aria from *Hiawatha* by Coleridge-Taylor, based on Longfellow's poem.

The following month, on 5 February, the Harold Wood Music Society in north-west London held its last concert of the season. Robert performed with the singer Frank Phillips, who later gave up singing to become a BBC radio announcer and TV compère.

February also saw Robert and Cecilia entertaining the Masons at the Connaught Rooms, Covent Garden; the occasion was the 23rd Festival of the Royal Masonic Benevolent Institute. The instrumental fare was supplied by the violinist De Groot and Shakespeare and Rutterford, who played cornet and concertina respectively. The vocal part of the programme was duets and solo pieces by Robert and Cecilia.

On 9 June 1927 *The Times* announced that 'The Old Vic Opera will appear next week at the Chelsea Palace Theatre in *Faust* and *Il Trovatore*. Mr Charles Cori will conduct the orchestra and the singers will include Mr Robert Naylor.' Robert played the part of Dr Faust and Harry Brindle that of Mephistopheles. *Faust* was performed on Monday, Tuesday and Saturday, while *Il Trovatore* was heard on Wednesday, Thursday and Friday.

There was a Masonic date on 11 November at Pagani's Restaurant on Great Portland Street when a 'capital programme of entertainment' was arranged for the members by the organist Frederick Arthur. The vocalists were Robert and Cecilia. Pagani's was a select establishment run by Giuseppe Pagani. During the war it was bombed, but it survived for a time afterwards as a single bar with a restaurant above it. Restaurants like Pagani's went out of their way to cater for the Masonic trade, having their own Masonic temples and offering rooms where lodges could store their equipment.

During 1927 and 1928 Robert studied at the Guildhall School of Music, which was at John Carpenter Street, Victoria Embankment, London EC4, near Blackfriars Bridge. The Guildhall School of Music differed in many important particulars from the Royal College of Music and the Royal Academy of Music. It was established by the Corporation of London in 1880, with the aim to enable all those desirous of obtaining a musical education, whether professional or amateur, to have lessons from professors of the highest ability. In order to meet the requirements of those who

29

worked during the day, instruction was given daily from 8.30am to 8.30pm. In this way the school brought affordable musical education within the reach of many who would otherwise have been unable to take advantage of it, and this flexible provision enabled Robert to study while fulfilling his various professional engagements. The school year consisted of three terms of twelve weeks each, beginning on the fourth Mondays in September and April, and the second Monday in January, but students could join at any time, lessons thus missed being made up or allowed for.

Robert attended the Guildhall from October 1927, having been awarded a scholarship of 12 guineas by the Federation of British Music Industries.[33] He not only received a scholarship but also had his entrance fees waived by order of the college principal, Sir Landon Ronald. His studies included coaching, singing and elocution; he began his voice studies under Professor M. Mirsky, who specialised in German lieder. He was also a pupil of the eminent tenor Walter Hyde, famous for his Wagnerian roles; before taking up his professorship he had performed at Covent Garden and with the Metropolitan Opera of New York.

In November 1927 the students of the combined Grand and Light Opera classes presented a revival of the rarely heard opera *Martha* (or *The Richmond Market*) by Friedrich von Flotow (1812–83), which had been presented at the Theatre Royal, Drury Lane, in 1849; Robert played the part of Lionel. Von Flotow's tuneful score, which crosses the genres of ballad opera, light opera and romantic serious opera, was accompanied by the Guildhall School of Music Orchestra under the direction of Sir Landon Ronald. The students' last performance was on 25 November, a Saturday afternoon, when the concert was attended by the Lord Mayor and sheriffs. *The Stage* noted that Robert, 'whose tenor of generally pleasing timbre was employed successfully in the air, one formerly knew as "*M'appari tutt'amor*", also let himself go in the rejection of Nancy's efforts at a reconciliation in the fourth act'.[34]

Landon Ronald is a name that will weave itself in and out of this narrative. Born Herbert Russell in London in 1873, he was the illegitimate son of Henry Russell (1812–1900) and Hannah de Lara. His father led an eventful life on both sides of the Atlantic as a pianist, baritone singer and composer. He wrote the song 'A Life On The Ocean Wave' and the music for 'Woodman! Spare That

Tree!', a song made popular on record many years later by the American comedian Phil Harris. He was educated at St Marylebone and All Souls Grammar School and the high school in Margate.

Landon Ronald went on to study at the Royal College of Music, where he was taught composition by Sir Hubert Parry. He made his first professional appearance in Gounod's *Faust* in 1896 at Covent Garden. Between 1898 and 1902 he took conducting jobs wherever he could find them, appearing in musical comedy in the West End and at concerts in Blackpool during the summer months. An early advocate of the gramophone, he argued strongly that the new medium of sound recording had the potential both to educate and to entertain. As a result of his interest he acted as musical advisor for the Gramophone Company (HMV), becoming a director of the company in 1930. He made a number of important signings for the label, including the soprano Dame Nellie Melba. Ronald was appointed principal of the Guildhall School of Music in 1910. During his tenure he was able to bring about a number of changes to the curriculum and management of the school, and in doing so he raised the status of the Guildhall and increased the quality of the education on offer there. Ronald composed various orchestral works and over 200 songs. He was knighted for his services to music in 1922.

On 14 January 1928 Robert was once more to be heard on the BBC in a 'Popular Concert' from the Kingsway Hall, Holborn. The programme was arranged by Gatty Sellars, who was organist at the Kingsway Hall, and featured the Kingsway Hall Choir. The Kingsway Hall was built in 1912 as the Methodist West London Mission, not as a concert or recording hall. It was considered, however, to have the finest acoustics in London for the recording of orchestras and choirs, more by accident than design, and as result it became the most sought-after recording venue for orchestral music in England and was extensively used by HMV. The London Symphony Orchestra alone made 421 recordings there from 1926 to 1983, making it second only to the Abbey Road studio in popularity. After its sale by the church in 1984 various schemes for refurbishment and alternative use came to nothing, and the derelict building was demolished in 1997 to make way for a hotel. Among the numbers performed by Robert at the concert, and heard by radio listeners in the London and Daventry reception areas on that winter's Saturday evening, was 'A Sheepfold Song', composed by Landon Ronald. The rest of the bill included Megan Thomas (soprano) and the duo Rickards and Stevens (entertainers).

During 1928 Robert's appearances with the Old Vic Company included a further run of Gounod's *Faust,* with Robert sharing the lead with Edith Coates. Miss Coates was a mezzo-soprano who also began her career with the Old Vic and sang alongside Robert in all his Old Vic appearances; later she was a founding member of the Covent Garden Opera Company. In 1977 she was awarded the OBE for her services to music, six years before her death at the age of seventy-four.

Robert played Doctor Faust on 8 and 11 February. Sandwiched in between these dates, on the 10th, he starred as Lieutenant B.F. Pinkerton in Puccini's *Madam Butterfly.* Set in Japan at the turn of the century and reputedly based on a true incident, this tale of an American naval officer and his young Japanese bride has remained one of the world's most popular operas since its 1904 premier at La Scala in Milan.

Twenty-five wards make up the City of London; one of them is the Coleman Street Ward. The Ward Club organised about half a dozen functions every year, including formal dinners and civic luncheons. This club had a long history, having held its inauguration dinner at the Old King's Tavern, Old Jewry, on Tuesday 8 April 1862. On 21 February 1928 the club members met at the Moorgate Street Restaurant, and dinner was followed by 'an excellent concert, arranged by Frederick Arthur. The singers were Robert Naylor and Cecilia Farrar: Jean Butt delighted everyone with her violin playing . . . W.T. Best was the accompanist.'[35] W.T. Best, though described as something of an eccentric and a recluse, was the leading organ recitalist of his day.

The round of after-dinner entertainment continued. The Worshipful Company of Girdlers held a livery dinner on 15 March at Girdlers Hall, which was followed by a recital by Robert and Cecilia. Historical trade guilds are known as livery companies in the City of London, and the Girdlers Company remains today as a charitable trust. Medieval girdles once had symbolic importance; one is still presented to the sovereign at the Coronation.

Robert and Cecilia performed together again on Sunday 18 March and Tuesday 20 March at the Café Royal on Regent Street. They were part of a programme of acts, arranged again by Frederick

Arthur, for the members of the Bon Frères Club. The club's membership was exclusively theatrical and musical artistes; the 'Good Brothers' provided mutual support by attending each others' first nights and subscribing to charity causes within the profession. It was reported that Robert and Cecilia 'were received with delight for some capital singing'.[36]

On 3 April Robert was on the radio once again, this time in the company of contralto Muriel Morgan and the orchestra from the Marble Arch Pavilion. The Marble Arch Pavilion was opened as an 'electric cinema' in 1914; there was also a tea-room attached. In the days before 'talkies' – the film *The Jazz Singer*,[37] released the previous year, was an early example of the use of synchronised sound – it was usual for cinemas to provide music to accompany the silent films. Towards the end of the 1920s the more prestigious cinemas had moved from a solitary pianist to small orchestras, and even when the 'talkies' arrived live musicians still formed part of the entertainment in many cinemas. This was because the main film might be a 'talkie', but the rest of the programme would most likely be silent films, and music was still required to accompany those. Orchestras were gradually replaced by organists, and sometimes the two co-existed for a brief period. There also existed for a time cine-variety, which I will come to later.

On 3 May 1928 Robert appeared with the Old Vic Opera Company in *Rigoletto*, which was staged at the Old Vic Theatre on Waterloo Road. The tragic play by Victor Hugo, which centres upon the scandalous goings-on in the royal household in the duchy of Mantua, inspired Verdi to produce one of his great works, which immediately became a staple of the operatic repertoire.

On the evening of 1 June Robert was heard on the radio again, this time in the company of the contralto Margery Phillips and the Wireless Military Band, conducted by B. Walton O'Donnell. Among the songs Robert sang were 'Yearning' (Eric Coates), 'Clorinda' (John Bledlowe and R. Orlando Morgan) and 'Had I The Heaven's Embroidered Cloths' (Landon Ronald). On 29 June Robert was in a further radio broadcast, this time with the Ernest Leggett London Octet and the soprano Maud Nelson. He performed 'Romance', written by J. Herbage, the winner of the BBC Staff Music Composition.

The Concert Artistes Association Cricket Team played its first full season in the summer of 1928, on Sunday 15 July playing the London & North Eastern Railway team. It is quite likely that Robert was a member of the CAA team. After the match everyone adjourned to the Pavilion where, following refreshments, a concert was given and Robert performed. These events always included a collection for the CAA Benevolent Fund.

On 20 September Robert's recording career began somewhat inauspiciously when he recorded at least one song, 'Sigh No More', for the rather eccentric Duophone label. The company had been founded in 1925 as the Duophone Syndicate Ltd of 63 Victoria Street, London EC4, and went through a number of incarnations in its first few years. In August 1928 the Duophone and Unbreakable Record Co. Ltd, as it was now known, gained control of British Brunswick Ltd and moved once again, this time to 15–19 Cavendish Place, W1. The company made a number of recordings during this period, but none was ever released, though test pressings exist of some of them. Robert's record was given the number DB 45-1, which may indicate that a test pressing exists somewhere. Further details about this début recording session can be found in the discography at the end of the book.

Professionally things were going very well for the Naylors, and Robert in particular was in much demand. By this time he was represented by the concert agents Ibbs & Tillett, who had offices at 19 Hanover Square, EC1, and were largely responsible for arranging his professional bookings. This old-fashioned company apparently never had a written contract with an artiste; a gentlemen's agreement and a shake of hands was seen as sufficient. If a relationship didn't work the artiste was free to look elsewhere. Ibbs & Tillett was founded by Robert Leigh Ibbs and John Tillett, and it was for many years the foremost concert agency in Britain, responsible for the provision of soloists to music clubs, societies and festivals, and for the management of international stars such as Fritz Kreisler and Kathleen Ferrier. Almost everybody performing in the classical music world was represented by the agency. In 1929 they had seventy-five tenors on their books in addition to Robert, as well as scores of other vocalists and instrumentalists.[38]

On Saturday 20 October Robert performed at a Ladies' Night held in the Abercorn Rooms at the Great Eastern Hotel, Liverpool

Street, London. This was a Masonic function for the Danehurst Lodge, and Robert appeared with two fellow artistes, Olive Tyson and Cecil Johnson.

The Guildhall School of Music held its Students' Annual Concert and Prize Giving Ceremony on Saturday afternoon, 27 October. Robert was one of only nine students selected to perform in the concert before distinguished guests, including the Rt Hon. the Lord Mayor, Sir Charles A. Batho, Bart, and Alderman and Sheriff Sir William A. Waterlow KBE, JP. He performed 'Onoway, Awake Beloved' by Coleridge-Taylor.

At the presentation of prizes by the Lady Mayoress, Robert was awarded the Mercer's Scholarship for the term ending April 1929. This had been established by the Worshipful Company of Mercers, the premier livery company of the City of London, to offer financial incentive to talented students. The scholarship value was £52 10s 0d. This was not a tremendous amount, but as with most scholarships awarded primarily on merit the monetary value was secondary to the recognition it conferred. Robert was also awarded the Alfred and Catherine Howard Prize – which is still awarded annually to the student who is the best tenor singer. The scholarship and prize clearly illustrate the success that Robert was experiencing in his studies.

The Concert Artistes Association held an 'At Home' concert on 1 November at the Cecil Hotel. These regular events, held in various banqueting rooms in the capital, were organised as an opportunity for members to socialise and to help raise money for the association's benevolent fund. Robert was one of a handful of performers on this year's concert programme. The CAA's benevolent fund provided relief for distressed members of their association, or their dependents, in necessitous circumstances, providing assistance in cases of extreme hardship caused by illness or misfortune.

During November 1928 Robert appeared in *La Bohème* with the Old Vic Opera Company. The *Times* reviewer felt that the work was a welcome addition to the Old Vic's repertory: 'It presents no insuperable problems of any sort and no difficulties of production . . . the really important things like the casting of the six principal parts were admirably done. Mr Robert Naylor has the right style of Italian tenor for Rudolph, and if his vocal production was a little freer, and his words a little clearer, he would be very good indeed. The customary enthusiasm of the Old Vic audience was well justified.'[39]

The City of London Printers' Musical Society held a concert for members on 22 November at Anderton's Hotel on Fleet Street; there was a very large attendance. The entertainment was arranged by the society's musical director, George J. Harrison. Robert was among the artistes who appeared, accompanied on the piano by Charles Hardy. Others on the programme included Violet Houghton, Victor Lodge, Dudley Barrington and the variety star M'Lita Dolores who scored with the audience.

Two days later, on Saturday the 24th, Robert was again on the radio, this time with Muriel Southern (contralto), D. Wise (violin) and B. Mason (piano). The items performed on this occasion were not listed.

Before 1928 ended Robert and Cecilia moved from 19 Boundary Road to Wembley Park. They bought a property at 76 Oakington Avenue, a tree-lined residential road located off Wembley Park Drive. In the 1920s it must have felt like moving to the countryside. The property was a newly built, double-fronted detached bungalow with a large garden. It had white rendered half-timbered walls in the mock-Tudor style and a red tiled roof. There was a short driveway and a garage built to match the bungalow's design. The couple named their new home Red Roofs, and Robert lived there until the outbreak of the Second World War.

Just four years earlier Wembley Park had hosted the British Empire Exhibition, by which time Wembley UDC was 'a beautiful and salubrious little suburb' complete with a landscaped park. This was a remarkable event, with fountains, lakes, gardens and many pavilions, each representing the architectural style of the countries exhibiting. It was opened by King George V on 23 April 1924 and was an immediate success. After the exhibition the buildings were sold and many demolished – but the stadium was saved, and became the home of English football. Many visitors decided to settle in the area, and a lot of houses were built to satisfy the demand, roads and sewerage being improved. During the 1930s Wembley High Road became a major suburban shopping centre, with constantly growing housing development, social facilities, churches and schools.

When he was relaxing at home Robert's recreational interests included gardening, golf, cricket, riding and association football. In a publicity blurb at the time he was described as 'a keen lover of his garden . . . at his home in Wembley Park he spends happy hours amongst a wealth of roses'. He played golf regularly and was a member of the Stage Golfing Society. This was founded in 1903, and membership is open to all those involved in the theatre and music business. In Robert's day it had its headquarters in a top room of the Salisbury, a Victorian pub at 90 St Martin's Lane, WC2. Robert was also a member of the Savage Club, a gentlemen's club founded in 1857 and in the 1930s based at Carlton House Terrace in St James's. The club has always been a favourite among the theatrical set. Past 'Brother Savages' have included Charlie Chaplin, W.S. Gilbert, Sir Henry Irving, Carl Rosa and Henry Wood, as well as the likes of Earl Mountbatten and HRH Prince Philip, Duke of Edinburgh.

The Concert Artistes Association held its third concert of the season on 4 January 1929 at the New Hall, Eagle Hotel, London. W.J. Lawson was in the chair. Among the artistes who contributed to the programme were Harry Brindle (born in Chorley, Lancashire, and principal bass with the Old Vic Opera Company) and Robert Naylor. The accompanist was George Ison, who recorded with Isobel Baillie.

On 12 March Robert was on the radio in a concert with the baritone Herbert Simmonds and the Birmingham Studio Orchestra. The conductor was Joseph Lewis, who was born in Dudley, Staffordshire, and was the founder and conductor of various choral societies in the Midlands, conductor of the City of Birmingham Choir and assistant conductor of the City of Birmingham Orchestra. His first broadcast was from Birmingham in 1923, and in 1928 he joined the staff of the BBC as a conductor.

Robert did a season with the Carl Rosa Opera Company from 15 April, appearing at the Royal Theatre in Nottingham for a fortnight. The programme included *La Bohème, Cavalleria Rusticana, Pagliacci, Rigoletto, Carmen* and *Tannhäuser*. Robert starred as Rudolfo in *La Bohème* with Pauline Brindley, and it was reported that he 'sang delightfully'. On 29 April the company opened at the Royal Court, Liverpool, for a week, performing

Bizet's *Carmen*, Joseph Holbrooke's *Bronwen*[40] and Wagner's *Siegfried*.

Towards the end of the month Robert was back with the Old Vic, and on 25 and 27 April they presented *Otello*, a four-act opera by Verdi. The plot, based on Shakespeare's play *Othello*, centres upon the Moorish general Otello, who has married Desdemona against her father's wishes. A mercenary in the service of the Venetian army, Otello has been sent to Cyprus to repel an invasion by the Turks. Iago, his ensign, feels slighted because of Otello's captain Cassio's promotion over him. Iago plots and manipulates events and feelings to his benefit, in order to destroy Otello's marriage and eventually his life. Robert played the part of Cassio.

From 6 May Robert was once again with the Carl Rosa Company at the Opera House in Manchester. Again one of the featured operas was Bizet's *Carmen*. The libretto, written by Meilhac and Halévy, was based on the story of the same title by Prosper Mérimée; having been first produced in Paris in 1875. The fiery story of love and jealousy has made it one of the world's most popular operas. Several well-known pieces from this opera have taken on a life separate to the work: the 'Prélude' (overture), the 'Toréador Song' and the 'Habanera'. As lead tenor with the company, Robert played the part of the doomed lover Don José. *The Stage* reported that 'the tenor Robert Naylor sang with brilliancy'.[41]

In July, eight months after the Old Vic production, Robert appeared with the Carl Rosa Company in Puccini's *La Bohème*, once again playing the part of Rudolfo, at the Lyceum Theatre on Wellington Street, just off the Strand. *The Times* noted that 'the company gave a spirited performance of *La Bohème* at the Lyceum Theatre last night. Messrs Robert Naylor, Hubert Dunkerley, Phillip Bertram and Frederic Collier made a capital quartet of Bohemians singing with alternative gaiety and sentimental fervour, and acting with a full appreciation of the differences in characters of the four friends.'[42]

Later that same month Robert was the star of the Carl Rosa production of *Madam Butterfly*. The *Times* observed that 'Mr Naylor (as Pinkerton) and Miss Olive Gilbert (playing Suzuki) have good voices and contributed much to the high level of the performance. Last night's performance of *Madam Butterfly* sent me away thinking that Puccini was a good composer. A mediocre performance invariably sends one away thinking how bad he is.'[43]

On Sunday 21 July the Concert Artistes Association Cricket Club met the Exiles Cricket Club for a match at Twickenham. The CAA won the match by 165 runs to 81 runs, and the game was followed by a concert at which Robert performed. The following month he was again on the radio, this time with Dorothy Robson, soprano, and Andrew Brown's Pianoforte Quintet, in a programme broadcast on 12 August.

On Saturday 2 November the London and North Eastern Railway (Great Northern Section) held its twenty-eighth annual concert on behalf of their benevolent fund at the Northern Polytechnic, Holloway. Bernard Barker was in charge of the programme, which included Mabel Adeane ('whistling and comic character numbers') and songs 'sung effectively' by Robert.

Since his arrival in the capital Robert's singing career had flourished. He had proved to himself, and to those back home in Yorkshire, that he had the talent and ability to succeed. His appearances at the Promenade concerts and with the Old Vic and Carl Rosa companies must have been gratifying and professionally rewarding. However, the numerous short radio broadcasts, after-dinner concerts and performances in grand opera are not likely to have provided him with a huge income. Cecilia had more or less stopped performing with her husband, and by 1930 she appears to have virtually relinquished her own career. It is possible that Robert was feeling the financial pinch and was looking for engagements that provided a better income than the classical concert platform.

This is a common predicament facing musicians who, above all else, have to earn a living. The tenor Webster Booth was offered advice on this point while he was still with the D'Oyly Carte Company. When Dr Malcolm Sargent was engaged as musical director at the Prince's Theatre for the 1926 season, he advised Webster that opera singing was poorly paid and that if he did not have a supplementary private income he should concentrate on trying to obtain more lucrative singing engagements.[44] More lucrative singing engagements were, of course, to be found in variety and on the West End stage – and Robert turned increasingly to these avenues of entertainment to earn his living.

CHAPTER THREE
The West End Stage and the Recording Studio

*I*n the autumn of 1929 Robert made his West End début in a revue written by Ronald Jeans and Douglas Furber, with music by Ivor Novello, called *The House That Jack Built*; it starred husband and wife team Jack Hulbert and Cicely Courtneidge. The show opened at the Adelphi Theatre on 8 November 1929. The Adelphi is on the Strand, in the City of Westminster. The original theatre was founded in 1806, but the present building is the fourth on the site. It was reopened on 3 December 1930, designed in the Art Deco style by Ernest Schaufelberg, with seating for 1,500 people. The Adelphi has a reputation for specialising in comedy and musical theatre.

The show's male star Jack Hulbert (1892-1978) was an undergraduate at Cambridge and appeared in a number of shows and revues. He later studied at the Central School of Speech and Drama and rose to become an immensely popular entertainer in musicals and light comedies. Together with his wife Cicely Courtneidge, a talented comedienne in her own right, he co-starred in a series of London musical hits. Esmeralda Cicely Courtneidge (1893-1980) was born in Sydney, Australia; her father, Robert, was a British theatrical manager-producer and playwright. She made her

41

professional stage début in 1909 in *The Arcadians,* produced by her father at the Shaftesbury Theatre. She married her stage partner in 1916, and their innocent clowning kept theatre audiences amused throughout the thirties. In 1962 she gave a wistful performance as an ageing music hall star in Bryan Forbes's film *The L-Shaped Room.* In more recent years she became a television actress, playing the role of Mum in the first series of the London Weekend Television comedy *On the Buses,* opposite Reg Varney.

A revue is a multi-act popular theatrical entertainment that usually combines music, dance and sketches. Though most famous for their visual spectacle, revues frequently satirised contemporary figures and topical news items. *The House That Jack Built* contained a number of such sketches. For example, one was set in a doctor's consulting room, another was set in a branch post office, and a third sketch was set in the parlour of a semi-detached villa in Harringay, North London. Robert's cameo appearance in the show occurred shortly after the interval in Scene 12. This was set in a doge's palace in Venice on the evening of a betrothal festival, and the heroine was taking a fond farewell of her young lover, played by Robert, tenderly singing 'Tear Drops From Her Eyes Are Pearls'.[45]

The show transferred to the Winter Garden Theatre, Covent Garden, from Monday 14 April 1930, where in an effort to compete with cinema entrance charges the theatre's manager Paul Murray offered tickets from 1s to 7s 6d (plus tax). *The House That Jack Built* finally closed in the first week of June that year.

On Friday 25 October 1929 the Chough Musical Society held their second concert of the season in the Cannon Street Hotel's Great Hall in the City of London. The concert provided a couple of hours of delightful entertainment. The Chough Musical Society concerts had been going on for over fifty years, the origin of the society stretching back to mid-Victorian days. The Irish tenor John McCormack had sung at the Chough Musical Society in 1907. At this afternoon concert Peter Dawson was principal singer, but Robert Naylor and Edward Holland were heard in duets and well-applauded solo items. Peter Dawson was an Australian bass-baritone who gained world-wide popularity. He was a prolific recording artist and made his first sides for Edison Bell on wax cylinders in 1904. It has been estimated that by the Second World War his record sales had exceeded 12 million.

The 1930s are often viewed as an era of economic depression. Although the overall picture for the British economy in this decade wasn't good, the effects of the depression were uneven: some parts of the country fared better than others. In London and the southeast of England the later 1930s were relatively prosperous. There was a housing boom, encouraged in part by the prevailing low interest rates and the growing population. While many traditional industries in the north had suffered, the south was home to new developing industries. These factories were booming thanks to the new electrification of housing and industry and their mass production methods. New products, such as electrical cookers, washing machines and radios, were brought within reach of the new affluent consumer, and the industries that produced these goods prospered. Nearly half of all new factories which opened in Britain between 1932 and 1937 were in greater London.[46] As the region remained relatively affluent, theatres and concert halls also prospered – and new revues, shows and operas were staged to capacity audiences.

For Robert the new decade got off to an auspicious start when, on the afternoon of 28 January 1930, the Lady Mayoress held her first reception of the year at the Mansion House. The guests included many of the members of the delegations to the Naval Conference and their ladies. Also in attendance were the Portuguese, Italian and Belgian ambassadors, Baroness de Cartier de Marchienne and Susan Seymour, Duchess of Somerset. A programme of instrumental music was performed by George Newman's band, and Cecilia and Robert were the vocalists.

The following month, on Monday 3 February, there was a Ladies' Night at the Smithfield Lodge, which took place at the Connaught Rooms on Great Queen Street, Covent Garden. As usual entertainment was on hand: 'Gladys Knight and Robert Naylor sang to the delight of everyone. Frederick Arthur's Orchestra played during the dinner and later provided music for dancing.'[47]

On Sunday 13 February Robert took part in a Concert Artistes Association Benefit Concert held at the Palladium. Also on the bill were Ernest Rutherford's Concertina Band and comedian Arthur Askey. Henceforth there would be fewer engagements like this: already it seemed that Robert was riding the crest of a wave, and 1930 was to see the start of a string of stage successes.

On 24 March 1930 *The Times* announced: 'The Drury Lane Theatre will re-open on Friday with the musical version of Dumas' ever popular romance, *The Three Musketeers*, which has been adapted for stage by William A. McGuire. The story, which follows closely the original, is told through twelve elaborate scenes, accompanied by twenty-five musical numbers and three ballets.' The music was by the Bohemian-American composer Rudolph Friml (1879–1972). He was born in Prague, where he studied piano and composition at the Conservatory before moving to the United States. Alongside other immigrants from Europe, such as Victor Herbert and Sigmund Romberg, he helped to establish a strong school of Viennese-style operetta. His most famous works are *Rose Marie* (1924) and *The Vagabond King* (1925). Friml's works were enormously popular but are seldom performed these days. However, even in the 1930s he was often criticised for the sentimental and insubstantial nature of his compositions, and he was never able to adapt to the new styles that started to dominate the musical theatre. *The Three Musketeers* was his last real stage success.

The lyrics to the show were by Clifford Grey and P.G. Wodehouse. Sir Pelham Grenville Wodehouse was born in 1881, the son of a British judge in Hong Kong. He grew up in privileged surroundings in Guildford, Surrey. His witty prose was quintessentially English, although from 1914 he spent more time in the United States, eventually becoming an American citizen in 1955. He was a prolific author, writing over ninety books, numerous plays, screenplays and lyrics in a career spanning seventy-three years. The Jeeves and Wooster stories are perhaps his most famous creation. In the writing of the lyrics for *The Three Musketeers*, he was assisted by an equally fascinating wordsmith called Clifford Grey.

Clifford Grey (sometimes spelled Gray) was born Percival Davis in Birmingham in 1887 and became another prolific songwriter, his most successful song being 'If You Were The Only Girl (In The World)', which was sung by George Robey and Violet Loraine in the 1916 musical *The Bing Boys Are Here*. Grey, in addition to being a songwriter, film actor and composer, was also a successful sportsman. He competed for the United States in the 1928 Winter Olympics in St Moritz, winning a gold medal in the five-man bobsleigh event. At the 1932 Winter Olympics in Lake

Placid, New York, he won another gold medal in the four-man event. He also won a bronze medal (using his American persona Tippi Grey) in the four-man event at the 1937 FIBT World Championships in St Moritz. Despite his achievements he was by all accounts a modest man, and his children did not discover his gold medals until after his death in 1941 from a heart attack and complications of asthma.

The Three Musketeers starred the dynamic English actor Dennis King, who had played the role of D'Artagnan in the 1928 New York production at the Lyric Theatre on Broadway. He was supported by Miss Lilian Davies as the Queen. When the show opened on 28 March 1930 the Duke of Buckingham was played by Webster Booth, whose main number was 'Queen Of My Heart (Here In The Night)'. Booth was a well-known singer who possessed one of the finest English tenor voices of the twentieth century. His career as a performer soon blossomed in a number of genres: grand opera at Covent Garden, musical comedy in the West End, over 1,000 radio and television broadcasts, and several films. His appearance at the Drury Lane Theatre was a major attraction.

The Three Musketeers was a big success, but as the show got underway there was a major problem looming. Webster Booth was committed to appear in a Blackpool summer show that year and, try as he might, he could not get out of his contract.[48] The manager of the Theatre Royal was Sir Alfred Butt MP, who represented the London wards of Balham and Tooting. Butt's career was built around the management of some of the most prestigious variety theatres in London; he also had a lengthy parliamentary career. This ended in disgrace in 1936 when he was forced to resign from the House of Commons after a scandal in which it was alleged he obtained personal financial gain from leaked budget proposals. It was said he was able to insure himself against the forthcoming rise in the duty on tea when the chancellor of the exchequer, J.H. Thomas, with whom he was playing golf just before the budget, said 'Tee Up!' – the remark being accompanied by a wink.

In 1930 Butt was a powerful figure in the West End; even so, not even his intervention held sway with the Blackpool promoter. Someone else had to be found to take over Webster Booth's role in *The Three Musketeers*. In the end Booth's successor was Robert Naylor, and this unexpected opportunity gave him his second major exposure on the West End stage. The show ran for 240 performances, finishing on 26 October 1930.

The Three Musketeers, like many of the successful shows during this period, was an operetta – perhaps best described as a light opera. It is said that the emergence of operetta in the mid-nineteenth century was largely the result of economic and social changes. As the middle classes, and subsequently the working classes, became increasingly affluent and in a position to dictate their entertainment needs, there arose a demand for operatic entertainment of a more approachable and tuneful kind, tailored to suit less high-brow tastes than the chiefly Italian grand opera.[49] Normally some of the libretto of an operetta is spoken rather than sung: instead of moving directly from one musical number to another, the singers intersperse their arias, recitatives and choruses with dialogue. Usually there is no accompaniment, although sometimes music is played quietly under the spoken section. Operettas are often considered less serious than operas – but this has more to do with the often comic and far-fetched plots than with the calibre of the music.

Operettas like Franz Lehár's *The Merry Widow* swept the public away, inspiring imitations by other European songwriters such as Rudolf Friml and Sigmund Romberg. As writer Tony Palmer observed, 'Operetta scores were complex and elaborate, partly because musicians such as Friml and Romberg were operatic composers by inclination who had resigned themselves to what may have seemed the second-rate task of achieving something more than vaudeville, although less than opera. For the ambitious songwriter, the extended form operetta entailed was the perfect opportunity for fulfilment.'[50]

Robert made a further radio broadcast on Tuesday 30 March, when between 3.45pm and 5.00pm listeners could hear a programme featuring him with Margaret Bissett (contralto), J. Pessach (violin), and Edith Gunthorpe and C. Baumer (two pianos).

On Good Friday, 18 April, Robert appeared again on the stage at the Old Vic in a concert given in aid of the St Giles Home for British Lepers. The charity home, which no longer exists, was founded in 1914 in Bicknacre, near Chelmsford, Essex. Also on the bill at this fund-raising concert was a twenty-five-year-old John

Gielgud, destined to become arguably the greatest Shakespearean actor of the twentieth century. The young Gielgud very much led the Old Vic Company during these years. Robert's contribution was 'Strange Harmony Of Contrasts' (*Recondita Armonia*), an aria from *Tosca* by Puccini. Also on the bill were Arthur Cox, Adele Dixon, Winifred Kennard, Frank Sale, Peter Taylor-Smith, Constance Willis and Jack Wright.

On Sunday 11 May the Concert Artistes Association held a musical evening at the Palladium in aid of the CAA Benevolent Fund. The artistes included Robert Naylor, the baritones Ashmoor Burch and Dennis Noble, and the entertainers Leslie Sarony and Arthur Askey. Also on the bill were Vera Florence, May Thomas, Gladys Knight, Lucas Bassett, Arthur Cox, Trevor Watkins, Reginald Morphew, Dorothy Gadsden and Richard Harris, Pauline and Diana, the Maestros, Mona Grey, and Ernest Rutterford's Band with Charles Forwood.

Robert was on the radio again on 14 May. The BBC's London Regional station broadcast a performance of *Dorothy,* a pastoral comedy opera in three acts, with music by Alfred Cellier and written by B.C. Stephenson (revised by Avalon Collard). This opera had first been produced at the Gaiety Theatre in London in 1886. Cellier had been the conductor at the Savoy Theatre, and apparently composed the opera in the hope of rivalling the success of his ex-associates Gilbert and Sullivan. He was pretty successful, as *Dorothy* ran for over 900 performances. One of the show's songs, 'Queen Of My Heart' (incipit: 'I Stand At Your Threshold Singing'), published by Chappell, became popular as a drawing room ballad.

The BBC broadcast of *Dorothy* starred Robert, with among others Robert Chignell, George Baker, Esther Coleman, and the Wireless Orchestra and Chorus conducted by John Ansell, whose nautical overture *Plymouth Hoe,* composed in 1914, used to be very popular. *Dorothy* was based on *The City Heiress,* a comedy by Aphra Behn, and was first produced in 1886 at the Gaiety Theatre, London. The story tells of a scoundrel who falls in love with his disguised fiancé. The script makes use of mistaken identities and social class distinctions to create a series of amusing situations.

In 1930 Robert's recording career began in earnest, with three 78rpm records issued on the Piccadilly label; the first of these had been recorded nearly twelve months before in about March 1928. After many months with no sign of his recordings in the catalogue, one wonders whether he gave up hope on his early sessions with Piccadilly – assuming the company did not keep him informed of their intentions. Since his earlier session for Duophone had ended in rejection, this would have been a second big disappointment for him regarding his gramophone career. Piccadilly was a budget line for Metropole Records, although no mention is made of this on the label; the records originally sold for 1s 6d each. Robert's recordings were released on the Piccadilly 'Celebrity Series', which sold at the slightly higher price of 2s. The label was short-lived, disappearing in April 1932.

Robert's three Piccadilly records also appeared on the Octacros label, owned by Syncrophone Ltd. They were produced in response to a dispute between cinema operators and the Performing Rights Society, whereby cinemas were prevented from playing records to the public without paying a fee. Octacros records were made for use exclusively in cinemas: the label typically stated, 'This record may be played in public without further charge by holders of the appropriate contract with Syncophone Ltd.' These records first appeared in 1934, using old masters from the defunct Piccadilly label. On the labels of Octacros records the artistes performing were not named.

The Piccadilly recording studio was based at the Highbury Athenaeum, 96A Highbury New Park, North London. Opened in 1882 as a literary or scientific club, the Highbury Athenaeum was also licensed for music until 1889, having a concert hall that held an audience of 1060 on the ground floor and a music hall above. It closed in about 1920, becoming a recording studio for Piccadilly in 1926. The building was acquired by the Rank film company in the late 1930s to make second features and to train young directors and actors. Associated with it was a charm school for young actresses. The studio closed in about 1950, and the building was taken over to make ITV programmes for a few years. It was demolished in 1963 and replaced by flats appropriately named Athenaeum Court.[51]

Robert's first Piccadilly release in May 1930 was 'For You Alone' by Henry Geehl, written in 1909 (incipit: 'Take thou this rose, this little tender rose'.) Henry Ernest Geehl was born in London in 1881. In 1919 he was appointed a professor at Trinity

College of Music, and he composed a symphony, a violin concerto, a piano concerto and numerous works for brass bands – including *Oliver Cromwell* and *On The Cornish Coast*. The song 'For You Alone' became a bestseller and was widely recorded by the likes of Enrico Caruso and Richard Tauber. On the B-side was an uncredited song called 'The Star'. A music critic reviewing the disc wrote, 'It will be to Piccadilly's advantage to print composer's names on their labels. With 'For You Alone' we hardly expect to find another song on a very high level; but 'The Star' is by no means uninteresting. It suggests Coleridge-Taylor. I advise everyone who can hear this record to do so, especially as Naylor is far from dull. I shall look with interest for other records of his. I doubt if his production, at any rate his breath control, is quite finished.'[52] In fact 'The Star', published in 1912, was by the American composer James Hotchkiss Rogers (1857-1940). An organist, teacher and music critic as well as composer, Rogers wrote more than 550 works: over 50 compositions for the organ, 5 cantatas, over 130 songs, as well as instruction books for piano and organ.

Robert's second Piccadilly release[53] followed in July 1930, and included 'Sigh No More' by W.A. Aitken, which he had recorded in September 1928 for Duophone. The words are Shakespeare's, from *Much Ado About Nothing*, and it laments how men can deceive women but women are expected to remain chaste and not be troubled by men's infidelity. 'Sigh no more ladies . . . but be you blithe and bonny, converting all your sounds of woe to Hey nonny, nonny.' It is not the kind of sentiment that would go down well with women today. There was a fad among songwriters at this time for composing tunes to fit Shakespeare's words. Many were pieces put to music for original theatrical productions, but others were penned as popular songs. Robert already had in his concert repertoire 'It Was A Lover And His Lass', by Richard Walthew, who was professor of music at Queen's College, London.

Robert's recording of 'Sigh No More' was backed by Wilfrid Sanderson's song 'Until'. Wilfrid Ernest Sanderson (1878-1935) was born in Ipswich. He studied with Frederick Barge at Westminster Abbey, where he became assistant organist. In 1903 he moved north to Doncaster as organist at the local parish church, and became conductor of the Doncaster Musical Society. It was here through the encouragement of Arthur Boosey of Boosey & Co.

that he turned his hand to writing ballads. He was to compose over 170 in all, and Robert and Cecilia included his duet 'The Voyagers' (1912) in their repertoire. The words to 'Until', which are by Edward Teschemacher, are typical of their time: 'No rose in all the world until you came/No star until you smiled upon life's sea/ No song in all the world until you spoke/No hope until you gave your heart to me.'

In September 1930 came Robert's third Piccadilly release.[54] The main side was 'I Attempt From Love's Sickness To Fly', an English Baroque aria from *The Indian Queen* by Henry Purcell – a work usually referred to as semi-opera and first performed in 1664. The libretto was by John Dryden and Sir Robert Howard. The recording was coupled with 'The English Rose', from Edward German's comic opera *Merrie England*.

While Robert was a classically trained singer and regularly performed in opera and oratorio, all his gramophone recordings were of light music; they were issued on 10in discs and aimed at the popular market. Recordings of classical works were typically (though not exclusively) issued on 12in discs. However, much of what passed as being popular music at this time would be regarded as 'highbrow' by today's listeners.

Franz Lehár's operetta *Frederica* was performed at the King's Theatre, Glasgow, during the week beginning 31 August 1930, before its début in the West End. It tells the true story of the younger days of Goethe, Germany's most famous poet, and his tragic love for Frederica, daughter of the Vicar of Sesenheim. Easily staged with only two sets, the operetta is one of Lehár's loveliest and includes the well-known song 'Oh Maiden, My Maiden'.

Frederica starred Joseph Hislop, the great Scottish tenor, who was reportedly paid £1,000 per week. The son of an Edinburgh housepainter, Joseph Dewar Hislop was born in 1884. He made his début with the Swedish Royal Opera in 1914 and was later decorated by the King of Sweden. During his career he made over 180 recordings and sang in 29 operatic roles, including appearances at Covent Garden, La Scala and the Chicago Opera House. In the 1930s he was a major concert artiste. He died at home in Fife in 1977.

During rehearsals for *Frederica* Robert was Hislop's understudy. An understudy learns the lines (and songs) of a leading actor. If through illness or accident the lead is unable to appear the understudy takes over the part, often at short notice, thus allowing the show to continue. For aspiring actors and actresses being engaged as an understudy can be an invaluable experience, and may be the first step towards a successful career. The position allows them to work alongside well-known performers and observe at first hand their skills and technique. It is not uncommon for an understudy to be asked to learn the lines of three or more parts, because this helps producers to keep a show's costs down. It can be a stressful position, and even more difficult than playing the lead role.

By the Thursday of the Glasgow run, Hislop had developed a severe cold and was indisposed. As his understudy Robert stepped into the part at an hour's notice, never having rehearsed with the other principals. He sang for the rest of the week and received much acclaim. On Saturday the local newspaper reported:

> The closing performance on Friday of *Frederica*, the operetta which played during the week in the King's Theatre, Glasgow, was noteworthy for the cordial reception given to Mr Robert Naylor who scored so remarkable a success on Thursday evening as deputy for Mr Joseph Hislop. It may be recalled that owing to indisposition, the famous tenor was unable to appear, and Mr Naylor was called upon at short notice. His success was satisfying in the extreme and among those who sent felicitations was Mr Hislop who telegraphed – 'All good wishes and thanks for holding the fort.' Mr Naylor has received instructions from Drury Lane to be in readiness as deputy in London this week should the need arise.[55]

Not for the first time fortune had smiled on Robert, and allowed him to unexpectedly step into someone else's shoes. The following year it would happen yet again, to even bigger acclaim.

Frederica opened at the Palace Theatre, Shaftesbury Avenue, on 9 September, with Hislop fully recovered from his cold. Once again Robert acted as his understudy and received a three-figure sum weekly contract. Unfortunately *The Times*'s review of the show was not entirely positive, the reviewer feeling that the show's storyline 'led to nothing more than pretentiousness'. There was praise for the leading lady, Miss Lea Seidl,[56] for whom the audience expressed its gratitude with 'real enthusiasm when the curtain fell'. But the paper considered that '[Hislop's] singing and acting hardly rose above the commonplace'.[57] The *Daily Telegraph* was much more favourable, praising Hislop's singing. In the end *Frederica* – in spite of Felix Edwards' delightful staging – ran for only 110 performances, finishing its run at the Palace Theatre on 14 December.

The score provided Robert with some strong material, and he recorded four of the numbers from *Frederica* during his début sessions for Parlophone during September and October. The label released all four sides in December 1930, hoping no doubt to take advantage of the Christmas market. The first was 'I Live For Your Love' coupled with 'O Maiden, My Maiden',[58] and the second disc coupled 'Wayside Rose' with 'Wonderful'.[59]

Around this time Robert bought his first motor car. It was a Talbot 14/45 (14 for the RAC Road Fund rating and 45 for the target brake horsepower), manufactured by Clement Talbot Ltd, Barlby Road, London W10. It had a 1666cc six cylinder overhead valve unit engine producing 45bhp and giving a top speed of about 60 mph. It was the only model produced by Talbot at this time and it sold for the relatively inexpensive price of £395. In a family photograph he proudly stands alongside it with Cecilia. Car ownership has always been closely related to income, and in the 1920s owning a car was way beyond the means of the average working man. The number of cars on the roads began to rise during that decade as manufacturers started to make small, lightweight and cheaper vehicles for a wider market. However, those owning their own car were still predominantly middle-class professional people. In London the number of driving licences issued rose from 100,000 in 1920 to 261,000 in 1930.

Robert appeared with the Wireless Military Band in a BBC London Regional broadcast on 10 October. The conductor was Charles Leggett, who began as a cornet player after joining the Scots

Guards Regimental Band. He rose to become principal professor of cornet at Kneller Hall, the Royal Military School of Music. He was one of the first musicians hired by the BBC in 1927 and he stayed with the organisation until his death. He became principal cornet, deputy conductor and general supervisor of the BBC Wireless Radio Orchestra, as well as of the Wireless Military Band.

The Concert Artistes Association held their first reunion and concert of the winter season on Sunday 19 October. The event drew a record crowd to the Café Royal. All seats were booked in advance, and even standing room was difficult. Music was provided by Robert and Cecilia (in what was by now a rare joint concert appearance) and another couple – David Jenkins and his wife, the versatile comedienne and singer Suzette Tarri. David Jenkins was a graduate of the Royal Academy of Music; in addition to singing bass in grand opera at Covent Garden, he was a pianist and songwriter.

As already noted, Robert had begun recording for the Parlophone Company Ltd, who had issued his first records in December 1930. The New Year saw a further release.[60] The two songs were 'Someday I'll Find You', from Noel Coward's musical play *Private Lives,* a number Coward had written especially for Gertrude Lawrence to sing, and 'The World Is Waiting For the Sunrise'. This was written by the Canadian pianist-songwriter Ernest Seitz and published by Chappel in 1919. The tune was a favourite with jazz musicians and, when played at break-neck speed, became a million seller for Les Paul and Mary Ford in 1949.

As the majority of Robert's recordings were issued on Parlophone between 1930 and 1933, it is worth looking at this label in some detail in order to see the part it played in the history of gramophone recording. The British Columbia Graphophone Company, originally an off-shoot of the American Columbia company, took over the German Lindstrom group, which included the Parlophon, Odeon and Phonotipia labels in early 1923. The group's £ trademark is not a British pound symbol but a German L for Lindstrom.

On 8 August 1923 Parlophone, with an 'e' added, was established in the UK; the label was headed by Oscar Preuss who had originally worked for the Lindstrom Company in Germany. Jumping ahead for a moment, in 1950 Preuss hired George Martin as an assistant A&R man (Artist and Repertoire). In 1955 Oscar Preuss retired and Martin succeeded him as head of the label.

When Martin took over from Preuss he inherited Judy Lockhart Smith as his PA; she had been PA to Oscar Preuss. Judy helped George Martin through the collapse of his first marriage, and they themselves got married in 1966. Through his signing of the Beatles and other pop groups, Martin turned Parlophone into one of the world's most famous and sought-after record labels.

The original Parlophone studio at 81 City Road, London EC1, while satisfactory for acoustic recording, was deemed unsuitable for the emerging system of electrical recording, and so by 1926 the company began looking for new premises. Preuss and his co-workers were already very familiar with the acoustic process, but they knew little or nothing about the new electrical process. Preuss recruited a young university student named Cyril Francis as his recording engineer, specifically to develop an electrical recording studio. It took nine months for them to find a studio and install and test equipment suitable for electrical recording. The place they found was on Carlton Hill between Maida Vale and St John's Wood, a former Presbyterian church that had opened in 1851 and was built in the Romanesque style. It ceased to be used for religious purposes in 1922 and was converted into a house and artist's studio in 1924. The building originally had no number, having been a place of worship, but was given the number 72A Carlton Hill.

The Parlophone recording studio at Carlton Hill became operational in about September 1927. Batteries were used to run the recording equipment. All of one vestry was required for two sets of batteries, a main set and a backup, while the other vestry housed the recording equipment. Batteries had to be used on the fixed installation because the studio was direct current.

The introduction of electrical recording (using microphones instead of horns) was a gradual one, with the changeover starting towards the end of 1924. During the next six years various labels stated that their content was 'Electrically Recorded' as a selling point. At Carlton Hill Parlophone used one microphone and did not have a mixer. They also only used one cutter per take. There were no equalisers, just a level control, and the balance was left to the engineer's skill and discretion. Levels were set by a meter calibrated in decibels. Normally a recording session lasted for about three hours, the aim being to produce four tracks in that time. This was no easy task: musicians had to get their performance right all the way through; if not, they had to repeat it from the beginning until they did. This cumbersome process put them under considerable strain.

In those 78rpm days, before the introduction of magnetic tape after the Second World War, recordings were inscribed on wax masters. The hard wax, prepared at the factory, was in vats, filtered to keep the mixture as smooth as possible and, after cooling and hardening in circular moulds, turned on a lathe in order to produce a smooth surface. The resulting wax blanks were packed in cases and sent out to the studios, where they were stored at the right temperature in a heated cupboard until they were needed. For recording, the wax was placed on the turntable of the recording machine where, in theory though by no means always in practice, it rotated at 78 rpm. A cutting head was then used to cut a groove from the outer edge of the wax disc towards the centre. This was originally done by a Westrex Moving Magnet cutter, which was licensed to most recording companies. However, in 1931 the brilliant Columbia engineer Alan Blumleim (1903–42; he died young in an air accident in the Second World War) invented the Moving Coil Disc Cutter. EMI went over to the new system as soon as they could: it gave cleaner recordings and saved the fees to Western Electric. The system was used first in the Columbia studio at Petty France, and became the standard at the new EMI studios in Abbey Road when they opened in November 1931.

In 1930 George Scott-Wood was appointed director of light music for the Parlophone label under Oscar Preuss. Scott-Wood was a former dance band pianist who provided arrangements and supplied accompaniments to a wide range of artistes, including Larry Adler, Webster Booth, Elsie Carlisle, Bebe Daniels and Ben Lyon, Gracie Fields, Flanagan and Allen, Hildegarde, Beatrice Lillie, Richard Tauber and Sophie Tucker.[61] It is more than likely he was also involved as the producer and arranger of many of Robert Naylor's Parlophone sessions. Because Scott-Wood was on the company's payroll, however, his name did not normally appear on the labels of records that he conducted.

George Scott-Wood was also regarded as one of the country's leading piano accordion experts. This instrument has gone out of fashion in recent decades, but there are still many brilliant exponents of the instrument. Scott-Wood was the author of the first ever comprehensive accordion tutor, *A Complete Detailed Method for the Piano Accordion*, which was published by Keith Prowse in 1930. Indeed, he is credited with having introduced the piano accordion to Great Britain, becoming its first professional exponent; his Accordion Band broadcast regularly throughout the war years and beyond. He was appointed chief advisor of light music at EMI in 1935.

The gramophone industry had been largely founded on middle-of-the-road operatic arias, but as sales of gramophones increased the record companies poured on to the market hundreds of releases in the belief that rich pickings were theirs to be had. On scores of different record labels could be found, for example, boy sopranos, military bands, Hawaiian groups, song and dance artistes, symphony orchestras, organists, choirs, accordion bands, folk singers, jazz musicians and novelty outfits of every conceivable kind. It was, in short, a musical cornucopia aimed at entertaining the masses and catering for as wide a market as possible.

In towns and cities across the country gramophone societies flourished. One such was the Bradford and District Gramophone and Phonograph Society, which on 28 May 1924 held its annual general meeting at the Society Rooms, Church House, Bradford. The report and balance sheet were presented, showing that the society was in a very sound position with an ever-growing roll of members and substantial financial funds. A survey of such societies carried out by *The Gramophone* magazine at this time noted that there was often a lack of light and shade in their musical programmes, with an over-emphasis on serious music at the expense of music of the lighter kind.[62] It would appear that these early societies were often run by middle-class intellectuals who used the new medium of the gramophone record purely for the advancement of highbrow culture.

Throughout the 1920s and until the 1930s sales of records showed a steady upward curve, until the effects of the Depression hit the recording industry like a tidal wave. Before the decade was out, sales of records had plummeted by over 80 per cent.[63] As a result of the contracting market the Columbia Graphophone Company and the Gramophone Company (HMV) agreed to a merger in March 1931. The new company was called Electric & Musical Industries, which became known as EMI. To begin with the creation of this new parent company did little to affect Robert's recording activities, although (as we shall see) it did later.

In February 1931 Robert was appearing at the Coliseum Theatre in Charing Cross, three times a day, in a show called *A Novel Interpretation of Liebestraum*. The music was by Franz Liszt (*Liebestraum*,[64] c. 1850). The show had its premier on 16 February 1931, and was produced by Sir Oswald Stoll, the Coliseum's managing director. The theatre business made Stoll a wealthy man. In 1898 he merged his business with that of Edward Moss, one of his competitors, to form Moss Empires. By 1905 almost every large town in Great Britain had an Empire or a Coliseum theatre, run by Stoll.

Liebestraum appears on programmes for the weeks beginning 16 and 23 February and 2 March – along with 'other dances produced by George Balanchine' (Director of Sergei Diaghilev's Russian Ballet). The Coliseum was distinguished by having 'the finest revolving stage in the world'. In his setting of *Liebestraum* Balanchine used the stage as a giant phonograph record, with a small dog in the centre as 'His Master's Voice' and the women as phonograph needles. The show included a personal appearance of Pola Negri (real name, Barbara Apolonia Chałupiec), a Polish film actress who achieved notoriety as a *femme fatale* in silent films between the 1910s and 1930s. Also on the bill was the Scottish comedy and revue act the Houston Sisters – Renee and Billie. In her later years Renee appeared as a battle-axe mother in the film *Carry On At Your Convenience* (1971).

In the week beginning 16 February Robert headlined at the London Palladium with the American soprano Edith Day. Miss Day was a beautiful dark-haired actress and singer born in Minneapolis on 10 April 1896. She became a major star, playing the title role in *Irene*, a musical comedy in two acts that had been written especially for her. Edith originally starred in the show on Broadway and left the New York cast to take the lead in London. The show opened at the London Empire Theatre on 7 April 1920 (produced by J.L. Sacks), where it ran for 399 performances. The show became a popular favourite, especially Edith's rendition of 'Alice Blue Gown', with music by Harry Tierney and words by Joseph McCarthy. The song has survived its original setting and has been recorded over the years by artistes as disparate as Duke Ellington and his Orchestra and organist Reginald Dixon. Edith was enthusiastically received in London by both audiences and critics ('a theatrical star of rare brilliance' said the *Daily Mail*) and decided to stay in England. She went on to have triumphs in *Rose Marie*, *The Desert Song* and *Showboat*, and became known as 'The Queen of Drury Lane'. At the time, such was her stardom, that she even had a cocktail named after her: the Edith Day comprises dry gin, grapefruit juice, sugar and egg white, and is best served over shaved ice in a champagne flute! While appearing in *Irene*, which was produced by her husband Carle Carlton, Edith developed a relationship with the show's male star Pat Somerset, which led to divorce proceedings by both parties. Retiring from acting in the 1930s, she briefly returned to the stage in 1960 in Noel Coward's *Waiting in the Wings*. Edith died in London in 1971, aged seventy-five.

Edith Day was the first of a number of female singing partners with whom Robert undertook sustained work. His partnership with her was particularly successful and lasted for many months.

On 28 March Robert broadcast an hour-long programme from London with the BBC Orchestra, conducted by Joseph Lewis. At this time Lewis was the senior conductor with the BBC; he later became conductor of the New Light Symphony Orchestra.

The following month produced a further dinner date. The Oil Industries Club is a prestigious organisation which was founded in 1925 and provides managers of the oil industry and allied trades with the opportunity to get to know each other outside normal business relationships. On Friday 17 April they held their annual dinner at the Mayfair Hotel, which had been opened by King George V only four years previously. Robert was among those engaged to provide the evening's entertainment.

Life and careers are full of the unexpected. This is especially true in show business, where a lucky-break is often dependent upon an artiste being in the right place at the right time. For Robert, who had already experienced his share of good fortune, the coming month would see the start of a chain of events that was destined to have a major impact on his career and future reputation.

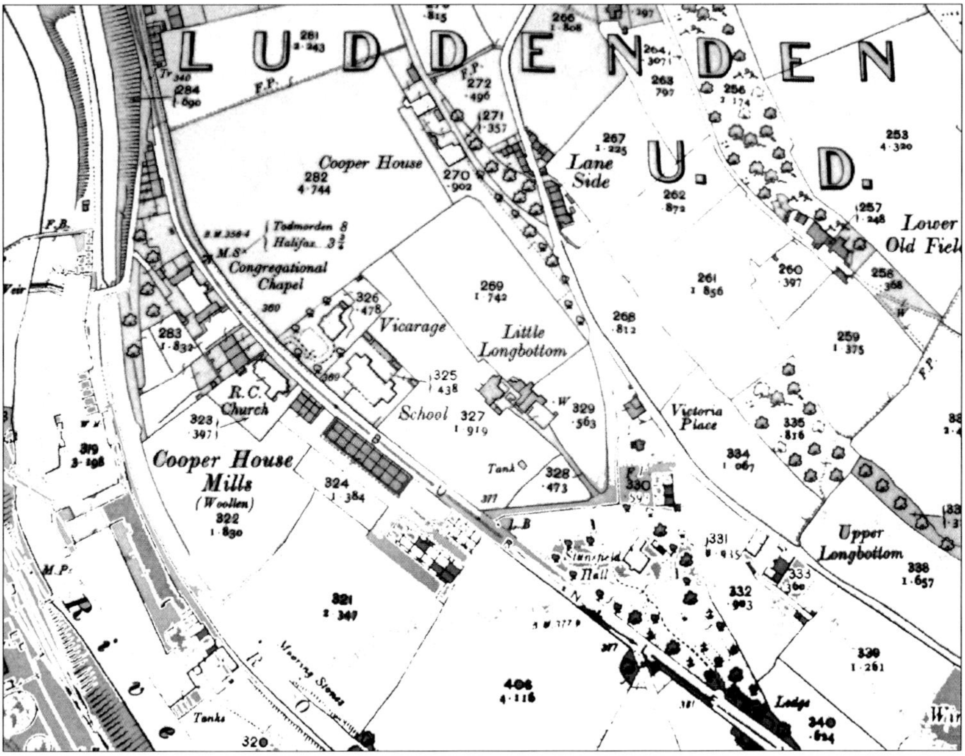

Map of Luddenden, Halifax, *c.* 1900. (Calderdale Library)

Robert helping his uncle at Shepherd House Farm, *c.* 1912.
(*Halifax Courier*)

Robert in *Cupid & the Ogre*, c. 1920. (Author's collection)

Herbert Teale, Robert's first music teacher. (Author's collection)

Fred Sutcliffe. (Author's collection)

Walter Widdop. (Author's collection)

Naylor family portrait, *c.* 1916. (Author's collection)

A certificate awarded to Robert at the Plymouth Festival, 1918.
(Author's collection)

Medal awarded to Robert at the Plymouth Festival, 1918.
(Author's collection)

Scottish Engineering Choral Festival medal, 1919.
(Author's collection)

Glasgow Choral Festival medal, 1919. (Author's collection)

Cecilia Farrar, aged about eighteen, photographed by Brigham Photographers of Scarborough and Bridlington. (Author's collection)

HIPPODROME,

TODMORDEN.

Lessee and General Manager, Mr. H. HARTLEY; Resident Manager, Mr. ALBERT E. NICHOLLS.

By kind permission of R. D'Oyly Carte, Esq.,

Gilbert & Sullivan's Opera THE

Yeomen of the Guard.

WILL BE GIVEN BY

The Todmorden Amateur Operatic Society,

FOR SIX NIGHTS,

JANUARY 17th to 22nd, 1921.

Commence at 7-30 p.m. (Overture 7-20).
Doors open 6-45 p.m.

Producer and Stage Manager, Mr. J. W. Helliwell. Musical Director, Mr W. Mitchell. Business Manager, Mr. A. Woodhead.

Dramatis Personæ.

Sir Richard Cholmondeley (Lieutenant of the Tower) .... Mr. W. P. FARRELL.
Colonel Fairfax (under sentence of death) .... Mr. R. NAYLOR.
Sergeant Meryll (of the Yeomen of the Guard) .... Mr. W. WOODHEAD.
Leonard Meryll (his son) .... Mr. J. H. THOMAS.
Jack Point (a Strolling Jester) .... Mr. J. W. HELLIWELL.
Wilfred Shadbolt (Head Jailor and Assistant Tormentor) .... Mr. F. GREENWOOD.
Elsie Maynard (a Strolling Singer) .... Miss CECILE FARRAR.
Phœbe Meryll (Sergeant Meryll's daughter) .... Miss JULIA GIBSON.
Dame Carruthers (Housekeeper to the Tower) .... Miss ADDYCE SHUTTLEWORTH.
Kate (her niece) .... Miss NORAH MASON.

Wardens.—Messrs. Woodhead, Peel, Simpson, Crossley, Ounliffe, Eastwood, Stansfield, Butterworth.

Citizens.—Messrs. Howarth, Mitchell, Veevers, Davis, Firth, Greenwood, Davis: Mdlles. Garner, Hasselby, Holden, Proctor, Bailey, Lever, Crabtree, Tamblin, Atkinson, Fielden, Greenwood, Heyworth, Baldwin, Woodhead, Firth.

ORCHESTRA.—Messrs. Ounliffe, Bentley, Ackroyd, Pavis, Nuttall, Crowther, Shuttleworth, Marshall, Lord, Helliwell, Marshall, Ackroyd, Ashworth, Clegg; Mdlles. Mitchell, Ashworth, Mitchell.

Costumes and Wigs by Messrs. F. A. Smith, Manchester.
Scenery by Messrs. Barrett and Sons, Pendleton.

PRICES OF ADMISSION (including Tax)—Dress Circle & Orchestra Stalls, 3s. 6d.; Pit Stalls, 2s. 4d.; Upper Circle, 1s. 6d.; Pit, 9d.
No extra charge for booking. Seats booked at the Hippodrome. Seats not guaranteed unless previously booked.

Tickets may be obtained at HIPPODROME and from Members of the Caste.

Busses for Portsmouth, Eastwood and Walsden will leave the Hippodrome at the close of the performance each evening (Tuesday, Wednesday, Thursday and Friday).

SPECIAL NOTE.—THE SERIALS. "SMASHING BARRIERS," Monday, Tuesday and Wednesday. "BLACK SECRET," Thursday and Friday. "LOST CITY," Saturday. Will be shown each evening respectively at 7 p.m. prompt, and there will be the usual Pictures Matinee on Saturday Afternoon.

Poster for *The Yeomen of the Guard*, Todmorden, 1921.
(Author's collection)

Robert as Colonel Fairfax in *The Yeomen of the Guard*, 1921.
(Author's collection)

Cecilia as Elsie Maynard in *The Yeomen of the Guard*, 1921.
(Author's collection)

Montana, Robert's home from 1921 until his marriage. (Bob Naylor)

Robert, *c.* 1922. (Author's collection)

Cecilia, *c.* 1922. (Author's collection)

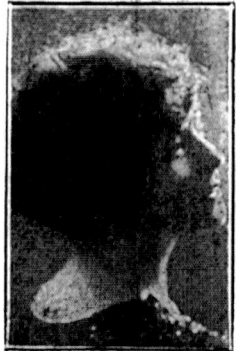

Robert and Cecilia's wedding
portrait, 22 September 1922.
(Author's collection)

Robert and Cecila's wedding,
reported in the Halifax paper.
(Author's collection)

VOCALISTS' WEDDING.

Mr. R. Naylor and Miss C. Farrar, well-known local vocalists, were
married at Cornholme yesterday.   Block: "Courier."

A studio portrait of Robert, early 1920s. (Author's collection)

Cecilia in a portrait taken at the Knightsbridge Studio, Brompton Road, London, 1925. (Author's collection)

The Queens Hall, London: the original venue of the Promenade concerts. (Author's collection)

Landon Ronald, composer and Principal of the Guildhall School of Music. (Author's collection)

CHAPTER FOUR
The Land of Smiles

On 30 April 1931 *The Times* reported: 'Herr Franz Lehár, the well known composer, is expected in London within the next few days to attend the final rehearsals of his new musical play *The Land of Smiles*, which is to be staged at Drury Lane Theatre on Friday May 8th. This will be Herr Lehár's first appearance in London since 1907, when he came here for the opening performance of *The Merry Widow*. It is possible Herr Lehár will stay in London throughout the run of the play. Mr Ernest Irving will be in charge of the orchestra, but Herr Lehár may conduct at least part of each performance.'

Bringing *The Land of Smiles* to London was the brainwave of a young businessman named Stanley H. Scott. In the early part of 1931 he went to visit Lehár in Vienna, not only to secure *The Land of Smiles* but also to secure the services of the tenor Richard Tauber. It was felt that nobody could sing Lehár's music quite like Tauber and the combination of composer and singer had proved a winning combination abroad. Scott was apparently an extremely self-confident young man given to wishful thinking and grandiose schemes, and saw himself in the role as a successful impresario. He was, to use the well-known expression, tall, dark and handsome, and like many of his generation high-spirited and hedonistic; his life revolved around having a good time. He knew a lot of theatrical people and he thought he knew a thing or two about the theatre.[65]

So confident was Scott of the show's success that he persuaded George Grossmith, general manager at Drury Lane, to promise him that he could have London's most famous theatre for *The Land of Smiles,* and it was being able to offer such a prestigious venue that enabled Scott to secure the deal with Lehár.[66] Scott may have been a novice at the game, but George Grossmith was, by contrast, from a theatrical family. He was a very experienced theatre producer, as well as being an actor, playwright and songsmith. For many years he had been the senior half of the production firm Grossmith and Laurillard, which had many successes to its credit. He had only just been appointed as Drury Lane's general manager, at a tiime when the theatre was not doing very well. Grossmith was looking for a successful production to prove his worth, and *The Land of Smiles* seemed to be just the ticket.

The Theatre Royal, Drury Lane, lies in Covent Garden, although the building actually faces Catherine Street (earlier named Bridges or Brydges Street) and backs onto Drury Lane. It is London's oldest theatre, having been originally erected in 1663 under a charter granted by 'the merrie monarch' Charles II. Steeped in history, and alleged to be haunted, for its first two centuries it was London's leading theatre and therefore one of the most important theatres in the English-speaking world. Today's building, Grade I listed, is the fourth to stand on the site, and opened in 1812. It is a four-tier house with a capacity of 2,283, a proscenium opening of 42ft, and a stage depth of 80ft. Today it is owned by composer Andrew Lloyd Webber and generally stages popular musical theatre.

Stanley Scott took offices in the Strand and started to work on bringing the production to fruition. The producer was Felix Edwardes, who had produced many shows at Drury Lane.For the London premier Scott hired an eccentric journalist, writer and poet named Harry Graham to write English lyrics for the show. Graham was educated at Eton and Sandhurst and served in the Coldstream Guards. During the First World War he turned to writing lyrics for English operettas and musical comedies, including *Tina* (1915), *Sybil* (1916), the hit operetta *The Maid of the Mountains* (1917) and *A Southern Maid* (1920). He also wrote English adaptations for

European operettas such as *Madame Pompadour* (1923) and *Victoria and Her Hussar* (1931).

Scott also hired a publicity man to generate interest in the forthcoming production and to create a buzz of expectation around the arrival of the show's star, Richard Tauber. As a result, in the spring of 1931 Tauber, *The Land of Smiles* and of course Lehár all became newsworthy. Scott himself never lost an opportunity to shout about the glories of his forthcoming show, and in his over-active imagination he was convinced he could already hear the first night cheers and the sound of money pouring into the box office. He also took pains to ensure his photograph – in which he looks for all the world like a brooding Hollywood film star – was included when the theatre programmes were printed.

The Land of Smiles's composer, Franz Lehár, was an Austro-Hungarian who in 1931 was at the height of his fame. He was the son of a band sergeant major in the Austrian Army, who gave him his first music lessons. Lehár later studied violin and composition at the Prague Conservatory. International fame came in 1905 with his operetta *The Merry Widow*; this tuneful and vivacious musical comedy was destined to become a stage classic. It was followed by various other successes, including *Gypsy Love* (1910), *The Count of Luxembourg* (1911), *Eva* (1911), *Frasquita* (1922) and *Frederica* (1928). Lehár had celebrated his sixtieth birthday the previous year and there were some five hundred different productions of Lehár operettas in Europe, of which two hundred were *The Land of Smiles*.[67] These productions, staged in various European cities, had made him a very wealthy man.

The Vienna production of *Frasquita* in 1922 brought Lehár for the first time into contact with the young operatic tenor Richard Tauber. The effect on Lehár was electric, and between 1925 and 1934 he wrote six operettas especially for Tauber's voice, each with an endless flow of lyrical songs, duets and ensembles, and each including what became known as the 'Tauber-Lied' – a signature tune that exploited the exceptional qualities of the tenor's voice. On this occasion it was '*Dein Ist Mein Ganzes Herz*' (You Are My Heart's Delight), probably the most famous of all the Tauberlieder. *The Land of Smiles* (*Das Land des Lächelns*) was first performed at the Metropol Theatre, Berlin, in 1929, with Tauber in the leading role. It is considered to be the pinnacle of his long and successful association with the composer.[68]

Richard Tauber was the illegitimate son of the actor Richard Anton Tauber and the actress Elizabeth Seiffert. He was born in Linz (Upper Austria) on 16 May 1891. He had sung with the Vienna State Opera and the Berlin State Opera, and was acclaimed as one of the greatest singers of the twentieth century, with a lyrical, flexible tenor voice, excellent breath control and a warm, elegant legato. Tauber was elegant in appearance too, despite a slight squint in his right eye which he disguised by wearing a monocle; this, when accompanied by a top hat, added to the effect. For many people he was the epitome of Viennese charm. Tauber's career was interrupted by the war. He eventually settled in England for fear of Nazi persecution (he was of Jewish extraction), becoming a naturalised citizen in 1940. Dying from lung cancer on 8 January 1948, Richard Tauber is buried in Brompton Cemetery, London.

The Land of Smiles was Tauber's London début, and his appearance was eagerly awaited.

Unfortunately he had been very ill in 1929, paralysed by rheumatoid arthritis for three months; he was also being blackmailed by his first wife over his inability to consummate their marriage. *The Land of Smiles* was his first major show after his illness, and the costumes were designed to hide his infirmities. Although he lived in fear that his illness would return and incapacitate him further, no one, least of all Stanley Scott, seemed to be aware of the stress under which the star was living.

The leading lady was the beautiful soprano Miss Renee Bullard, a leading female singer from the Vienna State Opera Company who had been specially imported for the part of Lisa. She was an English-born artiste who had spent much of her life in Vienna and had become a member of the State Opera there. The part of Princess Mi was played by the equally attractive soprano Hella Kurty, a role which she had created in the original production of the show at the Metropol, Berlin and also at the first production at the Theater an der Wien in Vienna.

During rehearsals Robert Naylor was appointed as Tauber's understudy.

According to McQueen-Pope, on the day of Tauber's arrival Scott went down to Dover to meet him, and the pair returned by train to Victoria station. Later that evening a press conference took place, and as a result a lot of space was given to Tauber in the following morning's papers. Rehearsals began the next day. Tauber, who liked to play the big shot, arrived at the front entrance to the theatre, not the stage door, in a white limousine. During the rehearsals Tauber, when he chose to attend, neither acted nor sang a note. At the dress rehearsal everything was as it should be, with the magnificent Drury Lane orchestra under the baton of Ernest Irving (soon to become famous for his film scores) and everyone in costume and make-up – everyone except for Tauber, that is, who went through the motions of singing while wearing his street clothes.

Those who had seen the show in Berlin or Vienna raved about it, and as a result there was a big demand for seats – ranging from 12s 6d in the stalls, to £1 11s 6d for the best private box. On the opening night, Friday 8 May 1931, Drury Lane was packed with a smart and fashionable audience, and expectations were running high. When the curtain rose on the first act it displayed a beautiful scene set in 'The house of General Count Lichtenfels in Vienna'. Tauber's entrance was awaited with impatience. When he appeared – a short, thickly built man in evening dress – he was wearing make-up to make him look oriental, which gave his face a yellowish hue. He was not a handsome man and had a rather ungainly walk and gestures, which may have been occasioned by his rheumatoid arthritis. Tauber sang wonderfully, however, and was given a rapturous reception by the audience, some of whom had taken their places in the queues thirty-six hours before the curtain rose.

However, despite the audience reception, the illustrious cast and the show's previous success on the Continent, the English theatre critics were less than kind. Although *The Times* gave the show a fair review, it complained about 'the extreme stiffness of the action, particularly in the first act, which consists of solos by Herr Richard Tauber and duets for him and Miss Bullard. These, though charming in themselves, stand solidly in the way of the play's movement. Indeed the stage is an embarrassment to them, and the half-dozen irrelevant ladies who supply Herr Tauber with an excuse for one of his songs would have been better away.'[69] Other critics were less reserved in their comments. The *Yorkshire Post* unflatteringly described Herr Tauber as 'looking like Signor Mussolini' and felt that '*The Land of Smiles* is a far more pretentious work musically than Lehár's *Merry Widow* or *Frederica.* It is elaborately scored for a large orchestra, there are no dance numbers worth mentioning, the chorus has practically nothing to do, and substantial merits of the music do not include the quality of simplicity . . .' The reviewer added that 'the piece is without humour, and all the characters have an exasperating habit of referring to Chinese as Chinamen. They might as well, of course, say "Chinks" and be done with it.'[70]

On the second night Tauber arrived at the theatre complaining of a bad throat and said that he couldn't sing. Stanley Scott fumed at this, and summoned a throat specialist. McQueen-Pope recalls that in the audience this particular evening was the Princess Royal, daughter of the king. Scott warned Tauber that if he failed to perform it would spell ruin for his career. There was an angry scene, but in the end Tauber sang – just as well as he had done the night before. The following day, being Sunday, there was no performance, but on the Monday morning Tauber dropped a bombshell: he refused to perform that evening. Whether the cause was the poor notices in the press, home sickness or the throat trouble of which he was complaining, he was adamant. Monday evening was only the show's third performance, the house was sold out, and it was imperative to all concerned to keep the curtain up. There was nothing for it: despite the short notice, the understudy had to perform.

Despite the backstage crisis Robert was calm and collected; he knew the part – both words and music – and he confirmed he was ready to go on. It is disheartening to be an understudy, however good you may be: you go on knowing that the audience doesn't want to see you at all; that they will sympathetically applaud, but wish you weren't there. However, Robert's fine voice rang out that evening, and he soon had the audience enraptured. At the end of the show his performance was tumultuously received and he took encore after encore, singing 'You Are My Heart's Delight' six times. Whatever shock he must have felt in taking over after only two performances, he overcame his fears, and Robert left the stage that night to tremendous acclaim.

'I must confess,' he said afterwards, 'it was a great ordeal to follow such a wonderful singer as Tauber, especially as I had never been through the second and third acts before. I felt that the audience had come to hear Tauber, and my wife was even more nervous. She would not enter the theatre and sat in the car outside. But when it was all over the audience showed much appreciation, and I have quite recovered my confidence.' He received shoals of congratulatory messages of success.[71]

It appears that Tauber watched Robert's performance on the night of 11 May, because the following day he sent Robert a congratulatory telegram: 'Sincere Congratulations on your beautiful performance last night it makes me happy and quiet to know that during my indisposition the part of Souchong is being performed with such great success. Auf Wiedersehen – Richard Tauber'.[72]

On the Tuesday morning Tauber's absence from the show was front-page news. One paper reported that 'Drury Lane has never known, the theatre world has never known, such a startling, such a dramatic, such an unexpected withdrawal from a cast at short notice of so highly-paid an artiste as Richard Tauber.'[73]

Unperturbed by all the brouhaha, Robert stood in for Tauber from 11 to 16 May. During this week the show was seen by Sydney W. Carroll, the theatre critic of the *Daily Telegraph*, who told his readers that Robert gave a superb rendering of the role.

On Monday 18 May Tauber returned for the remainder of the week. Then in the week beginning 25 May he was ill again. *The Times* reported: 'Herr Tauber, the tenor of *The Land of Smiles* at Drury Lane Theatre was examined yesterday by a throat specialist, who advised him to rest. He will probably leave London today for Switzerland. His voice almost broke down during Monday night's performance, and his later numbers had to be curtailed. He is now leaving the cast. The inflammation of the throat from which he has been suffering appeared on the second night.'[74]

Consequently, from Tuesday 26 May Robert took over the lead role once more. The theatre critic in *Punch* caught Robert's performance that evening: 'On the occasion of my attendance, the widely-regretted indisposition of Herr Richard Tauber threw the burden of the long and exacting part of *Prince Sou Chong* on Mr ROBERT NAYLOR. Mr Naylor has a fine ringing tenor and won from the audience something much more than the friendly applause that is given out of sympathy for a courageous and competent understudy. He was compelled by our enthusiasm to sing the flagrantly romantic 'You Are My Heart's Delight' no fewer than four times (a little "plugging" and "reprising" imposed it upon him a few times more); and he won himself merit with a love-song in the (alleged) Chinese manner.[75]

Although the report that Tauber had 'left the cast' sounded permanent, Scott swore, in fact, that Tauber would return. Meanwhile the theatre had printed a new edition of the show's programme in which Tauber's name and picture were removed and Robert's name and picture were inserted. Three weeks later Tauber returned, brought back to London by Lehár himself, and resumed his part for a second time from Monday 15 June. Robert performed the starring role for the last time on the 13th. His appearance on stage at Drury Lane during the previous two weeks had been, without doubt, a personal and professional triumph, as the *Halifax Daily Courier & Guardian* reported:

> Mr Robert Naylor, England's great tenor, and a native of Halifax, scored another triumph at Drury Lane theatre on Saturday when he ended his engagement as deputy for the German £1,500 a week singer, Tauber in Franz Lehár's *The Land of Smiles*. Tauber was back in the theatre after his spell of recuperation in Germany, but the occasion was perhaps more notable for the presence of Herr Lehár himself who occupied the Royal box and who frequently showed his appreciation of the tenor's voice. It can be truthfully said that Mr Naylor rose to the occasion and he said he never felt in such form. The audience after the final curtain, again and again, demanded his reappearance but when the cries of 'speech' were raised he gracefully pointed to the distinguished occupant of the box. Herr Lehár, speaking in English, thanked the audience for the wonderful reception of the opera and the artistes for so ably fulfilling their tasks.
>
> Behind the scenes there was another happy incident. Herr Lehár lost no time in

meeting the young singer, who had so courageously and ably filled the breach after Tauber's breakdown, and Mr Naylor provided a pleasant surprise. Speaking in excellent German, which with the help of his dresser Schultz, he had previously mastered, Mr Naylor said, 'I'm happy to have the opportunity of meeting you, Herr Lehár, and to have the honour of singing your opera in my native country.' To this the composer replied in English by saying he was very delighted to have heard Mr Naylor, whom he congratulated on the wonderful interpretation of the part, and also on the natural beauty of his voice. It is gratifying to add that two famous producers, who were among Saturday's distinguished audience, have made proposals to Mr Naylor for his services in the near future. These he is considering.[76]

Some days later it was reported: 'There has been a pleasant sequel to the meeting of Mr Robert Naylor, the Halifax tenor, and Herr Franz Lehár, the composer of *Land of Smiles* at Drury Lane Theatre. Yesterday, Mr Naylor received by post a medallion, and in the same box a personal note of congratulation in the handwriting of Herr Lehár, thus showing his further appreciation of Mr Naylor's talent.'[77]

A correspondent in the Halifax paper wrote: '. . . we went to Drury Lane last Saturday. It was Mr. Naylor's last night, and we felt that would be the best time to help to give him a rousing reception and farewell.' When he arrived to book tickets he was told he ought to wait until the German tenor returned, as there was only an understudy at present. The correspondent continued:

I suppose it would be bad business to allow it to be known that an English-man could do the job as well. I have not heard Mr. Tauber – but several people in the foyer in

67

the interval had done so – and expressed
their indignation at the way Naylor was
being treated, for they said he was quite as
good. Perhaps national prejudice swayed
them a little in this judgment, but,
personally, I cannot imagine any singer
giving me greater pleasure than he did.
Never have we enjoyed singing so much.
Naylor's voice has improved marvellously,
also his stage technique. We were really and
truly entranced, and our applause was the
very sincere outburst of our enthusiasm. He
was encored and encored – his great song in
the second act was encored five times and in
the end he had seven curtains...others in
different parts of the house were shouting
'Naylor!' 'Bobby Naylor!'[78]

Despite Tauber's return to the show, the cast disruptions and the
poor reviews meant that the show had lost its momentum: what
should have been a glittering success began to fade. Business fell
away, as nobody could guarantee when Tauber was going to sing.
As a result of poor ticket sales the show became 'evenings only'
from 11 June, and the matinée performances on Wednesday
and Saturday afternoon at 2.30pm were dropped. Not even the
attendance at the theatre of their Majesties King George V and
Queen Mary on Monday 22 June could halt the decline: the
damage was done. The curtain fell for the last time on Saturday
18 July, with a loss to the backers of thousands of pounds.

McQueen-Pope, who was there at first hand to witness this
theatrical episode, is somewhat unforgiving of Tauber and his
role in the débâcle. '*The Land of Smiles*,' he writes, 'a born
winner if ever there was one, ran at Drury Lane for a mere
seventy-two performances and all because of the temperament,
bad sportsmanship, and complete unreliability of a tenor . . . He
had no thought of his own reputation, of his companions in the
company, or of his manager Stanley Scott.'[79] McQueen-Pope's
indignation, while understandable, is perhaps a little unfair.

Tauber was, after all, a dedicated artiste who did not like to let his public down. He must have felt wretched about the Drury Lane fiasco. In the coming years he sang successfully in further productions of *The Land of Smiles* with Josie Fearon, both in London and on tour, and did much to redeem his reputation among critics and theatre management. He remained hugely popular with English audiences.

In Tauber's absence Robert was not given star billing; that privilege was given temporarily to the show's leading lady, Renee Bullard. Yet he bore no resentment, and many years later he recalled what a pleasure it had been to play opposite Renee Bullard as Lisa and Hella Kürty, whom he described as being 'A great little Mi'.[80]

Those weeks performing in the cathedral-like grandeur of the Theatre Royal, where he received both professional and public acclaim, were regarded, not least by Robert himself, as his crowning achievement. Stepping into the shoes of a £1,500-a-week man, and at a moment's notice, added a touch of glamour to his name. Of the seventy-two performances staged of *The Land of Smiles*, Robert had starred in thirty-four. For the remainder of his career he was always requested to sing 'You Are My Heart's Delight', and became resigned to hearing himself referred to as 'The English Tauber'.

CHAPTER FIVE
The Variety Circuit 1931-1934

uring May 1931 Robert recorded four selections from *The Land of Smiles* for Parlophone. The first disc[81] included, not surprisingly, 'You Are My Heart's Delight', which was coupled with 'Patiently Smiling', a song heard in Act 1 of the show. This was the best-selling record of his career and 'You Are My Heart's Delight' became the song most associated with him. The second disc,[82] released the same month, coupled 'Beneath The Window of My Love', a solo by Robert, with 'A Cup of Tea With You', a duet for the hero and heroine. At Drury Lane Robert sang this with his co-star Renee Bullard, but on the Parlophone recording Lisa's part is sung by the English soprano Olive Groves.

Olive Groves was born in Hampstead and began her musical studies as a child. She made her professional debut in 1925 at the Lyric Theatre, appearing in *Lionel And Clarissa*, a largely forgotten opera by Charles Dibdin (*c*. 1745-1814). She first broadcast in 1926. According to the information found on Radio Celebrity No. 19, a cigarette card published by W.D. & H.O. Wills, Olive came to the microphone through a coincidence. Her father was in the

Army of Occupation in Germany just after the First World War, and Miss Groves went over to Cologne to entertain the troops. Years later in the Strand someone stopped her, and asked if she was the young girl who had sung at Cologne. The man was a BBC official, and as a result of this chance meeting Miss Groves was booked as a singer. She was very famous in Britain throughout the '30s. She became the second wife of the singer George Baker, who made hundreds of recordings himself, most notably of Gilbert and Sullivan songs for HMV. He was the BBC's overseas music director from 1944 to 1947, and for thirty years served the Royal Philharmonic Society as committee member, treasurer and chairman.

On Thursday 25 July Robert was heard on the BBC's London Regional station in a concert with Fred Adlington's New Octet. Adlington was a violinist, arranger and composer of light music. He died three months after this broadcast, on 7 October, aged only thirty-nine.

In addition to recording and broadcasting, Robert's personal appearances continued. The *London Weekly Diary of Social Events* (a publication sponsored by hotels, restaurants and theatres in the capital and made available to customers) noted that on Sunday 16 August 1931 he was to sing at Alexander Palace in the evening, in a programme that included the Welsh Guards.

During the week commencing 14 September Robert was back with Edith Day at the Palladium Theatre, presenting *Songs from the Shows*. Also on the bill were Charles Austin and his company in 'a new sketch entitled *Parker's Irish Sweep*'. Charles Austin was a comedian, born Charles Reynolds in the East End in 1879. He was a highly popular entertainer in his day, and owned a houseboat moored at Cigarette Island, near Hampton Court. Houseboats were particularly popular with music hall artistes and with the gay young set of the times. Apparently the peace of a summer's evening was regularly disturbed by the sound of wild Bohemian parties on the River Thames.

During September 1931 ten thousand floodlights turned London into the world's brightest city, to honour Michael Faraday who, one hundred years before, had discovered the principles of electricity. In the greatest revel since Armistice night, crowds jammed the parks and streets. Robert and Cecilia themselves had much to celebrate, for after nine years of marriage Cecilia was three months pregnant.

Also during September Robert appeared at the Capitol Picture Theatre, 11–15 London Road, Forest Hill. When the theatre was not showing its current film (Sydney Howard in *Up for the Cup*), Robert was performing on stage, 'direct from Drury Lane', at 3.30pm, 6.00pm and 9.00pm with De Groot and his Famous Orchestra. Like many such noble establishments, the cinema spent its declining years as a bingo hall; it is now a J.D. Wetherspoon's pub.

In the first week of October 1931 Robert and Edith Day were again appearing twice-nightly on a variety bill at the Palladium. Sharing the bill were the dancing trio the Wiere Brothers, and Flanagan and Allen, the singing comedy double-act who became hugely popular in the Second World War, with songs like 'Underneath The Arches' and 'Run, Rabbit, Run'. While Robert and Edith always performed their musical numbers seriously, theirs was an act in which they used comedy and humour to engage with the audience between the songs. This was, after all, variety and not the concert platform.

The BBC presented a programme of Franz Lehár's music on 15 October 1931, with the BBC Theatre Orchestra conducted by Ernest Irving. It starred Robert Naylor and the soprano Tessa Deane. Miss Deane might have been a professional pianist instead of a popular radio singer. Winning the pianoforte scholarship at the Royal College of Music, she studied under Arthur Alexander before discovering that she had a voice, and turning her talents and enthusiasm towards musical comedy. She began broadcasting on the air in variety and in operetta. The show's conductor, Ernest Irving (1878–1953), is primarily remembered for his involvement in film music. He composed the score to the Ealing comedy *Whisky Galore!* and *Turned Out Nice Again,* starring George Formby.

Three days later, on the afternoon of 18 October, Robert performed at the Palladium in an all-star concert given in aid of the Newspaper Vendors' Benevolent and Provident Institution. Also appearing was the Shakespearian actress Phyllis Nielson-Terry, who was currently starring in *Elizabeth of England* at the Cambridge Theatre. Many years later she appeared in the Tony Richardson film *Look Back in Anger.* Other artists on the programme included

Edith Day, the comedienne Elsie Randolph, the actress Fay Compton, the American heavyweight xylophone player Teddy Brown, the actor Jack Buchanan, and Jack Hylton and His Band. Billy Caryll and Hilda Mundy, a variety double-act, acted as Masters of Ceremonies. The concert raised nearly £1,500.

On 20 October Robert performed with Edith Day on a BBC radio programme called *Vaudeville*, which included the vocalist Geoffrey Gwyther. He had appeared with Edith the previous year at the Prince Edward Theatre on Old Compton Street in *Rio Rita,* a romantic musical comedy set in Mexico. The show had been a big hit in New York, but sadly did not find similar success with London audiences and closed after fifty-nine performances. Day and Gwyther had also recorded two of the show's numbers for Columbia.[83] Also on the programme were the husband and wife comedy double-act Claude Hulbert and Enid Trevor and the comedy duo Clapham and Dwyer. In his previous life Clapham had been a clerk in the office of the King's Counsel, while Dwyer had been a commercial traveller. After their partnership was formed a booking came in the first week, for a private party before the Duke and Duchess of York (later King George VI and Queen Elizabeth). At their BBC audition they were asked to sing. Replying that they couldn't, they talked the first nonsense that came into their heads – and got the booking. Bill Dwyer, who tried to be sensible, was the fat one; Charlie Clapham, with monocle and moustache, the 'silly ass' who could never find the right word at the right time, was the thin one. Also on the bill were Paul England and Pat Patterson (comedy songs) and the Wireless Male Voice Chorus.

Around October 1931 Parlophone issued two new discs of duets, featuring Robert Naylor and the soprano Dorothy Bennett. The previous year Miss Bennett had sung with the BBC Symphony Orchestra conducted by Henry Wood. Both releases were designed to cash in on two shows currently being performed in the West End. For their first disc together they recorded 'Love Will Find You' and 'While You Love Me'.[84] These songs came from the stage production of *Waltzes from Vienna,* which had opened at the Alhambra Theatre, Leicester Square, on 17 August. Originally presented at the Stadttheatre, Vienna, the show was adapted for the London stage by Desmond Carter, Caswel Garth, G.H. Clutsam and Hubert Griffiths. The plot centres upon the tension between

Strauss the elder and Strauss the younger, a tension engendered by the son's ambitions to succeed his father as the Waltz King of Vienna.

On 9 November Robert and Edith starred in *Songs from the Shows* at the Bristol Hippodrome. The supporting cast included the variety artiste Bristol-born Randolph Sutton, who was one of the last of the latter-day *lions comiques* of the Music Hall. They were the heart-throbs of the Victorian era. Known as 'swells', these character singers dressed as fashionable, swaggering young men and sang songs about high life and drinking champagne. While their songs boasted about being seen at the most fashionable places, their attitude was distinctly laddish. Sutton became famous for his recording of 'On Mother Kelly's Doorstep'. Also on the bill were Hetty King (a famous music hall performer and male impersonator), Frank Tully, Jack and Lyle Jeffries, Bobby Orlac, the Yeates Sisters, Bert Hoppin, Frank and Betty Boston, and the Macari Brothers.

Robert and Dorothy's second release in November contained 'Goodnight' and 'Pardon Madam',[85] a couple of songs from *Victoria and her Hussar*, an operetta in three acts that had opened at the Palace Theatre, Shaftesbury Avenue, in September. *The Times* reported, 'The play has been a notable success on the Continent, and last year there were 34 companies playing it in Germany, Austria, and Hungary. The music is by a young Hungarian Paul Abraham, and the English book and lyrics have been prepared by Captain Harry Graham.'[86] The story was a romantic tale of a long-lost lover, with locations ranging from Tokyo to St Petersburg.

In November EMI opened their new recording studios at Abbey Road. The house at 3 Abbey Road, St John's Wood, had been purchased in 1929 with a view to transforming it into the world's first custom-built recording studio. Work began on the sixteen-roomed residence – which had nine bedrooms, five reception rooms, two servant rooms, a wine cellar and a 250ft garden – and in just under two years it was complete. Three varying sized studios were built in the garden and neighbouring garden spaces in order to accommodate the different sorts of music that were being recorded at that time – full orchestra, string quartets, choirs, instrumental soloists and singers. Abbey Road studios was the first custom-built studio complex of its kind anywhere in the world.[87] For the moment, however, Robert continued to record at the Parlophone studio at Carlton Hill.

On Saturday 5 December, between 9.40pm and 10.00pm on the BBC National Programme, Robert and Edith were heard together again in a performance relayed from the Palladium Theatre, where they were appearing in a variety show. *The Times* noted, 'The entertainment at the Palladium this week, apart from one or two interludes which allow artistes like Miss Edith Day and Mr Robert Naylor to give pleasure to the audience in their own way, is one continuous "rag". Through accident or enterprise, Nervo and Knox, Naughton and Gold, and Billy Caryll appear in the same programme, and this rare combination of comedians has been given a free hand to provoke laughter.'

In December Parlophone issued a recording of Robert singing 'Love Everlasting' (*L'amour, toujours l'amour),* words by Catherine Chisholm Cushing and music by Rudolf Friml, which had been recorded in September.[88] On the reverse was 'A Southern Song', an attractive number written by Landon Ronald and taken from a 1905 collection called *In Sunshine and Shadow,* which also included 'The Dove', 'Tis June', 'As A Dream', 'The White Sea Mist' and 'Peace And Rest'. A contemporary record reviewer felt that Robert scored well in his interpretation of 'A Southern Song'.

During December Robert was back in the studio, this time with Edith Day. They recorded two songs which she had sung hundreds of times on stage – 'The Desert Song' and 'Indian Love Call'.[89] Edith had starred in the original London production of *The Desert Song,* music by Sigmund Romberg, in 1927 at the Theatre Royal, Drury Lane. By this time, as the jazz age was sweeping in, it was an archaic survivor of the romantic era of Viennese-style operetta; but the melodramatic tale, set in the Sahara and inspired by the exploits of Lawrence of Arabia and the image of Rudolph Valentino, made it a box-office success. Edith had also starred in *Rose-Marie,* with music by Rudolph Friml and produced at Drury Lane in 1925. From this show comes the song 'Indian Love Call'. It was the first musical to be set in Canada, and it featured the Rockies and the Canadian Mounties. The writers of the book and lyrics, Otto Harbach and Oscar Hammerstein, made a trip to Canada to get it right, and came up with a heart-stirring love story between a singer, Rose-Marie, and a fur trapper. *Rose-Marie* ran for two years, and was London's most successful Broadway show after the First World War until it was surpassed by *Oklahoma!*, which opened at the Theatre Royal, Drury Lane, on 30 April 1947.

The year 1932 began for Robert and Edith with a week's variety show at the Victoria Palace Theatre from 18 January. Also appearing was the comedian Tommy Handley, later to find fame in the BBC show *ITMA* (*It's That Man Again*). *The Times* rather condescendingly noted, 'This week Mr Naylor and Miss Day sing before a background which does not seem quite decided whether it's intended to be an intimate, domestic interior, or a ballroom, in the third act of a musical comedy, but their well-known songs are at any rate enjoyable and honest enough in their sentimental intentions.'[90]

Also on 18 January Robert was heard on the radio again in another vaudeville programme for the BBC. Once more he sang duets with Edith. The show also included the northern comedian Stainless Stephen, whose real name was Arthur Clifford Baines. His hallmark was interrupting the flow of his intoned monologue by supplying the 'punctuation': 'This is Stainless aimless brainless Stephen, semi-colon, broadcasting semi-conscious at the microphone semi-frantic.' Perhaps it wasn't the greatest material ever, but the listening public loved it. Stainless Stephen also appeared in the Royal Command Performance in 1945. He died in Leeds in 1971. Also to be heard in the broadcast were A. McGill and Gwen Vaughan ('The Cheerful Chatterers'), Dorothy McBlain (*siffleuse*),[91] M. Lorenzi (harp), Scott and Whaley ('entertainers'), the Gresham Singers and the BBC Theatre Orchestra.

The New Year also saw further recordings by Robert made available. The first coupled 'The Song Of Songs' with 'For You Alone'.[92] 'Song Of Songs' (*Chanson du coeur brisé*), also called 'Song Of A Broken Heart', was written in 1919 by 'Moya', a pseudonym for the pianist and conductor Harold Vicars; the words were by Clarence Lucas and Maurice Vaucaire. The song was widely recorded during the '20s and '30s and was more recently covered by Perry Como. 'For You Alone' was a song that Robert had recorded two years earlier for the Piccadilly label. For this recording the orchestra was conducted by the song's composer, Henry Geehl.

The second release, in February,[93] featured two songs from *Good-Night Vienna*, a BBC operetta composed by Holt Marvell and George Posford and broadcast on 7 January that year to listeners in the London and Midland Regions. Later in the year it became a Herbert Wilcox film, co-starring Anna Neagle (Wilcox's wife) and Jack Buchanan. Holt Marvell was a pseudonym for Eric Maschwitz, who at the time was the editor of the *Radio Times* and later became the BBC's director of variety. He is largely forgotten today save for two songs that have earned him a degree of immortality: 'These Foolish Things' and 'A Nightingale Sang In Berkeley Square'. George Posford was a prolific writer and producer of stage shows and music broadcasts. The two songs recorded were the haunting tango title-song 'Goodnight Vienna' and 'Dear Little Waltz'.

At the beginning of March Robert was appearing in a further variety show at the Palladium Theatre with Edith Day. Sharing the bill was the magician Jasper Maskelyne, who came from a family of stage magicians. In 1905 his father John had bought St George's Hall in Oxford Circus and reopened it as Maskelyne's Theatre. This remained open until 1933, when the BBC took over the premises as a studio and concert hall. The building was destroyed by enemy fire in 1941. Jasper worked for British military intelligence during the Second World War, creating large-scale illusions and camouflages. He was praised by Churchill for his work but seemingly never received the recognition he thought he deserved, and died an embittered man in 1973.

The Palladium show also included Teddy Brown, tap dancers the Condos Brothers, the 'Cheeky Chappie' Max Miller and Harry Roy's Band. However, *The Times* was not over-impressed with the show: 'Although there are always some good individual turns, the Palladium programmes have not lately been quite up to the high standard they have always set. This week's is entertaining enough in its way, but it lacks anything to make it memorable. Miss Edith Day and Mr Robert Naylor fill the place of honour, although Mr Naylor is not free from some irritating mannerisms.'[94] Quite what these irritating mannerisms were the reviewer declines to say.

On 19 March 1932 Cecilia gave birth to a son. She and Robert named him Anthony Michael, and he was to be their only child. Michael grew up with no musical inclinations, and as we shall see he was to have an emotionally difficult childhood. Robert and Cecilia engaged the services of a nanny, a Miss Over, to help look after the baby. Despite the new arrival, Robert's work schedule continued unabated.

On 2 June Robert and Edith were on a variety bill at the Liverpool Empire with the usual assortment of acrobats and jugglers. The following week the show opened at the Edinburgh Empire. Robert had enjoyed a lengthy and successful partnership with Edith Day, but their professional association was now drawing to a close. June also saw the release of a further recorded duet by Robert and Edith: 'One Alone' from *The Desert Song* and 'Love, What Has Given You This Magic Power?' from *The Land of Smiles*.[95]

Around July 1932 Parlophone released Robert's recording of the popular ballad 'Gipsy Moon', words by Frank Eyton and music by Igor Borganoff.[96] 'Gipsy Moon' is also known as 'Hand In Hand', 'Mustalainen' and 'Zigeunerweisen'. The song, which had just been published in 1932, was also recorded by, among others, Richard Tauber. Robert's recording made in March was coupled with 'I Want Your Heart', composed by fellow Yorkshireman Haydn Wood. *The Gramophone*'s reviewer noted of the record, 'Everyone is recording Haydn Wood's "I Want Your Heart". The best version I have heard is Robert Naylor's.'[97] Wood was born on 25 March 1882 at the Lewisham Hotel, Station Road, Slaithwaite, near Huddersfield. His parents, Clement and Sabra Sykes Wood, owned and ran the pub and hotel; his father conducted the local brass band. The family moved to Douglas on the Isle of Man in the summer of 1885. Wood won a scholarship to the Royal College of Music and became a prolific composer of light orchestral music, as well as writing a number of popular tunes, perhaps the most enduring being 'Roses Of Picardy'. He died in a London nursing home on 11 March 1959, two weeks before his seventy-seventh birthday.

In August Robert made another variety tour, this time with the accomplished and popular Yorkshire actress and singer Annie Croft. She was born in Skirlaugh, Hull, in 1896. She starred in the show *Brighter London* at the Hippodrome in 1923, and appeared in the 1927 film *On with the Dance*; she also starred in a revival of *The Maid of the Mountains* at the Palace Theatre in 1931. Six photographs of Annie Croft, taken by Bassano in 1916, are to be found in the photographic section of the National Portrait Gallery, London. Bassano was a famous London studio that had taken pictures of Queen Victoria – and also the image of Kitchener used on the 'Your Country Needs You' recruiting poster. Annie was the mother of David Croft OBE, the writer and producer of such hit shows as *Dad's Army, Hi-De-Hi!* and *Are You Being Served?*

During the first week of August Robert and Annie were at the Palladium Theatre, with Roy Fox and his Orchestra. Also appearing was the wonderful Billy Bennett, usually billed as 'Almost A Gentleman'. A big man with a painted-on moustache, Bennett appeared in irresistibly funny stage attire – shrunken dress-suit, flapping dicky-bow and seedy collar, red silk handkerchief tucked into waistcoat top, and hobnail boots. The rest of the bill contained the usual eclectic mix of long-forgotten performers, including Senator Murphy, a famous American political comedian; Mills and Bobbie, a comedy duo comprising Nat Mills and Bobbie, his female partner both on stage and off; Darlene Walders, an American acro-tap dancer; and Tex McLeod, a rope-spinning vaudeville entertainer 'from the Wild West'.

The Dorchester Hotel, Park Lane, W1, was the venue for a 'Sunday After-Dinner Concert' in the restaurant on 9 October 1932, with Robert and Irene Scharrer providing the entertainment. Miss Scharrer was an English classical pianist who had studied at the Royal Academy of Music. Her London début was at the age of sixteen, and she gave concerts regularly until June 1958. She toured both Europe and the US, performing a wide repertoire but with the emphasis on Chopin and Schumann, and made recordings for HMV and Columbia.

Parlophone released two further discs by Robert during October and November. The first coupled 'In the Garden of Tomorrow' with 'You Loving Me'. 'In the Garden' dates from 1924, with words by George Graffe Jnr and music by Jessie L. Drepen. Gardens were a common subject for songs during this period: among countless others published are 'Walking In Her Garden' (1904), 'In The Garden Of My Heart' (1908), 'Life's Garden' (1914) 'A Cottage In God's Garden' (1917), 'Garden Of Dreams' (1909) and 'In A Little Old Garden' (1919). 'You Loving Me' is a sentimental waltz by the German composer Nicholas Brodsky, the English words by Ralph Stanley.[98]

These sentimental songs were turned out by countless songwriters, who hawked their songs round music publishers' offices, based mainly in Denmark Street near Covent Garden – an area known as 'Tin Pan Alley'. This was originally the name given to those music publishers centred on West 28th Street in New York. The nickname's origins are unclear, although credit for its invention is generally given to the composer Monroe H. Rosenfeld, who, in his newspaper column, likened the noise going on there to the clashing of tin pans.[99]

During the 1930s musicians congregated in this renowned area in central London, near the theatres and drinking spots of Soho. Music publishers had set up their businesses here in Victorian times, because rents were cheap, and they supplied sheet music to the various instrumentalists and singers who worked at local theatres and music halls.

In 1914 the Performing Rights Society had been formed, and in the 1920s it was looking after the interests of 40,000 composers. In 1924 the society's president, William Boosey of Chappells, predicted that the popularity of gramophone records would see a drop in sheet music sales, and that performing rights fees would be the composer's biggest, and perhaps only, source of income. His remarks were viewed as alarmist talk, but his prediction was to be accurate.[100] *Melody Maker*, founded by music publisher Lawrence Wright, was first published at 19 Denmark Street in January 1926. It was originally established to promote Wright's printed catalogue of sheet music and only began to cater for the growing dance band craze in the 1930s, when it was taken over by Odhams Press.

Robert's second release that autumn saw 'Somewhere A Voice Is Calling' coupled with 'Serenade'.[101] The first, written in 1911, is a Victorian parlour song with music by Arthur F. Tate and words by Eileen Newton. According to Professor Scott, this twentieth-century ballad turns away from a concern with morality and dwells on emotion for its own sake. It offers an example of the shift in ethos as a reaction to Victorian morality took root. However, it is difficult to deny the argument that expression of sentiment was turning into self-indulgence.[102] This didn't stop Frank Sinatra from cutting the number with Tommy Dorsey in 1942. The second song on the disc is from *Frasquita* (incipit: 'When the moon is shining bright, in the darkness of the night'), an operetta by Franz Lehár, first performed in London in 1922 at the Prince's Theatre. Lehár's lilting melody suits Robert's voice perfectly. *The Gramophone*'s reviewer was impressed: 'There is a very alluring record of "Serenade" from *Frasquita* by Robert Naylor with orchestra. With it is one of the best recordings of "Somewhere A Voice Is Calling".'[103]

Newspapers have always looked for ways to increase their circulation, and on 24 November 1932 the *Daily Mail* accepted a challenge from EMI, on behalf of its readers, to name the twenty-seven artistes on a Mystery Record. On 29 November 1932 the newspaper announced the issue of copies of the record for 2*s* 6*d* each, together with details and rules of the competition. A total of £1950 in prizes was offered for the correct, or most correct, list of artistes appearing on the record. As an aid to identifying the artistes, the *Daily Mail* printed on the entry form the names of dozens of stage stars, vocalists, organists, instrumentalists, orchestras and bands, a list that included the names of the twenty-seven artistes on the record. Robert Naylor was one of those featured. In an interview with Bradford's local paper the following year, Robert revealed that he was in Barrow at the time of the *Daily Mail* recording session and had to make a journey to London to sing just six bars from his famous song 'You Are My Heart's Delight'. At Carnforth he missed the connection and had to be motored to Carlisle to catch the Scottish Express. It was a tremendous rush for only six bars of music.[104]

The results of the competition were announced in the *Daily Mail* on 26 January 1933. As it turned out, no competitor had correctly named all twenty-seven artistes, but seven had managed twenty-three; the winner was chosen on the basis of the best slogan submitted. The first prize-winner of £1,000 (a princely sum in 1933) was Wilfred Pool of Hull. Surprisingly many people remember the *Daily Mail* Mystery Record, and copies of this 78rpm disc are still in existence.

Early 1933 saw the release of '*Iche Liebe Dich* My Dear' (I Love You My Dear) backed with 'You, Just You'.[105] Jack Hart and Tom Blight wrote the former for the 1932 Ealing Studios film, *Perfect Understanding,* starring Laurence Olivia and Gloria Swanson. The film is one of five that Gloria Swanson made in her early 'talkie' period and is a romantic comedy-drama about a couple of *modernes,* whose marriage is an open relationship in which they have a 'perfect understanding'. The song was performed on screen by Miss Swanson, who also produced the film. The record's flipside was a song from the operetta *Wild Violets,* produced at the Theatre Royal, Drury Lane, on 31 October 1932. It contains some lovely music by the composer of *White Horse Inn,* the Austrian orchestral conductor Robert Stoltz (1880–1975). *Wild Violets* traces the courtships, assignations and misunderstandings of a group of characters in the unlikely settings of a finishing school and a university. Originally set in the fairytale half-timbered Rhine town of Bacharach, it was moved to the Swiss Alps as it was thought this would be more familiar to audiences at Drury Lane. The production achieved a run of 291 performances. Robert recorded 'You, Just You' on 10 December 1932, but this master take was rejected. He returned to the studio on 20 December, just five days before Christmas, in order to re-record the number.

In February 1933 Parlophone released Robert singing '*Ave Maria*' by Pietro Mascagni. Mascagni did not actually compose an *Ave Maria*; Fred Weatherley arranged the intermezzo from the opera *Cavalleria Rusticana* as a vocal solo, setting the *Ave Maria* text to it. Fred E. Weatherley (1848–1929), was an English High Court judge, poet, radio entertainer, writer of children's books and a passionate songwriter. It was he who penned the words of 'Danny Boy' to the tune *Londonderry Air.* The other side of the record was 'The Great Awakening', written by Gordon Johnstone and Arthur Walter Kramer. Kramer was born in New York in 1890 and trained as a violinist. In addition to a number of songs, he composed extended works such as *Two Symphonic Sketches* for violin and orchestra. He eventually became involved in the business side of music, rising to become president of the Society for the Publication of American Music in 1934.

Robert's next major show was *The One Girl,* billed as a new Ziegfeld musical comedy. Florenz Ziegfeld, Jr, known as Flo Ziegfeld, was an American Broadway impresario. He is best known for his series of theatrical revues, staged from 1907 to 1931, called the Ziegfeld Follies. *The One Girl* opened on 24 February at the London Hippodrome on Cranbourn Street, starring the comic actor Lupino Lane. The book was by William Anthony McGuire, with the English version by Herbert Sargent, Clifford Grey and Frank Eyton.

Henry William George Lupino or Lupino Lane (1892–1959) was a British-born actor and theatre manager. He appeared in a wide range of theatrical and film performances but is best known for playing Bill Snibson in the play and film *Me and My Girl*, written by Noel Gay (1937), which popularised the song 'The Lambeth Walk'. The success of *Me and My Girl* made Lane a wealthy man.

A phenomenal acrobat, rivalling Buster Keaton, Lupino Lane made many comedy shorts in the UK during the 1920s. His film career reached a larger audience after he temporarily moved to the US in 1922 with his brother Wallace Lupino; together they made shorts for Fox. Lane returned to London to appear in more stage work, and then returned to the US in 1924 to make the film *Isn't Life Wonderful* for D.W. Griffith; this also starred Lionel Barrymore. Lane returned to England in the '30s and continued with his stage career. After the war he bought the bomb-damaged Gaiety Theatre in the Aldwych, hoping to create a permanent venue for comedic performance. Unfortunately he was unable to gain financial backing for its rebuilding, and sold the premises four years later. The theatre was demolished in 1956.

The One Girl was a musical comedy about the trials of a Salvation Army girl, with the chorus dressed accordingly for part of the evening. Variety appears to have been the essence of the show. It begins on the Western Front in a front-line trench, where a French girl, who happens to be strolling that way, is adopted as a daughter by four soldiers. From here the action moves to the Bowery district of New York, then to China and then to the splendour of the Hotel Crillon in Paris. *The Times*, in its favourable review of the show which it called 'a gay and amusing piece', noted, 'One must not forget Mr Robert Naylor's voice , which is more than equal to all the demands placed upon it.'[106] Also in the show was the comedy actor Arthur Roscoe, who was born in Sherburn-in-Elmet near Leeds. Despite this praise the show appears to have had a short run.

On 3 March Robert recorded two songs from *The One Girl* – 'Tell The Stars I Love' and 'Dreams (The Night I Made You Mine)'.[107] Accompaniment was by the London Hippodrome Orchestra and Chorus, conducted by Samuel Rogers. It is probable the recordings were made at the Hippodrome Theatre using Parlophone's mobile equipment

The Victoria Palace Theatre held a concert on Sunday 26 March, in aid of the Entertainment Artistes Benevolent Fund. A full programme included Robert Naylor, Rose Perfect, Nervo & Knox, Naughton and Gold, Anna Rogers, Neville Sydney, the Corona Babes, Flanagan and Allen, Irene Cowden, Maynard Grover, Jose Collins, Little Teddie, Dick Henderson and Elsie and Doris Waters. The concert was expected to raise over £200.

On Good Friday, 14 April, at the National Sunday League Concert[108] at the Palladium, Robert shared vocal honours with the soprano and actress Kathlyn Hilliard and the popular West End baritone Raymond Newell. Other artists on the bill included Seymour Hicks, Jane Carr (impressionist), Keith Wilbur, and Geraldo and his Orchestra.

Back in West Yorkshire, Robert's uncle James Naylor died on 21 April 1933. The Rev. James William Naylor was the vicar of St Paul's Church, Buttershaw, in Bradford. He was ordained in 1907, when Robert was eight years old. At the time of his death he had served his parish loyally for twenty-six years. His first wife was Annie Watkinson, the daughter of Samuel Watkinson of Shelf Hall, near Bradford.[109] She died during the Spanish flu epidemic in 1918. They had a son named James Watkinson Naylor. The Rev. James got married for a second time when he was fifty-four years old to Miss Dorothy Watson – one of his parishioners, whose family lived at Oakdene, 93 Harbour Road, Wibsey. Dorothy was the daughter of Harold Alderson Watson, a dress goods manufacturer who had a business, Harold A. Watson (Bradford) Ltd, at Prospect Mills, Holroyd Hill, Wibsey, Bradford. At the time of their marriage, in 1925, Dorothy was aged twenty, some thirty-four years younger than James.

The following year Dorothy gave birth to a son, John, born on 11 July. John became a school teacher before following in his father's footsteps and being ordained as a vicar in 1966. As a result of the great age difference between husband and wife, Dorothy became, in 1933, a widow aged just twenty-eight. Robert Naylor would eventually marry Dorothy himself, and in doing so make his aunt his wife. For the present, though, along with other members of the family, and a great many parishioners, Robert attended his uncle's funeral at St Paul's Church. In his funeral address Canon Watson said of the Rev. James Naylor,' The parish was his home: in fact he rarely left it.'[110] After James's death, Dorothy and her son John moved out of Buttershaw vicarage on St Paul's Avenue, Bradford and went to live at Fernmere, on Halifax Road, Bradford.

Back in London, on 18 May 1933, Brentford Football Club held their Jubilee Dinner at the Greyhound Hotel, Richmond. Brentford's most successful period was in the 1930s when they reached the First Division. Robert Naylor helped provide the after-dinner entertainment, accompanied by Kathleen O'Hagan on the piano. In 1958 the same Miss O'Hagan played piano in a *Hancock's Half Hour* radio episode entitled 'The East Cheam Drama Festival', where her over-enthusiastic hammering of the keys causes Hancock to retort, 'Turn it up, mate! This is a drama festival, not a music festival. We've all heard you, we know you can play.'

The life of an entertainer has always been a precarious way to earn a living. Employment can be intermittent, and illness or disability can have a devastating effect on a performer's income. In earlier years music hall entertainers were often at the mercy of unscrupulous managers, who demanded extra matinée performances without additional pay. In 1907 there had been a music hall strike; Joe Elvin, a Cockney comedian and musical hall entertainer, was a leading force behind it. The strike leaders persuaded less well-paid music hall artistes to strike for better pay and conditions and to picket the theatres that broke the strike. Their action was supported by the Variety Artistes' Federation, founded in 1906. In December 1907 Elvin helped found, and became the first president of, the Variety Artistes' Benevolent Fund, which was set up by performers to provide aid and welfare to artistes in need of charitable assistance. In 1909 Elvin was the prime mover in a scheme that eventually led to the building of Brinsworth House.

Brinsworth House at 72 Staines Road in Twickenham was opened in 1911 to care for retired members of the variety and music hall profession, and is one of the entertainment industry's most exclusive retirement homes. The brown-brick building sits back off a main road, set in an acre of land. It was the last home of such notable entertainers as Dame Thora Hird and Charlie Drake. Today the Entertainment Artists Benevolent Fund maintains Brinsworth House as a residential home for retired members of the entertainment profession and/or their dependents. It is supported by income from the Royal Variety Performance and other fund-raising events.

Before the war Brinsworth Weeks became an annual event. In 1933 the Brinsworth Week Scheme was held from 1 July to help raise money for the Variety Artistes' Benevolent Fund and Institution. Various charity concerts took place in London, including one held at the Victoria Palace Theatre, where the audience was entertained by Robert Naylor, Rose Perfect, Naughton and Gold, Dick Henderson and the Victoria Palace Orchestra under Reginald Moore. As a result the Victoria Palace was able to donate £160 19s 9d towards the fund. The total amount raised during the week was £3084.

The Court Circular is the official record that lists the engagements carried out by the Monarch and various other members of the Royal Family. It is issued by Buckingham Palace and is printed daily in *The Times*. On 29 June 1933 it was announced that Lady Newnes had held a meeting the previous day, regarding a concert she was organising in aid of The Guild of Singers and Players. This was a group of musicians who often gave free concerts in the capital. Lady Newnes (who incidentally had a bay in the Western Ross Sea named after her) was the wife of Sir George Newnes, a wealthy publisher. The concert took place on 6 July with Princess Marie Louise in attendance. Among those performing were Robert Naylor, Daisy Kennedy (an Australian violinist), Ray Lev (an American classical pianist), Thea Phillips (an English actress and singer), Violet Vanbrugh (an English actress) and Ivor Newton (pianist).

On 7 July 1933 Robert was in another BBC radio programme, this time devoted to the music of Franz Lehár. For the programme he had acquired a new co-star, the soprano Josie Fearon. Miss Fearon started her career in grand opera with the Carl Rosa Company, when she was nineteen years old, playing the lead role in *Madam Butterfly*, and she was the leading lady with Maurice Chevalier when he appeared in *White Birds* in London in 1927. It is said that when she hit a high note during a BBC broadcast a heavy 'unbreakable' glass tumbler shattered to bits in the home of radio listener Philip Mansel, 60 miles away.[111] Whether or not this was during her broadcast with Robert Naylor we do not know.

The Stage soon got wind of the new partnership: 'Neither Robert Naylor nor Josie Fearon are by any means unknown to variety audiences, but they have not been heard in association. Next week at the Manchester Hippodrome, they will join forces in a vocal act that will embrace various numbers from shows in which the artistes have enjoyed much success in recent times.'[112] At the end of the month Robert and Josie were sharing the stage with the actor Edwin Styles and the Andree Trio at Finsbury Park Astoria.

The first week in August saw Robert and Josie at the Plaza Theatre, New Regent Street, where the film *Bedtime Story,* with Maurice Chevalier, was showing. Today these two forms of entertainment are entirely separate but this was not always the case. In the 1930s the variety theatres that had been adapted to show films, and indeed even the new purpose-built cinemas, often included live acts as part of their admission price, known as cine-variety. Opened in 1926, the Plaza on Piccadilly Circus originally had its own orchestra, and the films were supported by the Plaza Tiller Girls.

It's difficult for modern audiences to appreciate what 'an evening at the pictures' meant to their predecessors some seventy-five years ago. Many theatres, and not just in London but in towns and cities across the country, went out of their way to provide a luxurious evening's entertainment and perhaps, too, a little escapism. For a few hours mundane day-to-day existence and cramped conditions at home, which was the lot of the vast majority of people during the inter-war years, could be forgotten and the opulent grandeur of the theatre enjoyed.

The grandest of the theatre foyers were often designed in the Palm Court style, with an exuberance of greenery, gilded trellis, nymph water fountains, glittering chandeliers and alcoves with decorative cut-glass mirrors. In the middle of this great hall was the pay box. Having bought their tickets patrons would climb the thickly-carpeted marble staircase to the vast auditorium where, following the beckoning torch of an usherette, they would be politely escorted to their plush velvet seats. The ornate and gilded décor was intended to resemble that of a stately home. The Finsbury Park Astoria,[113] for example, which opened in 1930, was famous for its Moorish style, the frescoes in the auditorium being redolent of an Andalusian village at night. In most theatres the great semi-circular arch of the proscenium was adorned with imitation clusters of fruit, doves or trailing vines. Many of the purpose-built super-cinemas of the '30s were designed, both inside and outside, in the ultra-modern Art Deco style. No wonder so many were named Picture Palaces: palatial is what they often were. Once seated in this heady atmosphere, thick with perfume and cigarette smoke, the audience would wait with a hush of expectancy as the great curtain was drawn back.

A cine-variety programme opened with the theatre organ rising majestically from the depths of the pit. A couple of coloured spotlights pierced the darkness to illuminate the ascending spectacle. These magnificent instruments were specially designed to imitate a whole orchestra. To make them even more eye-catching, the console was often gilded or painted white, to reflect the coloured spotlights. The organist was always dressed in tails. (The Granada Circuit insisted that all their organists appeared in white dress suits.) Many of the theatre organists were gifted players who became celebrities themselves, each with their own signature tune. For some years the BBC had included in their radio programmes relays from cinema theatres, which had become one of the most popular broadcast entertainments. The majority of these relays took place while the films were being shown: what listeners heard was the music that the organist had selected to provide suitable accompaniment to the picture. The dance suites of Edward German and Arthur Wood and the ballet music of Delibes and Gounod were frequently drawn upon. However, at the start of the evening the organist would play popular tunes of the day, and the audience was often encouraged to sing along. Sometimes the words to the song were projected on to a screen, a forerunner of today's karaoke.[114]

This was followed by the appearance on stage of well-known variety acts. Comedians were always popular, and the bill often included singers like Robert Naylor and Josie Fearon. There might even be a dance troupe, such as the Plaza Tiller Girls mentioned above. The final item on the programme was the screening of the evening's feature film.[115]

The following week, away from the capital, Robert and Josie were delighting audiences at the Hippodrome in Coventry. Later the same month they undertook an extended variety tour. En route to Scotland the show played the Newcastle Paramount, then in the week beginning 21 August they opened at His Majesty's Theatre, Aberdeen. The number three act on the bill that week was London comedian Tommy Trinder. The local press noted that, 'Although Tommy rattles on agreeably, it was felt perhaps his style was too intimate for a large theatre such as His Majesty's, or – perhaps it was the fact that the Aberdeen audiences found it difficult to keep up with his Cockney patter.'[116]

Also on the bill at Aberdeen was the beautiful songstress Nina Mae McKinney. Nina Mae McKinney, who was born in South Carolina in 1912, was one of the most successful African-American artists of the period. As well as being a singer she was also a gifted actress. Barred from opportunities and stardom in Hollywood, she soon departed the United States and took her great talents to Europe. In Greece she was known as the 'Black Garbo'. She performed all over Europe, singing in nightclubs and cafes in cities such as London, Budapest, Dublin and Paris. In England, she starred with Paul Robeson in the film *Sanders of the River*. She died in New York City in 1967. *The Stage* noted of the show, 'Robert Naylor and Josie Fearon are top of the bill with their delightful solos and duets, such as "You Are My Heart's Delight" and "My Hero" etc.' The newspaper then added, in the racially discriminatory manner of the time, 'Nina Mae McKinney, accompanied by Garland Wilson at the piano, wins applause for coon numbers.'[117]

The variety tour eventually reached Bradford, where from Monday 11 September 1933 Robert and Josie appeared for the week at the Alhambra Theatre. The bill here included the Tom Dawes Trio, a motor-cycle stunt team that used a tea cup track; Felovis, an expert juggler from Switzerland; Ernest Shannon, an impersonator; Bob, Tina and Jean, 'graceful acrobats'; Earl and Eddie Franklin, expert dancers; and a talented group of youngsters called the Twenty Four Corona Babes.

During the week's stay Robert was interviewed by a local news reporter, who wrote:

> I found him as modest and unassuming as anyone one could wish to meet . . . not in the least temperamental like many opera stars with far worse voices, but still a sound, level-headed Yorkshire man. Indeed, I think many people must take advantage of his charm of manner, for in his dressing room I saw a huge stack of autograph

albums waiting to be signed, the bulk of them I should think, from persons who have not the slightest claim to ask for his signature. When I remarked upon this he remained good-natured about it, though, with native-shrewdness, he remarked that they could become a nuisance when people posted them to one and expected one to parcel them up again and pay the return postage. I can see a time coming when he will have to do like other stars whom I know, and keep a secretary to sign the autograph books for him. For I can assure you that many autographs are cherished that have been signed by proxy.[118]

On 21 September 1933 Robert recorded 'Love Is Mine' and 'I Know A Lovely Garden', accompanied by a trio consisting of piano, violin and cello.

Around this time EMI had decided to close Carlton Hill and centre its operations at Abbey Road. As already mentioned, the new Abbey Road studios opened in November 1931, following the merger of HMV, Columbia and Parlophone into EMI earlier that year. It was intended that these studios – equipped from the start with Blumlein disc-cutting technology – should become the principal recording venue for the united company. Certainly the studio at Carlton Hill – which still used the Westrex disc-cutting technology – closed sometime before November 1933, by which time Robert was recording at Abbey Road.

Research into the Parlophone matrix numbers indicates that this was the last time Robert recorded there, and suggests it might also have been the final day of operation at Carlton Hill. (Matrix numbers are alphanumeric codes that are usually stamped into the run-off groove of a gramophone record. They are intended for the internal use of the record manufacturing plant but are studied and documented by record collectors.) However, owing to the complex technicalities around matrix numbers and recording sessions, some researchers feel the studio may have been vacated by Parlophone as early as April 1933. Although opinion is divided on this matter, 21

September 1933 looks, on balance, to be the likely closure date. Later research may throw further light on this.

What we do know for sure is that on the final day of recording a number of the label's artistes were present, including Robert Naylor, the pianist Patricia Rossborough, the comedy double-act Elsie and Doris Waters and the comedian Ronald Frankau. Frankau recorded various songs and skits for Parlophone, some of which, like 'Winnie The Worm' and 'Everyone's Got Sex Appeal For Someone', were banned by the BBC. Despite, or more likely because of, this flavour in his songs, Frankau sold over 100,000 records in 1932. He was usually accompanied on his recordings by Monte Crick, who found later fame playing the character of Dan in the long-running BBC radio serial *The Archers*.

After the final day's recording sessions were finished, the above artistes and musicians together with staff at the studio, held a farewell party where in the course of the festivities a private recording was made. It opens with the announcement, 'This is positively the last recording to be made at the Parlophone studios at Carlton Hill.' The recording is just under three minutes long and consists mainly of silliness. Robert Naylor is to be heard on the disc singing a snatch of '*Vesti la Guibba*' (On with the motley) from *Pagliacci* by Leoncavallo. Interestingly this is the only recording of Robert singing opera, and reveals a far more robust tenor voice with more *squillo* (ring) than we hear on his recordings of operetta and popular songs. Robert finally leads the party guests in a riotous rendition of 'Auld Lang Syne'. A limited number of copies were pressed as a memento for the artistes and staff. Two are known to be still in existence, one copy being owned by the author.

Once Parlophone had vacated Carlton Hill, the studio was acquired by Trusound Pictorial Records Ltd. The company produced some of the earliest flexible picture discs and specialised in producing children's records. Trusound may have been recording at the studio on a sessional basis before Parlophone vacated the premises. The Parlophone recording engineer Cyril Francis decided to stay at Carlton Hill and work for Trusound, probably because Abbey Road had all the engineers it needed. However, the company was only active for a few months, during which time they released about thirty picture discs; today these are highly sought after by collectors.

In September 1933 a further recording by Robert was released, recorded in June that year.[119] The record coupled 'She That I Love' with 'Bless This House'. Robert was accompanied on piano by Horatio Dayn, a name that is possibly a pseudonym. The first song was composed by Maurice Besly, with words by Mordaunt Currie. Born in 1888 in the ancient parish of Normanby, near Kirkbymoorside, North Yorkshire, Edward Maurice Besly was educated at the Leipzig Conservatorium. He was an organist, conductor and teacher. From 1912 to 1914 he was an assistant music master at Tonbridge School in Kent, and between 1923 and 1928 was Director of Music at Queen's College, Oxford. He spread his net wide, writing orchestral music, songs, piano pieces and an operetta called *Forever After*. As conductor of the Scottish Orchestra he toured New Zealand in 1927. 'Bless This House' has been widely recorded since it was first published in 1927. The music is by the Australian composer May H. Brahe; the words were by an English poet called Helen Taylor. It was originally entitled 'Bless The House', but was changed to 'Bless This House' by John McCormack, who made it one of his most famous recordings. Unfortunately *The Gramophone*'s record reviewer was not taken with Robert's version: 'He seems to be singing less well than formerly. Apparently he is now aiming at that dire modern adjective, mere force, and to that end tightening his throat. One notices that his words, when unfamiliar, are not easy to follow, and when he relaxes his tone it is not perfectly placed. A record to hear before buying.'[120]

On Friday 6 October 1933 Robert and Josie appeared on the radio together with the BBC Theatre Orchestra, performing songs and duets in a programme entitled *Music Hall*. The orchestra was conducted by S. Kneale Kelly, who was given to billing himself as 'conductor of 5,000 broadcasts'. A violinist, he was also leader of the Wireless Symphony Orchestra, the forerunner of the BBC Symphony Orchestra. Along with Robert and Josie were Alec McGill and Gwen Vaughan, 'The Cheerful Chatterers'; Nelson Keys, comedian; Hetty King, male impersonations; Charles Austin & Co., performing a sketch; Scott and Whaley, entertainers; and the Eight Step Sisters, dance routines. The show's compère was Christopher Stone.

Throughout its early years the BBC attracted to its service a considerable number of men and women who believed in broadcasting almost as a social and cultural crusade. They included a high proportion of men who had served in the war and could not settle down to any old humdrum profession after the war was over.[121] Among these was Major Christopher Reynolds Stone DSO, MC. He was educated at Eton College and served in the Royal Fusiliers, then became London editor of *The Gramophone.* Stone approached the BBC with the idea of a radio programme based solely on the playing of records, which was accepted, and on 7 July 1927 he became the first English disc jockey. His relaxed, chatty style was refreshing at a time when much of the BBC's presentation was formal and stuffy. As a result his record programme became highly popular with listeners.

On 13 November 1933 Robert and Josie Fearon were appearing at the Torquay Pavilion – 'to a large and appreciative house' – in a show called *Radio Stars* presented by the Russian dancer-turned-variety promoter Ivan Kotchinsky, who was also responsible for booking variety for the Bournemouth Pavilion. Other artists engaged included Avon and Vale, Gordon Freeman, the Fayre Four, Ivor Vintnor, the Avant Bros, Clapham & Dwyer, Levanda and Tommy Handley.

November also saw the release of the two sides Robert had recorded in September at the Carlton Hill studio, 'I Know A Lovely Garden' and 'Love Is Mine'.[122] The music critic Herman Klein, writing in *The Gramophone*, noted: 'This young tenor deserves and wins hearty approbation for his voice is as true and genuine as his style is unaffected and sincere. Moreover, he sings a nice type of ballad, if not precisely a new one, and the treatment of Guy d'Hardelot's 'I Know A Lovely Garden' with obbligati for violin and 'cello lends it a novel aspect.'[123]

Guy d'Hardelot (1858–1936) was the pen name of Helen Rhodes, a French composer, pianist and teacher. Born Helen Guy at Chateau d'Hardelot, near Boulogne-sur-Mer, she spent most of her life teaching singing and diction at her home in London. She was singularly successful as a writer of songs, in which, it is said, 'She combined French delicacy with English solidity. Few women composers became more popular in the early twentieth century than did d'Hardelot.'[124] The second song, 'Love Is Mine', dated from 1911, with music by Clarence Gartner and words by Edward

Teschemacher. It was famously recorded by Caruso for RCA in 1921.

In December Robert and Josie Fearon appeared at the New Victoria Cinema, on Wilton Road, near Victoria station in London. In between screenings of a Gaumont-British production, *A Cuckoo in the Nest*, Robert and Josie performed on the stage. The New Victoria had opened on 15 October 1930, and was equipped with a Compton three-manual fifteen-rank theatre organ, which had been played on the opening night by Reginald Foort. The theatre also staged variety shows but, as with many such venues, variety quickly gave way to specialisation in film, with only occasional performances by dance bands. Also in December Robert and Josie were at the Dominion Theatre on Tottenham Court Road. Although the Dominion wasn't designed as a cinema, its early failure as a live theatre meant that in 1930, just a year after opening, it became a cinema, and in 1933 it was sold to Gaumont-British.

In January 1934 *The Stage* reported: 'On Monday and Tuesday (29–30 January) Hugh Ormond deputised for Robert Naylor at the Gaumont Palace, Lewisham. Mr Naylor had an attack of laryngitis, but was expected to be well enough to appear on Wednesday.' Laryngitis is an occupational hazard of professional singers. Robert would have received voice training on how to recognise the first symptoms of vocal fatigue and how to protect himself from stress-induced laryngitis. The most effective treatment is immediate rest for the vocal cords, which is what appears to have happened here.

Also in January Parlophone released its final record by Robert Naylor. It had been recorded on 11 November 1933 at his only session held at the Abbey Road studios, after which the company dispensed with his services. The orchestra was conducted by George Scott-Wood and the two songs were 'Two Little Words' and 'I Still Love Mary'.[125] (This was the record that first came into my collection and led directly to the research for this book.)

'Two Little Words' was written by May Hannah Brahe.[126] Born in Melbourne, Australia, she wrote a number of songs popular at the time, her most enduring work being the sacred song 'Bless This House', which Robert had recently recorded. 'I Still Love Mary' had words by Bruce Sievier, the first chairman of the Songwriters Guild of Great Britain, and music by Harold Arthur Ramsay, an interesting character. He was an organist, choirmaster, composer and teacher who was born in Yarmouth in August 1901 and spent a good deal of his career in North America. In the early 1920s he was a vocal coach for Paramount Studios in New York and Hollywood and organist at Broadway's Rivoli Theater. In 1932 he moved back to England, where he was Musical Director of Bernstein Theatres Ltd and became a leading theatre organist, performing on some one thousand BBC broadcasts and appearing weekly at London's Granada Theatre. He died at Salmon Arm, near Kamloops, British Columbia, Canada, in 1976.

It seems more than a coincidence that Robert's departure from the ranks of Parlophone's artistes occurs at precisely the time that Richard Tauber – permanently banished from Germany since March 1933 – began his association with the Abbey Road studios. Before this his recordings had been largely sung in German, which had little appeal to English record buyers. From the end of 1933, however, nearly all his popular records, and concert appearances, were sung in English, and thus were more acceptable to the UK audience. From now until the end of his life he continued to record at Abbey Road. Tauber's first UK recordings were conducted by George Scott Wood, who had worked previously with Robert.

Robert might have been seen by EMI executives as redundant. Why pay him to record cover versions, in English, of Tauber's German hits when Tauber himself was recording them for the company in English? The changing economic climate may also have played its part in the decision to let him go. Singers such as Isobel Baillie and Heddle Nash, who had both been prolific Columbia recording artistes, were also dropped by EMI around this time. No doubt the formation of EMI, itself a result of the economic situation, led to rationalisation and the cutting-down of duplication.

A concert was held at the Lyceum Theatre, London, on Sunday 18 February in aid of the Royal Free Hospital. Among the many artistes appearing were Robert Naylor and Sylvia Cecil, Flanagan and Allen, Dick Henderson, Geraldo, Webster Booth, Charles Austin, Florrie Forde, and Elsie and Doris Waters. As the name indicates, in those pre-National Health days the hospital offered free care for those unable to pay. The royal charter was granted by Queen Victoria in 1837, after a cholera epidemic in which the hospital had extended care to many victims. Regular fund-raising events were arranged by the hospital to meet its running costs. *The Stage* reported that there had been a big demand for seats, with only a few left in the stalls at £1 1*s* and 10*s* 6*d*, and in the grand circle at 7*s* 6*d*.

Dropped by Parlophone, Robert made a handful of recordings for Imperial-Broadcast, a fusion of two labels that was nearing the end of its life. The label was one of many produced by the Crystalate Gramophone Company – a company I will return to later. His début for the label was 'I'll Follow My Secret Heart',[127] from Noel Coward's *Conversation Piece,* which had begun at His Majesty's Theatre on 16 February 1934. The music critic Benny Green wrote: 'There is a strong case to be made that "I'll Follow My Secret Heart" is the loveliest of all Coward's pieces, the perfect marriage of words and music, the ravishing upward swoops of the melodic line matched by the deeply moving unspoiled sincerity of the words, proclaiming the resolve to defend the purity of romantic dreams from the inroads of reality . . . [it] transcends its environment, its time and place, to become one of the great standard songs of the modern era, its musical beauty melting into the depth of its poetic emotion.'[128] Robert's version of 'I'll Follow My Secret Heart' is sensitively performed and is among his most delightful recordings.[129] The record was coupled with 'Gay Vienna', one of many sentimental songs of the time describing the proverbial charm of the Viennese.[130] The tune is by the Austro-Hungarian composer Fritz Rotter (1900–84), who moved to England in 1936 to escape the Nazis and later went to live in the USA. His best-known composition is 'I Kiss Your Hand Madam', which has been recorded by Bing Crosby, Vic Damone and Spike Hughes, among others. The words are by Jimmy Kennedy (1902–84), a prolific lyricist responsible for such standards as 'Red Sails In The Sunset', 'South Of The Border' and 'The Isle Of Capri'. Kennedy, born in Omagh, Ireland, won two Ivor Novello Awards for his contribution to music, and received an honorary degree from the New University of Ulster. He was also awarded the OBE in 1983, and in 1997 was posthumously inducted into the Songwriters' Hall of Fame.

On Saturday 24 February Robert was heard once more on the radio in *Music Hall.* Among the other performers were Charlie Higgins, comedian; Walsh and Arnold, musical act; Beryl Orde, impersonations; and Lily Morris, comedian. Robert sang with his new partner, Miss Sylvia Cecil, who had appeared with him a week earlier at the Royal Free Hospital charity concert. Sylvia (*c.* 1898 –*c.* 1983) was born in London. Like Robert, she studied at the Guildhall School of Music. She began her career as an opera singer with the D'Oyly Carte Opera Company before switching to lighter music, including musical comedy. A statuesque soprano, she was to enjoy a long stage career achieving particular success in productions of shows by Ivor Novello and Noel Coward. In 1935 she did a summer season at the Opera House, Blackpool, in *Jump For Joy* with Albert Burdon and Randolph Sutton. Robert and Sylvia's stage partnership continued for the next year. Press advertisements announced 'Robert Naylor & Sylvia Cecil – The Famous Musical Comedy Stars in *Songs from the Shows*'.

Robert and Sylvia recorded four sides for Imperial-Broadcast. The first disc presented 'I'll See You Again' from Noel Coward's *Bitter Sweet* and 'I Give You My Heart'[131] from the opera *The Dubarry,* by the Viennese composer Karl Millocker. The musical weepy *Bitter Sweet* was first produced at her Majesty's Theatre in 1929. Set in Vienna, with a plot involving a poor musician, a lady, who through poverty becomes a dance hall hostess, an amorous count and a fatal duel, it can been seen as Coward's tribute to the world of Viennese operetta. The film of *Bitter Sweet,* starring Anna Neagle, was released in August 1933. *The Dubarry* was presented at His Majesty's Theatre in April 1932. It tells the rather fanciful version of the rise of the great eighteenth-century French courtesan Madam Dubarry. In the featured aria the young Dubarry vows that there is only one man in her life.

From Saturday 21 April, in a variety show at the Alhambra Theatre, Leicester Square, Robert and Sylvia shared the top billing twice-nightly for a week with vocalist Jack Doyle. He was an accomplished tenor, who in the past had been both a contender for the British Boxing Championship and a Hollywood actor. He was born in County Cork, Ireland, and initially rose to fame as a heavy-weight boxer. With his good looks he became the darling of the boxing ring, Hollywood society and the gossip columns. Doyle's last fight in London in 1939 attracted some 250,000 people. By the age of thirty, by all accounts, he had earned and squandered a huge fortune, probably worth millions today. In his heyday his playboy celebrity rivalled that of the Prince of Wales, and he and his wife –

the beautiful Mexican film star and singer Movita, who later married Marlon Brando – were as popular in the '30s as Burton and Taylor were in the '60s or the Beckhams are today.[132]

In the first week of May Robert and Sylvia were with Harry Gordon's Company at the Pavilion, Aberdeen. Born in Aberdeen in 1893, Harry Gordon was the most famous and successful comedian ever produced by the city – a prolific entertainer in the theatre and on radio. Between the 1920s and '40s he made dozens of recordings for Beltona and Parlophone, the two most popular labels with Scottish performers of the variety era; he also ran his own theatre, the Aberdeen Beach Pavilion, for fourteen years. Gordon's favourite role was the socially and usually sexually inexperienced 'little fellow' who cannot cope with modern life but somehow gets by, and even manages to make fun of it. His comedy, delivered in a broad Scottish accent, never transferred successfully to English audiences. He died in Glasgow in 1957.

In a radio programme called *Guest Night*, broadcast on Saturday 19 May 1934, Robert and Sylvia were heard alongside Rochdale lass Gracie Fields. Most readers will be familiar with 'Our Gracie', who became a huge star of the cinema and music hall. She made the first of ten appearances in the Royal Variety Show in 1928 and had a devoted following. Her most famous song, 'Sally' (written in 1931 by Will Haines, Leo Towers and Harry Leon), which became her theme, was worked into the title of her first cinema film, *Sally in Our Alley* (1931), which was a major box office hit. The late 1930s saw her popularity peak and she was given many honours, including a CBE (for services to entertainment) in 1938 and the Freedom of the Borough of Rochdale.

The programme also included the songstress Natalie Hall, the BBC Dance Orchestra and the comedy act Claude Dampier and Billie Carlyle. Dampier and his much younger wife were regular performers on the radio. Their partnership lasted for thirty years until 1955, when Claude died. Dampier, a tall and toothy village idiot in a bowler hat, completely misunderstood everything his partner said to him. He rambled on about his mysterious friend Mrs Gibson, and managed to get himself banned from the BBC when he referred to 'squeezing Mrs Gibson's oranges . . .'

By the mid-'30s, as Robert's engagements steadily changed from concert hall to variety stage, he was at the peak of his

99

popularity. He had begun his career singing with his wife Cecilia, and now, perhaps more than ever, he found it advantageous to appear on stage with a female singing partner. This approach allowed for solo and duet numbers, as well as the development of repartee and comedy between songs. While Robert's female partners changed, this was probably not because of personal differences but because of competing professional commitments – and because neither artiste wished to be seen as half of a double-act. In addition to his frequent stage appearances, Robert was heard regularly on the radio, and his many gramophone recordings of popular songs were in much demand. Ahead lay further opportunities, although, as we shall see, not all would provide him with quite the success he had enjoyed to date.

The Guildhall School of Music.

Founded by the Corporation of London 1880.

This is to Certify that

Robert Naylor

has been awarded

The Alfred and Catherine Howard Prize

for the year ending **July** 1928

Dated this 27ᵈ *October* 1928

_____
Chairman

Landon Ronald, Principal

H. Saxe Wyndham, Secretary

John Carpenter St.
Victoria Embankment.
E.C.4.

Alfred and Catherine Howard Prize, awarded to Robert in 1928.
(Author's collection)

THE GUILDHALL SCHOOL OF MUSIC,

JOHN CARPENTER STREET,

VICTORIA EMBANKMENT. E.C. 4.

Founded in 1880 by the CORPORATION OF LONDON, and under the Management and Control of

THE MUSIC COMMITTEE.

Chairman - - FITZHERBERT A. B. LORD, Esq., C.C.

Principal - - Sir LANDON RONALD, F.R.A.M., F.R.C.M., F.G.S.M.

PROGRAMME

OF

STUDENTS' ANNUAL CONCERT

(1803rd CONCERT)

AND

PRESENTATION OF MEDALS, PRIZES. SCHOLARSHIPS, AND DIPLOMAS

BY

THE LADY MAYORESS,

ACCOMPANIED BY

The Rt. Hon. The Lord Mayor, Sir CHARLES A. BATHO, Bart.,
Alderman and Sheriff Sir WILLIAM A. WATERLOW, K.B.E., J.P., and
Mr. Sheriff WILLIAM G. COXEN, C.C.,

IN THE

CITY OF LONDON SCHOOL.

VICTORIA EMBANKMENT. E.C. 4,

ON

Saturday Afternoon, October 27th, 1928.

2.30 p.m.

The programme for the Guildhall School of Music students' concert at
which Robert sang, 1928. (Author's collection)

Red Roofs, Wembley Park: Robert and Cecila's London home from
1928 to 1939. (Author's collection)

Robert and Cecilia in their garden at Red Roofs, early 1930s.
(Author's collection)

Robert as the Duke of Mantua in Verdi's *Rigoletto*, probably Old Vic,
May 1928. (Author's collection)

Robert in the garden at Red Roofs, early 1930s. (Author's collection)

Robert and Cecilia in the garden at Red Roofs, from a publicity feature, mid-1930s. (Author's collection)

ADELPHI THEATRE

Phone Temple Bar 2522 | Strand, W.C.
2523 |

JACK HULBERT

AND

PAUL MURRAY

PRESENT

THEIR NEW REVUE

"THE

HOUSE

THAT

JACK

BUILT"

6*d.*

The programme for *The House That Jack Built*, Adelphi Theatre, 1929.
(Author's collection)

Robert as the Duke of Buckingham in *The Three Musketeers*, Drury Lane, 1930. (Author's collection)

A signed publicity photograph, taken by Marian Lewis, 50 Queen Anne's Gate, London. (Author's collection)

Piccadilly Records, who released Robert's first gramophone recordings. (Maurice Robson)

Robert and Cecilia enjoying the trappings of success. (Author's collection)

Parlophone Records.
(Maurice Robson)

Interior of the Theatre Royal, Drury Lane. (Author's collection)

Edith Day, Robert's stage partner 1931–2.
(Author's collection)

The Land of Smiles theatre
programme.
(Maurice Robson)

THEATRE ROYAL DRURY LANE

The Land of Smiles

CAST of CHARACTERS
(in the order of their appearance):

GENERAL COUNT LICHTENFELS ...	GEORGE BISHOP
COUNTESS ROHEIM	LENA HALLIDAY
COLONEL FRANKENBERG	... J. NEIL MORE
CAPTAIN GUSTAVE VON PLOETZ...	GEORGE VOLLAIRE
LISA	RENEE BULLARD
BUTLER...	... WALTER WEBSTER
PRINCE SOU CHONG	ROBERT NAYLOR
LORE	...PHYLLIS EDWARDES
VALLI	... DOROTHY CROFTS
FRANZI	... GWEN MAY
TONI	DOROTHEA RONALD
FINI	... DOROTHY COOPER
FU LI (Secretary of the Chinese Legation)	DAVID HENLEY
PRINCE TSCHANG	...W. CRONIN WILSON
MI... ... ... :..	HELLA KÜRTY
CHI FU	BRUCE WINSTON

CONDUCTOR ... ... ERNEST IRVING

F2

The Land of Smiles cast list.
(Maurice Robson)

Richard Tauber. (Author's collection)

Robert as Prince Sou Chong in *The Land of Smiles*.
(Author's collection)

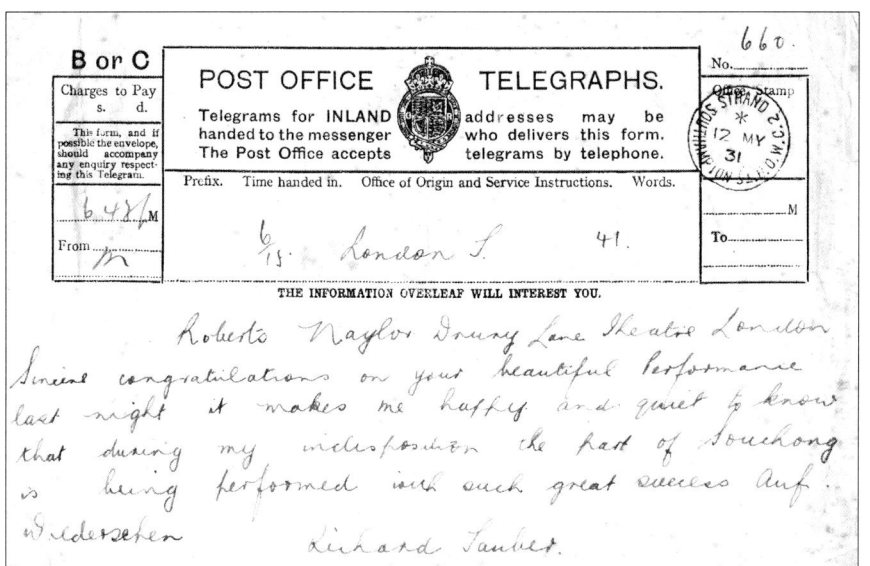

Congratulatory telegram sent to Robert by Richard Tauber.
(Author's collection)

THÉ CHANTANT.

Lisa . . . . Miss Renée Bullard.
Prince Sou Chong . . . Mr. Robert Naylor.

Pen and ink vignette from *Punch* magazine, 1931.
(*Punch* magazine)

Advertisement for Parlophone Records, 1931.
(*Gramophone* magazine)

Advertisement for Chappell music publishers, 1932.
(*Gramophone* magazine)

Robert: a studio portrait, *c.* 1932.
(Author's collection)

Olive Groves, who recorded with Robert in 1931, pictured on a Gallaher cigarette card.
(Author's collection)

Robert and Cecilia with their son Michael, born in 1932.
(Author's collection)

Annie Croft, with whom Robert toured in 1932.
(Author's collection)

Robert: a studio portrait, *c.* 1932.
(Author's collection)

Daily Mail Mystery Record
and solution.
(John Watson)

Josie Fearon, with whom Robert worked in 1933.
(Author's collection)

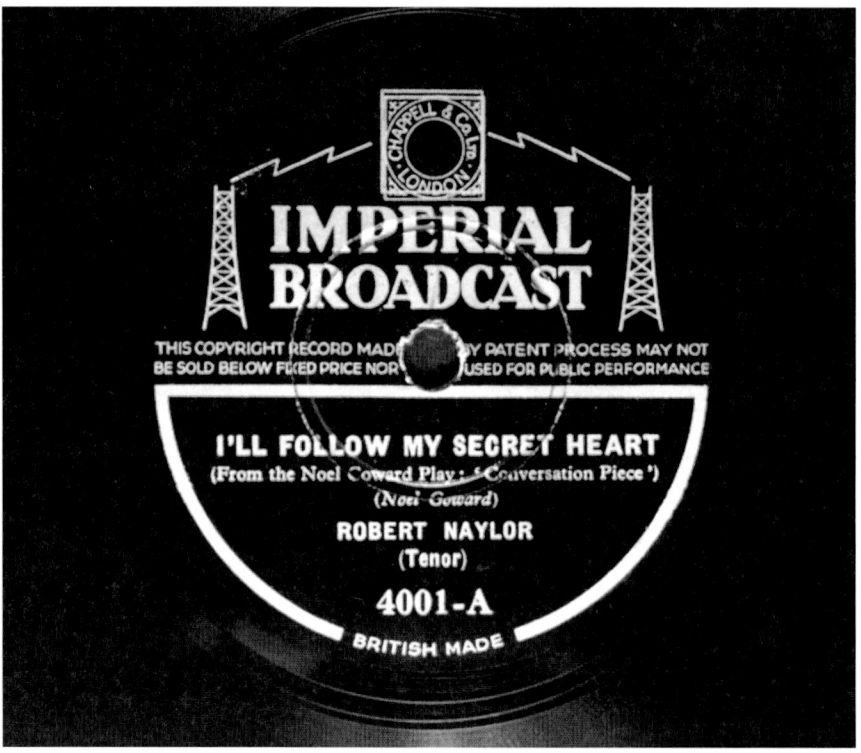
Imperial Broadcast label. (Maurice Robson)

Robert and Cecilia at home in their garden.
(Author's collection)

Robert performing for Pathetone, 1934.
(British Pathé/ITN)

Sylvia Cecil, with whom Robert recorded and undertook stage work, 1934. (D'Oyly Carte Opera Company)

Robert performing for Pathetone, 1934.
(British Pathé/ITN)

A Rex record. (Maurice Robson)

Anona Winn, with whom Robert recorded for the Rex label,
1934. (Author's collection)

CHAPTER SIX
Summer Shows and the Big Screen

In the summer of 1934 Robert and Sylvia starred in the summer season in Largs, Ayrshire, Scotland. The resort of Largs has a magnificent natural setting, with grand hills behind and the fine sweep of its bay running north and south; it had evolved as a genteel retirement resort. Long before the days of charter flights and an affordable fortnight in Spain, the summer holidays of many people were spent at the British seaside. In all resorts seaside entertainers were to be found. Whether it was a pierrot show on the promenade or a 'twice nightly' at the local theatre, these shows provided the resort's evening entertainment. In most holiday shows a resident company performed twice a night, with a weekly midnight matinée in some places, and the programme often changed twice a week. This meant that in a fifteen-week season everybody needed thirty different routines, costumes and music. The hectic schedule meant that a lot of the acts were put together at the last minute, and many comics learned to improvise and ad-lib.

The summer show with Robert and Sylvia started on 2 June 1934 'until further notice' at the Barrfields Pavilion. This had opened in 1930 as a variety theatre with seating for over a thousand, and became the centrepiece of the Largs Summer Season. The pavilion posters announced: 'Harry Kemp presents with pride, "Sunny Days" – A Bright Holiday Show, Twice nightly at 6:45pm and 8:50pm – Tickets 7d to 2/3.'

101

Harry Kemp was presenting the summer show for the fourth successive year. His father George was a travelling showman from Leicester who saw the potential in cinema and had opened a picture palace in Saltcoats in 1913. His son joined the business, extending their interests into concert parties and summer shows at Largs, Saltcoats and Dunoon during the 1930s.

The local paper ran a feature on the forthcoming summer show, which was destined to be one of the big assets of the Largs holiday season: 'Mr Kemp knows his public. He knows people have come to Largs from the big cities in Scotland, and further afield, and they know good variety. In Mr Robert Naylor from Drury Lane, Largs visitors will find an artiste who will give real pleasure to the most critical. Miss Sylvia Cecil, fresh from broadcasting triumphs, is in fine voice and twain sing together in numbers that have stood the test of time.'[133] Also on the bill was the usual collection of comedians and song and dance acts, including Scottish comedian George West, and the Clayton Sisters – Marjorie and Iris, 'tuneful harmony and clever stepping.' The bill was completed by Jack E. Raymond, light comedy; Gladys Watson, singer and dancer; the Jee Boys, a brother dance act; and Harry Carmichael and His Broadcast Boys, who provided the music.

I suspect Robert enjoyed the summer season. It was steady work, and allowed time for him to relax between concerts in surroundings more salubrious than the centre of London. No doubt he visited the Pencil Monument, which commemorates the Battle of Largs in 1263, and the nearby Kelburn Castle, which is believed to be the oldest castle in Scotland. Whether the opportunity to do a spot of sightseeing appealed or not, what we do know is that these summer seaside engagements now became a regular event for him.

After the summer Robert and Sylvia returned to London, and put together a new routine called *Memories from Musical Plays.* In September they found themselves as second billing at the Alhambra, Leicester Square. The variety bill was headlined by the distinguished dancers Anton Dolin and Wendy Toye, both members of the Sadlers Wells Ballet Company. Also on the bill was the American juggler Bobby May. He toured Europe during the '30s and played at the Palladium, as well as theatres in Paris and Switzerland, before returning to the US. One of his tricks involved throwing a cigarette behind his back and catching it in his lips. The cigarette was followed by a lighted match, also caught in his lips, which he used to light the cigarette. Rounding off the entertainment was the musical-comedy brother act, Val and Ernie Stanton.

Robert and Sylvia were together again on 8 October for an interesting radio programme called *Back In Town,* where among the artistes was the Liverpool comedian 'Big Hearted' Arthur Askey, who for the best part of forty years was a stalwart of the British entertainment scene. Robert and Sylvia were accompanied by the London Regional BBC Orchestra, conducted by S. Kneale Kelly. The other artistes on *Back In Town,* which was compèred by Davy Burnaby, were Mario de Pietro, mandolin and banjo; Richards and Dunk, entertainers; Ronald Gourley, *siffleur* and piano; Harley and Barker, duets; C. Hayes, comedian; K. and G. Western, cabaret artists; and the talented Mona Vivian.

Miss Vivian, as 'Wee Mona', had been a child star. She was introduced to pantomime by Francis Laidler, who presented her at the Princess Theatre, Bradford, in 1911 in *Dick Whittington,* from which point her stage career took off. Francis Laidler, 'the king of pantomime', who always presented a troupe of juveniles called the Sunbeams, was responsible for the building of Bradford's Alhambra Theatre. Mona appeared in countless pantomimes in the years to come and was a highly successful stage artiste. She married the wealthy businessman Joseph Hilton Crowther, who was the manager of Leeds United Football Club from 1919 to 1924. Upon marriage he expected his new wife to abandon her glittering stage career. When she refused he filed for divorce.

In the 1930s, as picture palaces became increasingly popular, a regular feature in the cinema programme was a newsreel produced by Associated British Pathé. The company was established in London in 1902, and was soon producing its famous bi-weekly newsreel, the Pathé Gazette. By 1930 Pathé was producing the Gazette, the Pathétone Weekly, the Pathé Pictorial and Eve's Film Review, covering entertainment, culture and women's issues. Fortunately preserved for posterity is a 2½ minute Pathétone film of Robert performing, recorded on 12 November 1934. The full opening credit reads: 'Pathétone has pleasure in presenting the celebrated English Tenor from Covent Garden etc – ROBERT NAYLOR – singing "For Love of You", accompanied by the composer Franz Vienna.'[134]

Franz Vienna's real name was Franz Steininger, a Viennese songwriter born in 1906. Franz Lehár named Franz Steininger his godson and gave him his early musical lessons at his knee. He came to London in 1931 as conductor at the Palace Theatre and composed numerous popular melodies. It seems that Vienna departed for Hollywood at some point in the late 1930s, reverting to his real name. He has over forty songs registered with ASCAP,[135] including one with lyrics by Johnny Mercer. He returned to Europe in 1970 and died in Vienna in 1974.

The Pathétone film short is the only extant footage of Robert singing in close-up. Filmed on an art deco stage setting, Robert appears in a suit of tails with a white bow-tie, a carnation and brilliantined hair. The song 'For Love Of You' was featured in the largely forgotten 1932 film of the same name, which starred the Yorkshire actor Arthur Riscoe, who had appeared with Robert in the West End show *The One Girl,* in 1933. Robert never made a commercial recording of the song. His performance on film is relaxed, skilful and reveals his commanding stage presence. Many popular performers, both singers and musicians, made these short films for Pathé. Some artists made several film appearances for the company, but this seems to be the only occasion on which Robert was invited to perform.

In 1934 further Imperial-Broadcast recordings by Robert were released. The first was 'Serenade' (incipit: 'Overhead The Moon Is Beaming') from *The Student Prince,* by Sigmund Romberg. The show opened at His Majesty's Theatre London in 1926. Romberg produced the music in the old operetta manner, which pleased audiences then and keeps the show a favourite with amateur societies today. The book and lyrics by Dorothy Donnelly tell the story of a prince who falls in love with Kathie, a waitress, in his student days. He then becomes king and must marry royally, but his true love will always remain Kathie. *The Student Prince* was turned into a film in 1954, and the voice of Mario Lanza was used on the soundtrack. In order to capitalise on Lanza's popularity, the producers tacked on to the soundtrack 'Be My Love' (words by Sammy Cahn, music by Nicholas Brodszky), which had been a huge hit for Lanza. Fortunately for them poor old Romberg wasn't around to complain, having died in November 1951. Robert's recording was coupled with the title song from Rudolph Friml's

1924 operetta *Rose Marie*, in which he collaborated with the American lyricist Oscar Hammerstein.[136]

Towards the end of the year, on Saturday 1 December, Robert and Sylvia Cecil starred in another BBC radio programme in the series *Music Hall*, this time alongside the Waters sisters, who, along with Robert, had taken part in the last Parlophone session at Carlton Hill the previous year. Elsie and Doris Waters were best known for their comic characters Gert and Daisy. They wrote all their own material and, an oddity on the comedy scene then, were actually women dressed as women. As Gert and Daisy they carried on a quick-fire conversation of one-liners. Their brother was Jack Warner, of *Dixon of Dock Green* fame. Robert and Sylvia were accompanied in the broadcast by Horatio Davies, who was official accompanist at the Royal Academy of Music and conducted various choirs, including the London Welsh Choral Society.

On *Music Hall* Robert and Sylvia performed 'Love Is A Song', a number written by bandleader Ray Noble for the 1934 film *Prince Charming* starring Evelyn Laye. During the year Robert and Sylvia also committed this song to wax, coupling it with 'Near And Yet So Far' from the same film.[137] Other songs featured in this radio broadcast were 'My Heart Was Sleeping', written by Jimmy Kennedy and the German composer W. Kollo (real name Willi Kollodzieyski), 'My Song For You', written by Mischa Spoliansky for the 1934 film of the same name, and 'Love For Ever I Adore You', a 1929 song with music by the Italian composer and violinist Giulio De Micheli, with an English lyric by Sonny Miller. Among those sharing the bill on *Music Hall* were Ross and Sargent, syncopated harmony; Norman Long, entertainer at the piano; Billy Merson, comedian; and the Dancing Daughters.

Robert's final Imperial-Broadcast record featured two songs from a 1934 film called *Blossom Time*, which starred Richard Tauber and Jane Baxter and was a fictionalised account of Franz Schubert's romantic life. The two songs recorded by Robert were 'Thine Is My Heart' and 'Once There Lived A Lady Fair'.[138] The show has something of a convoluted history. Schubert's original score was adapted for American audiences by Sigmund Romberg, named *Blossom Time,* and produced on Broadway in 1921. When it opened in London, however, at the Lyric Theatre on 22 December 1922, the show's title was changed to *Lilac Time*. To confuse matters further, the 1934 British-made film used the American stage title. The score for the film was further adapted by George Clutsam. 'Thine Is My Heart', based on music by Schubert, became the film's theme song. 'Once There Lived A Lady Fair' was written by Clutsam especially for the film. *The Gramophone* commented: 'Another welcome return is made by Robert Naylor in two songs from *Blossom Time* – 'Thine Is My Heart' and 'Once There Lived A Lady Fair' with Schubert's music. It is a superb voice, but the recording is fearfully forward, making it perhaps the loudest record of the month.'[139]

The recording industry popularised stage performers as never before, and music publishers, record manufacturers and retailers joined forces to capitalise on the developing medium. The F.W. Woolworth stores were in on the burgeoning music business, selling gramophone records ever since they began operations in the UK. In 1927 the company introduced an exclusive label called Eclipse. Their records were among the first to be electrically recorded, which gave a much better sound quality; they were presented on 8in discs, two inches smaller than most rivals. The discs were manufactured by the Crystalate Company, more of which later on. By 1930 a big price differential had opened up between Woolworths' exclusive Eclipse Records at 6*d*, and their main rivals, including Broadcast, also 8in but 1*s* 3*d*. As a result, sales of Eclipse records rocketed.

Woolworths was able to sell its records much more cheaply than the competition for two reasons. First, instead of paying a royalty each time a song was sold, the company bought the song outright, normally paying the artiste and copyright owner a fee up front. The plan relied on selling huge quantities – and because of the cost normally only one song on the record was bought outright. The second way in which prices were kept down was to record cover versions of popular songs, particularly from the movies or wireless programmes. A strong roster of artistes was built up but, often for contractual reasons, many of the vocalists who appeared on the Eclipse label used pseudonyms and were paid a flat fee. Robert Naylor was one such artiste who recorded two sides for the Eclipse label in about 1934, using the name Derek Powell. 'My Song For You' by Eyton and Spoliansky and 'The Isle Of Dreams' by Fenhow and McCulley (the bought song in this case), were issued on Eclipse 806.[140] Woolworths persisted with its own record labels into the 1960s, the last imprint being the Embassy label.

On 14 December 1934 the Court Circular announced, 'The Princess Royal attended a *Grand Divertissement* at the Hyde Park Hotel yesterday in aid of the "Not Forgotten Association". The proceeds were to buy Christmas gifts and treats for the "boys in blue", of whom there are over 2,500 still in hospital in the London area and over 5,000 in Great Britain and Ireland. Among those in attendance were the Duchess of Devonshire, the Marchioness of Hartington, and Lady Violet Astor.'

The programme of music, which included items by Sylvia Cecil, Robert Naylor and Elsie and Doris Waters, was arranged by Miss Marta Cunningham, herself a formerly well-known soprano who had established the Not Forgotten Association in 1919. In 1926 the association officially defined its task as being 'to provide comfort, cheer and entertainment for the wounded ex-servicemen still in hospital as a result of the Great War'.

From January 1935 Robert's official recordings were released on the Rex label – 'The King of Records'. Rex records were sold at Marks and Spencer, price 1s, and were the improved 10in successor of Imperial. Both these labels were owned by the Crystalate Record Company of Tonbridge, Kent, which had its London offices at 60–2 Clerkenwell Road, EC1.[141] Between 1920 and 1939 literally scores of labels associated with Crystalate were on the market. The company's musical director was Jay Wilbur, who assembled house bands from the cream of West End musicians. Most of his top-grade session men had a regular job with other leaders, including Ambrose, Carol Gibbons, and Sydney Lipton, at the same time. It is not known which musicians played on Robert Naylor's recordings, but session players from classical orchestras were probably most often used.

Crystalate's recording studio was at 165 Broadhurst Gardens, West Hampstead, north London – a stark red-brick building which had begun life in 1884 as the Falcon Works and was converted into a recording studio in 1933. Four years later the company was absorbed by Decca. The acquisition of this studio included the services of recording engineers, who would play a major role in the development of recording technology and established Decca as a world leader. These West Hampstead studios were rebuilt by

Decca in 1961 and became home to numerous recording artists involved in solo recordings, chamber music and other works that which did not require large venues. The studios remained in use until the beginning of the 1980s when, following the sale of Decca to Polygram, in 1981 the premises were converted to rehearsal studios for the English National Opera and renamed Lilian Baylis House.

Robert's first outing on the Rex label was *Gems from the Merry Widow*, recorded with the soprano Anona Winn – one of the busiest and most popular radio revue artistes. Born Anona Edna Wilkins in Australia in 1904, she was reading at the bar when one day the famous operatic soprano Nellie Melba (1861–1931; her real name was Helen Porter Mitchell) heard her singing and offered her a scholarship at the Sydney Conservatorium of Music. Anona Winn came to England in 1927 and appeared in *The Blue Mazurka*, music by Franz Lehár, at Daly's Theatre in London. The BBC was broadcasting from Savoy Hill at this time, and Winn rapidly made her name as a radio artiste; and she recorded for various labels. She had a major recording success in 1934 with 'What More Can I Ask', which was written by Ray Noble. She recorded it first alone and then, three weeks later, as a duet with Sam Browne (as Jack and Jill). Both sessions were made for EMI and released on the Regal-Zonophone label. Probably best remembered as a quick-witted panellist on the BBC's *Twenty Questions* for nearly three decades, Anona Winn was awarded an MBE in 1954 and died in 1994.

Robert and Anona's recording was a double-sided selection from the operetta *The Merry Widow*.[142] Recorded in about November 1934, the record was not released until January 1935. *The Merry Widow* (*Die Lustige Witwe*) was composed by Lehár. Often called the 'queen of operettas', it is certainly the most celebrated and successful show of its kind ever written. The melodies and songs are lovingly played and sung the whole world over, making it one of the surest box-office attractions of all time. The librettists, Viktor Léon and Leo Stein, based the story – concerning a rich widow, Hanna Glawari, and her attempt to find a husband – on an 1861 comedy, *L'Attaché d'Ambassade* (*The Embassy Attaché*), by Henri Meilhac. In its English adaptation by Basil Hood, with lyrics by Adrian Ross, the operetta became a sensation in London, from its first production in June 1907. In November 1933 MGM released a film of the show, starring

Maurice Chevalier and Jeannette MacDonald, which became popular when it was screened in England during the winter of 1933–4; the Rex recording was clearly intended to take advantage of this.

This musical format, minus Miss Winn, was repeated in the second Rex disc, called *Gems From Blossom Time*.[143] Robert re-recorded excerpts of two of the songs from the show that he had recorded the previous year for Imperial-Broadcast, 'Thine Is My Heart' and 'Once There Lived A Lady Fair', together with 'Red, Red Rose'. Further excerpts from the show were performed by the uncredited studio orchestra. As *The Gramophone*'s reviewer noted, 'On Rex 8345 [Robert Naylor] gives us some songs from *Blossom Time*, one of the many Schubert films. This is odd since Mr Naylor recorded two of these songs for us last month.' He did add, however, 'He sings well.'[144]

The third release on Rex was 'One Night Of Love',[145] the title song from Columbia's successful venture into movie opera, released in 1934. The film made a star of the American soprano Grace Moore – born in Tennessee in 1898 and known as the Tennessee Nightingale. Tragically, while still immensely popular she died in a plane crash at Copenhagen airport on 26 January 1947. Elvis Presley is said to have named his beloved Memphis home, Graceland, after her. 'One Night Of Love' was composed by Victor Schertzinger, an American of Dutch descent who was something of a child prodigy. As a child of eight he performed on the violin with several orchestras, including the Victor Herbert Orchestra. He studied music at the University of Brussels, and began to compose scores for the film industry as early as 1916. Schertzinger was closely associated with Paramount Films throughout the '30s and with 'One Night Of Love', which he not only composed but also directed, he was able to capitalise on his vast knowledge of the world of music. The film was a huge success and it won an Academy Award for original music score. Schertzinger's two best-known songs are 'I Remember You' and 'Tangerine', both with lyrics by Johnny Mercer. The lyrics for 'One Night Of Love' were by another contributor to the great American songbook, Gus Kahn.

Robert's recording of 'One Night Of Love' was coupled with 'Tell Me Tonight', a song lifted from the 1932 Gaumont British film of the same name that starred the Polish tenor Jan Kiepura. Set in Switzerland, it tells the unlikely story of an Italian tenor, dominated by his female business manager, who changes places with a fugitive con-man and falls in love with a mayor's adopted daughter. The music for the film was written by the distinguished Russian composer, Mischa Spoliansky. He moved to London in 1933 and was commissioned by film maker Alexander Korda to write the score for *Sanders of the River* (1935), starring Paul Robeson, which won the prize for Best Music at the Venice Film Festival. He went on to score over fifty movies. The lyrics to 'Tell Me Tonight' were by Frank Eyton, who is today best known as a co-writer of the standard song 'Body And Soul'.

At the Prince's Theatre, beginning on 28 February 1935, Robert appeared in a revival of *The Rose of Persia,* a two-act comic opera by Basil Hood and Arthur Sullivan. The Prince's Theatre was on Shaftesbury Avenue, Camden. In 1962 it was sold to EMI, and renamed the Shaftesbury Theatre. *The Rose of Persia* (subtitled *The Story-Teller and the Slave*), which was described as a combination of *Arabian Nights* and *The Mikado*, was first produced at the Savoy Theatre in 1899, where after good reviews it ran for over 200 performances. The major characters in the opera are Hassan, a wealthy philanthropist; Dancing Sunbeam, his first wife (they're still married – he has twenty-five wives in all); Abdallah, a priest; Yussuf, a professional storyteller; the Sultan of Persia; his Sultana, Rose-in-Bloom; Rose-in-Bloom's three slaves and companions. *Rose of Persia* is very much in the mould of earlier Savoy productions, with its farcical plot, mistaken identities, a domineering wife and a tyrannical monarch. Hood's libretto contains some amusing word-play, but critics felt the work was inferior to that of W.S. Gilbert.

Robert played the role of the storyteller, Yussuf. He sings in a number of chorus groups of different sizes, and he was also a soloist, singing 'Peace Be Upon This House', 'Our Tale Is Told' and 'I Care Not If The Cup I Hold'. A reviewer referred to it as 'an attractive production', with the comment, 'Mr Naylor can make sure of a double-encore for 'I Care Not If The Cup I Hold', the best solo number in the opera, by some good straight singing.'[146] Unfortunately the 1935 revival of the show was not able to repeat its original success, and closed on 23 March 1935 after only twenty-five performances.

Back in the recording studio, Robert continued his association with Rex. Around March 1935 he recorded two songs from the 1934 film *My Heart is Calling You*,[147] a Gaumont-British film produced by Michael Balcon. It starred the tenor Jan Kiepura and was released in France as *Mon coeur t'appelle*. The film's music was by the Austrian composer Robert Stolz, who provided the score for *Wild Violets*. The two songs recorded by Robert were the title song, with lyrics by Harry S. Pepper, and 'You Me And Love', with lyrics by Tommie Connor, who is much better known for writing 'I Saw Mommy Kissing Santa Claus'.

Robert had himself ventured into the world of movie-making when some months earlier he was given a supporting role in the film *Abdul the Damned*, made by British International Pictures at Elstree Studios, Borehamwood, Hertfordshire. Although a British production, there was a heavy input from exiled Germans. It was produced by Max Schach, directed by Karl Grune and had music by Hans Eisler. The film starred the Austrian-born actor Fritz Kortner, whose speciality was playing sinister and threatening roles. The female lead was played by the strikingly glamorous American actress Adrienne Ames. Aptly Robert appears in the film as an opera singer.

On the website www.allmovie.com, Sandra Brennan succinctly describes the film thus: 'An epic costume drama, from a story by Robert Neuman, it is set in turn-of-the-century Turkey and chronicles the ruthless reign of a paranoid ruler who begins killing everyone he suspects of treachery against him. The despot's loyal chief of police obediently enacts his master's bloody whims, until he too stands accused of conspiracy and is sentenced to die. To save him, his lover, a Viennese actress, offers to join the despot's harem.' Before the main filming started, a British International Pictures unit filmed exteriors in Constantinople for environmental atmosphere and back projection shots, to give the film a more realistic feel.

There was, it seems, some concern about the film being politically insensitive, because of recent Turkish history. Abdul Hamid II (1842–1918) became Sultan of Turkey in 1876, on the deposition of his brother. A subtle diplomatist, he cleverly played the European Powers against each other, but his empire was always in disorder and the Armenian massacres of 1896 earned him the title of Abdul the Damned. In April 1909 he was deposed and put in captivity; he died in Constantinople. However, when the film was viewed by Edward Schortt, the ex-home secretary and president of the British Board of Film Censors, together with representatives of the Foreign Office, on 26 February 1935, it was passed for exhibition with only two small deletions.

Abdul the Damned opened at the Regal Cinema, Marble Arch, in March 1935. *Film Weekly* described the film as 'A strong drama of a sinister Sultan tortured by fear of assassination, magnificently acted by Fritz Kortner. Interesting, impressive and, for the most part, gripping entertainment.'[148] However, *The Times*, always reserved in these matters, felt that the actors 'all do their best for a film that is technically excellent but which has lost its way in trying to be too impressive'.[149] Viewing the film certainly requires a degree of concentration; the pace is fast, making the story at times a little difficult to follow.

Also in *Abdul the Damned* was fellow Calderdale-born Eric Portman, playing the part of a conspirator. Portman was born in 1901 at Chester Road, Akroydon, Halifax, the third of four children. After leaving the private Rishworth School, he went to work in his father's outfitters shop in Halifax. A member of Halifax Opera Society, he made his début on the professional stage in 1924, appearing mainly in Shakespeare's plays, often with the Old Vic Company at the Lyric Theatre in Hammersmith. He died at his cottage in St Veep, Cornwall, in 1969.

Abdul the Damned was a runaway success at the box office. In 1935 the UK tobacco company Gallaher issued a set of cigarette cards of famous film scenes, and the thirtieth card in the series featured a scene from *Abdul*. The film was released in the United States in December the same year, by Alliance Films Inc.

In *Abdul the Damned* Robert is seen but briefly, appearing on stage in a club. He must have been disappointed to view the finished film and to find that most of his performance had ended up on the cutting-room floor. A number of other tenor singers in this period enjoyed varying degrees of big-screen success: John McCormack, Jan Kiepura, Webster Booth and, most notably perhaps, Richard Tauber. Whatever aspirations Robert had for a film career they were never realised, and this was to be his only film appearance.

In April 1935 Rex released a double-sided selection, entitled *Everybody's Songs*, of Robert performing alongside Sylvia Cecil and the bass Foster Richardson.[150] The recording session had taken place in July the previous year, when Robert and Sylvia were performing regularly together. Foster Richardson was born in Nottingham in 1890 and started singing as he walked behind the plough on his father's farm. He won a scholarship in an open competition, and studied at the Royal Academy of Music. The road to success was hard, but one day he sang to Sir Thomas Beecham and was engaged to sing in the Beecham Opera Company. Richardson became a popular and versatile broadcaster, making his first broadcast in an orchestral concert in 1927, and was equally at home in concert, opera and revue.

The selections on *Everybody's Songs* were: Part One (Side A): 'I Passed By Your Window', from *Song Pictures* by Helen Taylor and May H. Brae; 'Somewhere A Voice Is Calling' by Arthur Tate and Eileen Newton; and 'Down Vauxhall Way', from *Old Songs of London* by Herbert Oliver; Part Two (Side B): 'I Know Of Two Bright Eyes', from *Songs of the Turkish Hills* by George H. Clutsam; 'O Lovely Night', from the *Summertime* song cycle by Landon Ronald; 'Passing By' by Edward Purcell; and 'Come To The Fair' by Helen Taylor and Easthorpe Martin.

The Gramophone noted: 'Many will have seen Robert Naylor and Sylvia Cecil in their music hall act; they are now joined by Foster Richardson, that stalwart of old Zonophone days and one of the finest bass-barytones [sic] now singing, in *Everybody's Songs* on Rex 8388 (1 shilling). Good songs well sung, but why give 'Passing By' to the soprano and leave 'O Lovely Night' to the orchestra? Mr Naylor should have had the former, while Miss Cecil would have made a lovely thing of Landon Ronald's glorious melody.'[151]

On the morning of Tuesday 28 May, far away from the glitz and glamour of London, Robert's father passed away at his home, Montana, in Luddenden Foot. Robert Sutcliffe Naylor was aged sixty-six and had suffered a seizure the day before. He had worked at Messrs W.H. Boocock & Son, solicitors, in Halifax and Sowerby Bridge, for over fifty years: a lifetime spent dealing with the stresses of legal matters had earned him a short retirement. He had not enjoyed the best of health for some time and had recently gone to Morecambe to convalesce, only returning home three weeks earlier. The funeral was held at noon on Friday 31 May at St Mary's Church, Luddenden – which he had attended all his life. Through his work, Mr Naylor was held in high esteem in the district, and his role had brought him into contact with a great many people. In addition to family members, including Robert who had returned from London, a large number of friends and colleagues were present at the funeral. The service was conducted by the Rev. T.A. Craggs, and Mr Naylor's brother-in-law, Mr Thomas Mason, read the lesson. Robert's father was interred in the Naylor family grave in the church grounds. He had been immensely proud of his son's theatrical achievements.

In July Rex released Robert singing two newly published songs.[152] The first was 'Love Was A Song' (lyrics by Charles Dunn, music by Mischa Spoliansky) and 'For Love Alone (I Have So Little To Give)' (lyrics by Bruce Sievier, music by Pat Thayer). Patrick Thayer was a prolific writer of songs throughout the '30s and '40s. Unfortunately his wartime musical, *The Silver Patrol,* achieved only seventy-five London performances, but the summer of 1940 was scarcely a good time to launch a musical. The reviewer in *The Gramophone* said, 'Robert Naylor has strayed from Miscellaneous onto my list, and I am tempted to keep him there. Thayer's popular ballad 'For Love Alone' suits his charming voice admirably. It is coupled with 'Love Was A Song', delightfully sung.'[153]

The final release during 1935 from the Rex label was Robert singing two songs from *Glamorous Night* – a musical play in two acts by Ivor Novello, with lyrics by Christopher Hassall. The show was a huge box-office success when it opened on 2 May 1935 at Theatre Royal, Drury Lane, where it ran for 243 performances. The plot concerns the story of the young inventor Anthony Allen and the glamorous operetta star Militza Hajos, with whom he falls in love. Robert's disc features 'Glamorous Night' coupled with 'Shine Through My Dreams'.[154]

On 8 October Robert made an hour-long radio broadcast with the BBC Theatre Orchestra, conducted by Stanford Robinson, a conductor who had a long association with the BBC. Born in Leeds in 1904, his first wireless appearance, when he was still less than twenty years old, was when he conducted the Wireless Orchestra in March 1924. After conducting BBC choral groups, Robinson served as conductor of the BBC Theatre Orchestra from 1932 to 1946. In this post he was responsible for studio opera, and he made many distinguished radio and TV broadcasts and recordings. He made his Covent Garden début in 1937 and appeared in several other venues at home and abroad; later he was associate conductor of the BBC Symphony Orchestra (1946-9), conductor of the BBC Opera Orchestra (1949-52), and a BBC staff conductor (1952-66). In 1972 Robinson was awarded an OBE for his services to music.

One of the items Robert performed was 'A Southern Song', composed by Sir Landon Ronald and published in 1905 with words by Bertha Dean-Freeman. Robert had recorded the song for Parlophone in December 1931, some four years earlier, but here was a new arrangement of the song, probably by Stanford Robinson. The song's composer listened to the radio broadcast that evening, and the following morning wrote to Robert from the Guildhall School of Music:

> My dear Naylor, I feel I must write and tell you that last night I listened in to your singing, which gave me very great pleasure. What a fine artist you are today.
>
> I was so delighted with your rendering of 'A Southern Song' which I heard for the first time accompanied by the Orchestra. Who on earth did the orchestration? It is so exceptionally well done, that I am interested to know who did it. I thought Stanford Robinson followed you perfectly splendidly, and it isn't easy with the various pauses and rallentandos which you make and do so effectively.
>
> I thought it would please you to know that you gave me very great pleasure.
> Yours sincerely,'[155]

It is clear from this that Sir Landon Ronald was a great admirer of Robert's singing, and it is perhaps no surprise to discover that Robert was among the honoured guests invited to his Silver Jubilee Dinner, held to celebrate his twenty-fifth anniversary as Principal of the Guildhall School of Music. This was held at the Savoy Hotel on the evening of Sunday 3 November 1935. Among the distinguished guests were His Excellency the Persian Minister, Sir Thomas

Beecham, Catherine, Countess of Westmorland, Dr Malcolm Sargent and the Lady Mayoress of London.[156] The evening began at 7.15pm with a reception by the chairman, Sir Hugh P. Allen GCVO, MA, Mus. Doc. Dinner was served at 7.45pm. This was followed by speeches from the Lady Mayoress, Lord Justice Greer, Sir Thomas Beecham, Sir Seymour Hicks, and Sir Edward German. At 10.00pm a programme of music was presented by Clara Evelyn, Sterndale Bennett and Fred Gregory, and Elsie and Doris Waters.

Many of the guests attended with their wives, but Robert was at the function unaccompanied. Given that Cecilia was herself a concert artiste – and a more legitimate invitee than many of the other guests' wives – her absence from the celebration seems strange. However, it may be that by this time she was already unwell with the illness that would eventually shorten her life, and had declined to attend the dinner.

Landon Ronald was himself already ill at this point and had largely withdrawn from public life. His first marriage had ended tragically in 1932, when his wife committed suicide by taking poison. That same year he married his thirty-four-year-old former mistress. Though never a major international figure, Ronald made a substantial contribution to British musical life. He died from cancer at his home in Paddington, London, on 14 August 1938 and was cremated at Golders Green. His passing in some ways serves to mark the ending of a particular musical era.

By the mid-'30s people were besotted with dance bands that held residencies in all the top night-spots in London's grand hotels and supper clubs. These bands could be heard on radio throughout the country. Almost every night of the week at a turn of the dial you could hear, among others, Sydney Lipton from the Grosvenor House, Jack Jackson from the Dorchester, Carroll Gibbons from the Savoy, and Ambrose from the Mayfair. Henry Hall, the newly appointed leader of the newly formed BBC Dance Orchestra, could be heard on the radio throughout the day. These artistes sold gramophone recordings in large numbers. If there was a golden age of dance bands, it was those years between 1930 and 1939, when the West End thrived and prospered, and it seemed that the good times would never end.[157]

However, those attending such top-class venues were well to do and sophisticated. It was variety shows, summer shows, radio, films and records that gave the average person the chance to hear (and see) bands and singers. In the '30s radio broadcasts offered listeners a more varied output, so straight singers and musicians still had opportunities to perform and became known to a wider public than might otherwise have been the case. Straight singers of the era, like Robert, were more versatile performers than their successors. As we have seen, they could be performing opera and oratorio one week, and appearing in a variety show the next week.

As popular tastes were shifting, the style of music Robert performed was already beginning to lose favour as far as the general public was concerned. The emphasis was on a softer and more intimate manner of singing, using the subtle vocal nuances and phrasing found in jazz as opposed to the sheer volume to be found in opera houses. It was a vocal style that proliferated following the invention of the electric microphone, epitomised in this country by singers like Sam Browne, Chick Henderson, Denny Dennis and Al Bowlly. Highly popular too were cabaret artistes such as Leslie Hutchinson and Layton and Johnstone, who were black vocalists, and the white double-act B.C Hilliam and Malcolm McEachern, better known as Flotsam and Jetsam.

By the early '50s the variety halls, like the music halls before them, were in their twilight years. The post-war generation preferred calypso, skiffle and rock 'n' roll as musical entertainment and, as had occurred previously when tastes changed, many hitherto successful variety acts went into terminal decline. But in the years before the war there remained, for the moment, sufficient numbers of people who still admired 'a good voice' and popular tenors like Robert, while no longer quite as much in vogue as they once were, could still fill theatre seats.

At Eastbourne on 4 November 1935 many well-known artistes gave their services at a matinée at the Winter Gardens, Devonshire Park, in aid of the Heritage School and Hospital for Crippled Children at Chailey, Sussex. In 1903 Dame Grace Kimmings and her friend Alice Rennis took in seven physically handicapped children from the East End of London, providing accommodation and nursing facilities in an old workhouse; today Chailey Heritage School provides care for a few hundred handicapped children. Included in the 1935 benefit concert were Robert and Cecilia, the

117

English actress Marie Ney, and the Australian-born actress Madge Titheradge, together with the Eastbourne Municipal Orchestra.

On 17 December 1935 it was reported that Princess Alice, Countess of Athlone, was present yesterday at the *Divertissement* at the Hyde Park Hotel in aid of the 'Not Forgotten Association' to raise funds for Christmas gifts and treats for 'the boys in blue'. Among the distinguished guests were the Countess of Albermarle and the Duchess of Devonshire. Among those performing on this occasion were Robert Naylor, Olive Groves, George Barker, and the Frank Ivimery Band. Arthur Fagge, who had founded the London Choral Society, was musical director.

Robert made a further radio broadcast for the BBC on 27 January 1936, with the BBC Military Band. Today this combination of voice and military band may strike us as odd, but military bands as we know them are, in some respects, a shadow of their former selves. There was a time when they were accorded a huge following, when every self-respecting town had its own bandstand – a proud feature of the park. Open-air band concerts were very popular, and it was common for military bands to accompany vocalists. Not all bands were associated with the armed forces: there were, and happily still are, many fine concert bands, who augment their sound with woodwind players.

In the early days of British broadcasting the Wireless Military Band quickly built a fine reputation for its playing. Municipal orchestras sometimes performed as bands, and it has always been the custom for military band players to double on other instruments, including strings, thus allowing their ensembles to perform a more varied selection of works. The Wireless Military Band flourished from 1927 until its last performance on 16 March 1943. In 1936 it was renamed the BBC Military Band, and record labels and broadcasts reflected this change of name. It had its own staff arranger, Gerrard Williams, and the repertoire was largely made up of orchestral works scored with great virtuosity. Walton O'Donnell, formerly Director of Music of the Royal Marines at Deal, was the conductor, and he joined the BBC on 7 June 1927. He continued as conductor until 1937, when he took over the BBC Northern Ireland Orchestra, but sadly died two years later.

February 1936 saw Robert's penultimate record release. 'Vienna, City Of My Dreams' and 'My World Is Gold (Because

You Love Me)'.[158] Robert was accompanied on both sides by Fred Hartley and his Orchestra. Fred Hartley was born in Dundee in 1905. He was a prolific composer and arranger, as well as a conductor, pianist and regular broadcaster. Hartley was official accompanist at the Royal Academy of Music from 1922 to 1926, and went on to join the BBC as an accompanist. He made his first broadcast as a solo pianist in 1925, before founding his famous Novelty Quintet in 1931, which brought with it a weekly radio programme. A talented arranger, his skills were frequently heard on BBC radio either side of the Second World War. In 1946 he became the BBC's head of light music. His 'Scherzetto for Children' was the theme music for BBC Children's Television, and it could be heard each day, usually at 5.00pm, during the 1950s. Fred Hartley passed away in 1980 aged seventy-five.

Both songs on the disc were from the film *Heart's Desire*, which was showing at the time at the Stoll cinema, Kingsway, London. The plot concerns Oliver Desmond (Carl Harbord), who has written a new opera and is scouring Europe with Frances (Leonora Corbett) for a tenor to sing the lead. In Vienna they visit a street café where Josef Steidler (Richard Tauber) sings each evening for a few coins. They are impressed with his voice, in such an unlikely location, and invite him to London to sing in the opera, where he becomes famous. It is a predictable story, but of course it was written merely to showcase Tauber's singing. Of Robert's record, *The Gramophone* felt that 'Many people will like to have his manly singing on two such popular songs.'[159]

'Vienna, City Of My Dreams', lyrics by Edward Lockton and music by Rudolph Sieczynski, was published in 1916 as '*Wien, Du Stadt Meiner Traume*', long before the film. The song has remained popular, and has been recorded more recently by Harry Secombe and Placido Domingo among others. 'My World Is Gold' is credited to Richard Tauber and Clifford Grey.

March 1936 saw the release of Robert's final recording for Rex Records. It included what one reviewer felt was 'An extraordinary outburst from Horatio Nicholls [the composer] called "Here's Health Unto Our New King"[160] which somehow completely gives me the jitters, but it is appropriately presented by Robert Naylor and the band of H.M. Irish Guards and Organ.'[161] Horatio Nicholls was a pen-name for Lawrence Wright; the lyrics were written by

Edward Lockton. The song was meant to capture the patriotic fervour surrounding the accession to the throne of Edward VIII. His father, King George V, had died two months earlier at Sandringham, Norfolk, of influenza. He had not enjoyed good health for a long time, and during his final years he had spent much of his time pursuing his grand passion, philately. Edward succeeded him for a brief period before leading the country into an abdication crisis, fuelled in part by comments made about him by Dr Blunt, the bishop of Bradford. The reverse of the record featured 'The Old Songs Of Great Britain', a selection that included Edward Purcell's 'Passing By' and Landon Ronald's 'O Lovely Night'. Robert did not sing on this side of the disc.

The impresario Lawrence Wright organised his second annual 'Lights Out' ball at the Covent Garden Opera House on 26 March. This event was organised by Wright to plug his company's song catalogue. British Pathé made a short film of the event called *Let's Go Gay*. It opens with the Grenadier Guards playing, while Robert concludes by singing his latest recording, 'Here's Health Unto Our New King', finishing with a rousing crescendo as he raises his glass in the air. Crowds of people watch from the rear and balconies, and enthusiastically applaud at the end of the song. Others seen in the film include Joe Loss and his Band, pianist Billy Mayerl, orchestra leaders Mantovani, Debroy Somers, Geraldo and Maurice Winnick, and singer Florrie Forde. At the time of writing the film is available to view on the Pathé website.

At Easter 1936 Eastbourne did its best to make up for the inclement weather so far that year by providing a host of first-class entertainment for the diversion of the visitors. At the town's Winter Gardens on Good Friday there was a large audience of music lovers to hear the soprano Garda Hall. On Easter Sunday, 12 April, Robert sang at the Winter Gardens.

In the summer Robert appeared in *On with the Show* at Blackpool. This was the eleventh season (out of thirty-two) in which Lawrence Wright presented this show on the North Pier. Blackpool has three piers, of which the North Pier, designed by Eugenius Birch, was the first to grace the sea-front. It opened on 21 March 1863 amid much pomp and ceremony. Grade II listed today, it is considered the most traditional of the three piers, retaining much of its Victorian splendour and being devoted to the gentle pursuits of promenading and sun-bathing rather than the brash entertainment offered by its newer companions.

The impresario, composer and music publisher Lawrence Wright was born in Leicester in 1888. His father had a shop selling sheet music and instruments, and the young Lawrence followed him into the business. In 1906 he set up his own shop in the town and the Wright Music Company was established. Not content with selling other people's music, he began to write songs of his own. He became very much the doyen of the British 'Tin Pan Alley', which was clustered around Denmark Street in Soho. Although he was a prolific composer, the only one of Wright's songs that is heard regularly today is 'Among My Souvenirs' (1927), with words by Edgar Leslie. It was recorded by Louis Armstrong in 1942 and was featured by Hoagy Carmichael in the film *The Best Years Of Our Lives* (1946). The song was also a UK Top Twenty hit for Connie Francis in 1959. Wright often wrote using pseudonyms – including Paul Parce and Horatio Nicholls. In 1929, as Horatio Nicholls, he published a booklet entitled *How to Write a Successful Song*, in which he suggested that a lack of knowledge of music need be no barrier to achieving this. Wright was also shrewd enough to buy the British publishing rights to many jazz composers such as Duke Ellington and Fats Waller, all of which helped to make his company one of the largest music publishing houses in Britain. In 1962 he received an Ivor Novello award for outstanding services to British popular and light music. Lawrence Wright died suddenly in 1964 following a fall at his home in Blackpool. In 1965 the Beatles' company Northern Songs bought up the entire catalogue of the Lawrence Wright Music Company for £812,500.

In 1936 *On with the Show* opened on the North Pier on Friday 29 May, and was presented daily at 2.45 pm and 7.45pm. It starred, in addition to Robert, the attractive soprano Rose Perfect – which was actually her real name. She had appeared in concert with Robert twice before, during 1933. Born in Wandsworth, London, in 1902, until recently Rose had lived in the USA with her American husband and had taken out British naturalisation papers on her return. In 1929, while in the States, she had starred in a film musical entitled *Rose Perfect, The Girl with the Golden Voice*, which was directed by Murray Roth, a former tin-pan alley song plugger. She made her first stage appearance in this country at the

Palladium in 1930, in Will Hay's comedy *Out of Bounds.* She regularly featured the song 'Tears', written in 1930 by Frank Capano and Billy Uhr, which became a Number One UK hit for Ken Dodd in 1965. There is a British Pathé film clip from 1933 that features her with the Billy Cotton Band at the Adelphi Ballroom, Slough. In the film, after the Cotton band finish playing 'I'm Just Wild About Harry', the intertitle reads: 'Millions of Radio Listeners Have Heard This Famous Artist – Rose Perfect, The Celebrated Soprano.' She then stands in front of the band and sings 'The Song Of Songs', written by Moya (Harold Vicars). Before her Blackpool engagement Rose had starred for a week at the Trocadero Kinema on the South Bank, with much success.

In *On with the Show* the comedy was provided by Fred Wynne, and Revnell and West, a popular female double-act who began their career in concert parties. Their most popular variety characters were Ethel and Gracie, a pair of malevolent Cockney schoolgirls. Ethel was just over 6ft tall, while Gracie was considerably shorter, at just under 5ft. The bill also included Hal Swain and his Band, and the Five Sherry Brothers. The latter was a novelty act from Glasgow that included Sam Sherry on guitar. Their finale was an acrobatic dancing act – step-dances, acrobatic routines and a fast-winging routine. They wore tap shoes and evening dress and it was, by all accounts, a sensational show-stopping act. All this pier entertainment could be enjoyed for as little as 6*d* admission.

During the 1930s Robert bought a holiday home on the Fylde coast, which indicates his prosperity at this time, A second home is seen by many today as an indispensable accessory, but in the 1930s they were exclusively the domain of the rich. Robert's seaside retreat was a smart semi-detached property at Thornton Gate, Cleveleys. Cleveleys sprang up during the 1890s and owed its initial popularity to the tramway system between Blackpool and Fleetwood; it is often regarded as being a bit more select than its near neighbour Blackpool.

It was during the summer of 1936, while staying in Cleveleys, that Cecilia, who may have been unwell for some time, became poorly. Her illness was described as dropsy, an old term for the swelling of soft tissues owing to the accumulation of excess water. When *On with the Show* closed on Friday 2 October, Robert returned to London leaving Cecilia to recuperate in Cleveleys.

Perhaps it was felt that the sea air would be beneficial. As it turned out, she spent much of the next eighteen months as a patient in the Central Nursing Home at 230 Hornby Road, Blackpool, while Miss Over, the family's nanny, continued to look after Michael – as she had for the last four years. These domestic arrangements, in part necessary thanks to the demands of Robert's career, meant that Michael grew up never feeling close to his father.

Robert had little time in which to adjust to these new circumstances, for from Monday 5 October he was on stage at the Granada in Tooting with Serge Krish and his Orchestra. Krish was a Russian-Jewish émigré, born in 1887. A successful pianist and conductor, he founded the New Metropolitan Orchestra, with whom he made numerous gramophone recordings of light orchestra works. Further dates followed for Robert immediately in Walthamstow and Leytonstone.

In October *The Stage* carried the following announcement in their 'Variety Gossip' column: 'Following twenty weeks' summer season at the North Pier, Blackpool, Robert Naylor has been appearing on the Gaumont Circuit and singing about sixty songs a week. On Monday 26 October he opened at the Dominion, Tottenham Court Road, with a new act entitled "A Phantasy [*sic*] of Song" with Esther Coleman in association.'

The contralto Esther Coleman was born in Hampstead and, like Robert, studied at the Guildhall School of Music; she won the gold medal there in 1923. She worked extensively on radio and the brand-new medium of television, appeared in films and made numerous gramophone recordings. She recorded mainly for Zonophone, singing a number of duets with the bass Foster Richardson. She was, however, an adaptable performer, who was also known as Diana Clare, and she recorded under this name with Harry Roy and his Orchestra.

From 16 November Robert and Esther appeared at the old Hippodrome Theatre in Coventry. Others on the bill were the comedy double-act Murray and Mooney, Bower and Rutherford, the Gordon Richards Four, Jack Murray and Van Dusen. George Van Dusen's recordings were among the bestsellers of the 1930s. He used the title The Great Dutch Yodeller throughout his long career, although his stage name belied his East End origins.

Robert's second radio broadcast of 1936 was on 14 November with the BBC Theatre Orchestra, which had been formed in 1931 as 'an auxiliary to dramatic production'. The first conductor, Leslie Woodgate, was replaced within the year by Stanford Robinson, who remained as conductor until 1946. As well as providing incidental music for BBC plays, the orchestra performed its own light music concerts and appeared on variety and other programmes. For this radio broadcast with Robert, the orchestra was conducted by the Lancashire-born organist and choirmaster Harold Lowe, a Fellow of the Royal College of Organists.

From 23 November Robert and Esther were at the New Victoria Cine-Variety Theatre with their very successful act named *A Fantasy of Song*. On the opening night they sang five new numbers: 'Shine Through My Dreams' (Ivor Novello and Christopher Hassall), 'These Foolish Things' (Eric Maschwitz and Jack Strachey), 'You Are My Song Divine' (Edward Lockton and Horatio Nicholls), 'For Love Alone' (Bruce Sievier and Pat Thayer) and 'It's A Sin To Tell A Lie' (Billy Mayhew). The latter, introduced by Fats Waller, seems a surprising choice, but Esther was equally at home singing swing numbers. At the end of their performance, so insistent was the applause that they had to appear in front of the tabs for a well-deserved encore.

As 1936 drew to a close the constitution crisis that had rumbled on for the past months, caused by the desire of King Edward VIII to marry his mistress – the twice-divorced American socialite Mrs Wallis Simpson – reached its climax, when the king abdicated. On the day his reign officially ended, 11 December 1936, Edward made a BBC radio broadcast from Windsor Castle. No longer king, he was introduced by Sir John Reith, the director general of the BBC, as 'His Royal Highness Prince Edward'. Edward told a stunned nation of his inability to do his job without the support of the woman he loved.

As the decade rolled on, the growth of other forms of entertainment became an increasing worry to theatre managers, who were still begrudgingly paying the much opposed Entertainment Tax, which had been imposed on the industry as a temporary measure in 1916. The advent of 'talking films', the BBC's decision to broadcast live theatre on the radio and, by 1936, the first television broadcasts in the London area all caused concerned rumblings in Theatreland. The coronation of George VI which took place on 12 May 1937, the date originally set aside for Edward's coronation, highlighted the potential power of the new medium. The BBC broadcast the ceremony to 8 million people with wireless sets and to 50,000 television viewers in the London area. It was the first official outside broadcast and the first use of an outside broadcast van.

On Sunday 9 May 1937 Robert was heard again on the radio, in a concert broadcast from the Pavilion, Bournemouth. The Pavilion Theatre, then and now, is Bournemouth's traditional venue for year-round entertainment. It was opened on 19 March 1929 by HRH the Duke of Gloucester, having cost £250,000. In 1933 the stage was enlarged, but the venue still retains its elegant splendour and styling. For this concert broadcast Robert was accompanied by the Bournemouth Municipal Orchestra conducted by Richard Austin, the son of singer-composer Frederick Austin, who was one of the country's leading baritone singers. At the outbreak of war the BMO was cut from sixty-one to thirty-five, and then in 1940 to only twenty-four players. Austin felt unable to continue with a depleted ensemble and resigned. In 1954 the orchestra changed its name to the Bournemouth Symphony Orchestra.

Robert was re-united with Sylvia Cecil for the summer season of 1937, and the couple appeared in the Scottish resort of Ayr. The Gaiety Theatre, situated on Carrick Street, is one of Scotland's national treasures. For half of its lifetime the theatre was controlled by the Popplewell family. Ben Popplewell moved to Scotland in 1913 from Bradford, where he had worked as a stockbroker, to manage the Pavilion Theatre, Ayr – a municipally owned theatre that was not doing well and was known locally as 'the white elephant on the green'. In 1925 he took over the town's Gaiety Theatre, taking his two sons Leslie and Eric into partnership, and reopened the theatre on 5 October that year. Ben Popplewell retired in 1940 and died in 1950.[162]

Each summer, from 1931, the Popplewells presented a summer season variety show entitled *Gaiety Whirl*. The show that opened in June 1937, in addition to being headlined by Robert and Sylvia, also included Scotland's 'new star comedian' Jack Anthony; Arnaud, Peggy and Ready, a dance act; Robert Harbin, a South African conjurer and illusionist; the Four Brownie Boys, who offered vocals, instrumentals, dances and jokes; the John Tiller Girls, later to find fame on *Sunday Night at the London Palladium*, and Harry Broad and the Gaiety Rhythm Band. The show's finale was a Scottish pageant, with the whole cast appearing in highland dress. For some reason Robert left the show on Tuesday 17 August, before it had finished its run. He was replaced by the tenor Trevor Watkins, who had played leading parts in a number of West End productions.[163]

On Thursday 27 November Robert was heard on *Voices of Variety* in a radio broadcast from the Granada, Clapham Junction. Also on the bill was the wonderful Liverpool comic Robb Wilton. You may recall the fire station sketch, in which Robb, a bumbling fire officer, takes a call reporting a fire, but is sidetracked into trying to remember where it is instead of noting the details ('Grimshaw Street . . . No, don't tell me . . . Oh, I could walk straight to it . . .', finishing with the classic line to the long-suffering householder, 'Can you keep it going 'til we get there?'). The programme also included Bobby Howell and his Orchestra, Charles Higgins, and the comedy/dance double-act Brookins and Van.

In the spring of 1938 Robert starred as Canio in *Pagliacci*, presented at the State Theatre, Kilburn. The opera by Leoncavallo is a tale of adultery set in nineteenth-century Italy. Canio, the head of a small theatrical company, is distressed when a member of the audience suggests that his wife Nedda is having an affair with Tonio, the clown. His jealousy and uncertainty grow as the off-stage drama intertwines with the on-stage performance. The opera was first performed in 1892 and was an instant success. It contains the well-known aria '*Vesti la giubba*' (On with the motley), made famous by Enrico Caruso.

The State Theatre in Kilburn – so named because of its majestic tower inspired by the Empire State Building – had only been open a matter of months. Built as a super cinema, it had a large and fully equipped stage, workshops and dressing rooms. The orchestra pit had a raising platform for the Wurlitzer organ. The auditorium itself, designed in Italian Renaissance style, was capable of seating 4004 people on two levels. On the opening night of the theatre on Monday 20 December 1937 the artistes performing were Henry Hall and his Orchestra, Gracie Fields, George Formby, Carroll Levis, Vic Oliver, Larry Adler, Stone & Lee, Van Dam and

His Band, and Sydney Torch at the console of the Wurlitzer organ. The stage show was broadcast live by BBC radio from 8.00 until 8.45pm. Sidney Torch was the resident organist.

On 10 May 1938 Queen Mary visited the Royal Albert Hall to attend the Children's Union Jubilee and Founder's Day Festival of the Church of England Waifs and Strays Society. She was welcomed upon arrival by various dignitaries, including the Bishop of London, who had taken the chair at the annual meeting of the society for thirty-seven years. In 1938 the society had collected £300,000. Queen Mary received about 1,000 purses from child members of the Union, representing their local collections for the union. Afterwards she was entertained by a 'birthday cake ballet', where fifty performers carried fifty candles, one for each year in the history of the union. This was followed by a presentation of Hubert Parry's musical version of *The Pied Piper of Hamelin*. The production was on a large scale, with about 1,000 performers taking part in a spectacular presentation of the story. The cast included Robert Naylor as the Pied Piper and Harold Williams as the Mayor; the choir and orchestra were under the direction of Charles Proctor.

On 1 July 1938 the BBC broadcast a programme of gramophone records devoted to the music of Guy D'Hardelot and Eric Coates. The records played included those by Robert Naylor, the Spanish mezzo-soprano Conchita Supervia, the Australian contralto Essie Ackland and the English soprano Eva Turner, who became Professor of Singing at the Royal Academy of Music, a position she held until well into her eighties.

In the summer of 1938 Robert returned for a second season in Blackpool as a star attraction, alongside Tessie O'Shea, in *On with the Show* at the North Pier. It opened on Friday 3 June, and by July it was announced that 'owing to the demand for seats an extra matinee has been added and there are now three performances daily at 2.30, 6.30 and 8.45'.[164]

Teresa Mary O'Shea (1913–95) was born in Cardiff. Her background was in music hall, where she had developed her act of singing and playing the banjo. However, it was in Blackpool beginning in 1934 that she began to exploit her generous figure, introducing what became her theme song, 'Two-Ton Tessie from Tennessee', a song written in 1912 by Roy Turk and Lou Handman. She became a regular attraction at Blackpool for the next twenty years. She later went on to have a varied career on stage and screen, both in Britain and in America.

Sharing the bill was the Lancashire comedian Frank Randall; Bertini And his Famous Band (real name Bert Gutsell); the Five Sherry Boys, a dance act; Marietta, a soprano with her harmonising monkey; Alex and Dorrano, billed as the world's greatest Apache dancers; and the Six Health and Beauty Girls. Also to be heard was the pianist Peggy Desmond, who in addition to having her own spot, provided accompaniment for Robert.

In the programme notes for the 1938 show the producer Lawrence Wright wrote: 'It gives me a thrill to present once again the greatest of all British tenors ROBERT NAYLOR. Whilst rehearsing for this show he played lead in *Pagliacci* at the State Theatre, and *The Pied Piper of Hamelin* at the Albert Hall. In this show he will again feature "You Are My Song Divine",[165] which I wrote especially for him, and "Tears In My Heart".' Robert recorded neither of these songs, although the sheet music of 'Tears In My Heart', written by Leonard Whitcup and Teddy Powell, was published by Lawrence Wright featuring a picture of Robert on the cover.

Another of the songs featured by Robert in the show was 'When Granny Wore Her Crinoline', written by Roy King, Freddy Grant and Paul Paree (Lawrence Wright). The music was published again by the Lawrence Wright Music Co. Ltd, selling for 6*d* and with a picture of Robert on the cover. Robert never recorded this number either, but it was picked up by Al Bowlly among others.[166] In the Blackpool production the song was staged with the girls appearing in crinolines, and holding up a large crinoline in the centre of the stage. In the show's first half the company presented a mini-operetta called *The Romance of the Fan.* The girls in the troupe introduced fans of all ages and countries, and Tessie O'Shea appeared from behind a couple of huge ostrich feathers. Robert contributed to the spectacle by singing 'Lady of the Fan', probably another specially penned number by Lawrence Wright. In the grand finale the whole company assembled on stage in evening wear to sing 'Blackpool Is Saying Goodnight'. The summer season ended on Friday 1 October.

On Monday 24 October Robert was back on the variety circuit, appearing at the Theatre Royal, Edinburgh, with pianist Peggy

Desmond. The following week they were at the Glasgow Pavilion along with Espinosa's British Ballet Company and Leroy and Brown. The *Glasgow Evening Times* reported, 'Hit of the bill is the "Fantasy of Song" presented by Robert Naylor, England's famous tenor, with Peggy Desmond at the piano.'[167] The show also appeared in Liverpool. During the first week of December Robert and Peggy were at the Chiswick Empire, a huge auditorium with a seating capacity of 1,950. Designed by the theatrical architect Frank Matcham, the Empire was demolished in 1959. Peggy Desmond was a regular on the radio, billed as the 'Queen of the Ivories', and appeared in a number of Pathétone film shorts, such as *A Medley of Piano Harmony by Peggy Desmond of BBC Fame.* In these films she played anything from Chopin to jazz tunes.

The Press Club held their Ladies Dinner Night on 17 December 1938. The speakers were Gerald Dobson, Recorder of the City of London, and Sir George Franckenstein, Austrian ambassador to the Court of St James's. The Press Club was established in 1882; among its famous past chairmen is the crime writer Edgar Wallace. The artistes who entertained were Robert and the distinguished Australian contralto Essie Ackland.

Throughout the summer Cecilia's health had been in decline. Robert spent an increasing amount of time at the nursing home in Blackpool, comforting her. The year was to end on a sad note: on Thursday 29 December Cecilia died, just forty-one years old. The cause of her death was given as myocardial disease. Robert was at her bedside when she passed away, and he registered her death the same day. They had been married for sixteen years.

Throughout their marriage the couple had been close, and Cecilia's death would cause Robert to re-evaluate his life in the coming months.

Cecilia was brought back to Yorkshire and laid to rest two days later in the Naylor family grave at St Mary's Church, Luddenden. The funeral service, held on the Saturday afternoon, the last day of 1938, was conducted by the Rev. J.A. Kings. In addition to the relatives and friends, including Cecilia's parents Mr and Mrs Walter Farrar, also in attendance was Councillor Percy Sutcliffe, the Mayor of Todmorden. The local paper noted that 'Her death at the early age of 41 will be regretted by music lovers in various parts of the country . . . Mrs Naylor had a charming personality coupled with a voice of pure quality and excellent range. That she enjoyed singing was always evident to her hearers.'[168]

As 1939 dawned, Robert faced the new year alone. While it is likely his son Michael, now six and a half years old, had returned to live at Wembley with his nanny, there is little doubt that Robert must have felt bereft of the emotional support he had come to rely upon over the years. For people in the British Isles this was a time of tremendous anxiety, created by Germany's rush towards rearmament and what Churchill later described as 'the gathering storm'. Following a period of bereavement, Robert's stage work continued. Beginning on 6 February, he appeared in a production of Gounod's *Faust* at the Royal Albert Hall. The show was produced by T.C. Fairburn and half the profits went to the Lord Baldwin Fund for Refugees. Robert played the lead on the opening night, but this was shared during the short run with Benjamin Williams and Henry Wendon.

In the spring Robert travelled to the south-west for two weeks in variety, including shows at the Bristol Hippodrome during the week beginning 20 March and the Palace Theatre, Bath, from 3 April. Supporting acts at Bath included various barely remembered artistes such as Michael Moore, Walter Nildo, Reading and Grant, Nino Rossini, Freda Wynn and the Gerard Sisters. At Bristol Robert appeared with Les Allen, a saxophone player turned vocalist who had great success with his recording of 'Little Man You've Had A Busy Day', Hal Yates, a popular radio and variety singer who accompanied himself on the piano accordion, Stone & Lee, Mildred Kramer, the Gaillard Four and the comedian Charlie Chester.

On 18 May 1939 the Adair Wounded Fund held a social at the Scala Cinema, King's Cross, for wounded soldiers and their friends. The Barnet Town Silver Band played and the programme included songs by Robert Naylor. These concerts were organised by Basil F. Leakey, known in the entertainment world as Alan Adair. He organised concerts for wounded soldiers and their friends at the Wigmore Hall every Sunday afternoon throughout the winter. There were an estimated 3,500 wounded soldiers in hospitals in London, and some of them were taken by taxi to the concerts and afterwards returned to their hospitals.

On 5 July Robert was back at the Royal Albert Hall as part of a gala night of entertainment given in aid of the Radium Institute and the Mount Vernon Hospital for Cancer. Princess Helena Victoria was president, and Viscountess Harcourt chairman of the organising committee. The first part of the programme consisted of operatic excerpts conducted by Albert Coates. The climax of the programme was the presentation, with full rites, of the Mount Carmel episode from Mendelssohn's oratorio *Elijah*. *The Stage* noted that 'Mr Henry Gill, Miss Gwen Burke and Mr Robert Naylor with the chorus and ballet performed with enthusiasm.'

In August 1939 *The Stage* informed its readers that 'Robert Naylor succeeds Bruce Carfax as the Red Shadow in the *Desert Song* at the Garrick on Monday.'[169] There was no indication why Carfax was stepping down. This may just have been newspaper speculation, for if Robert was approached to take over the role, for some reason he didn't do so. The part was taken by Sanders Warren, who stayed until the curtain fell on the production at the end of the month.

The summer was an uneasy time for most people. The previous year Neville Chamberlain had returned from a meeting in Munich with a non-aggression pact signed by Adolf Hitler. Although this allowed Hitler to annex the Sudetenland, Mr Chamberlain said the accord signalled 'peace for our time' when he read it to a jubilant crowd gathered at Heston airport in West London. Everyone sighed with a sense of relief; but it was a false calm.

Re-armament was speeded up, and although the frenzy of sandbag filling was relaxed after the Munich crisis, the training for air raid wardens and the issue of gas masks continued as before. The Emergency Powers (Defence Act) of August 1938 authorised the British government to take certain steps in defence of the realm and to maintain public order, and the Military Training Act of 27 April 1939 made it compulsory for all British men aged twenty and twenty-one who were fit and able to undertake six months' military training. By this time most people felt that war was inevitable, and Londoners feared that the capital would take the brunt of the hostilities.

Unsurprisingly this period was a testing time for London's Theatreland. It was felt that the continuation of usual leisure facilities would be essential to maintain general morale and some sense of normality. However, the fear of immediate air attack led the government to close places of public entertainment, with a loss of employment for thousands of theatre people, as soon as war broke out to avoid putting large numbers of people at risk. The entertainment world had known this would happen, 'So that the grave dislocation of the theatre industry throughout the country, with its attendant distress and unemployment, was not unforeseen,' wrote the editor of *Theatre World* in October 1939. However, during those first months of 'the phoney war' – the period between September 1939 and April 1940 when seemingly nothing much happened – a gradual re-opening commenced, although blackout restrictions and earlier playing times made staging a production more difficult.

The government's fears were not entirely unfounded, and once the hostilities started the Shaftesbury, Queen's and Little Theatres were destroyed in the bombing, while the Old Vic, Duke of York's, Court and Sadler's Wells were damaged. Drury Lane, which was requisitioned to be used by the Entertainments National Service Association (ENSA) during the war, was hit by a bomb which failed to explode. Then on 8 March 1941, in the bright moonlight of a Saturday night, the Café de Paris received a direct hit from two 50K landmines which came through the Rialto roof and landed neatly in front of the bandstand. It killed a young bandleader from British Guiana, Ken 'Snakehips' Johnson (real name Kendrick Reginald Hymans), a tenor player named Dave Williams, and scores of guests. As one writer observed, 'The West End was never the same again.'[170]

By this time Robert had decided to relinquish his stage career and return home to Yorkshire. What factors lay behind this decision will never be fully known. John Naylor, Robert's stepson by his second marriage, said it was always something of a family mystery and that Robert himself never discussed his reasons.[171] It does, on the face of it, seem strange for Robert to abandon a thriving show business career, which had brought him fame, success and a degree of prosperity. I suspect that the decision was down to a combination of circumstances.

The loss of his wife was, I believe, the over-riding factor. Cecilia (always affectionately known as Cissie) had been the inspiration behind Robert's launch of his own professional singing career, and he owed his success to the great help, support and guidance he had received from her throughout their marriage. There is little doubt that he took her death badly, and now felt alone in the world. There was also uncertainty facing the professional entertainment industry with the outbreak of war; London stage productions, in particular, were to be badly affected. Perhaps Robert also sensed that it might be safer to move away from the capital, which was bound to be one of the main enemy targets. Emotionally weakened, faced with the increasing insecurity of a stage career and feeling isolated and unsafe, Robert disappeared from the national stage. He was always a modest Yorkshire lad at heart, and it seems that the bright lights were no longer so important to him.

"ABDUL THE DAMNED"

A Gallagher cigarette card. (Author's collection)

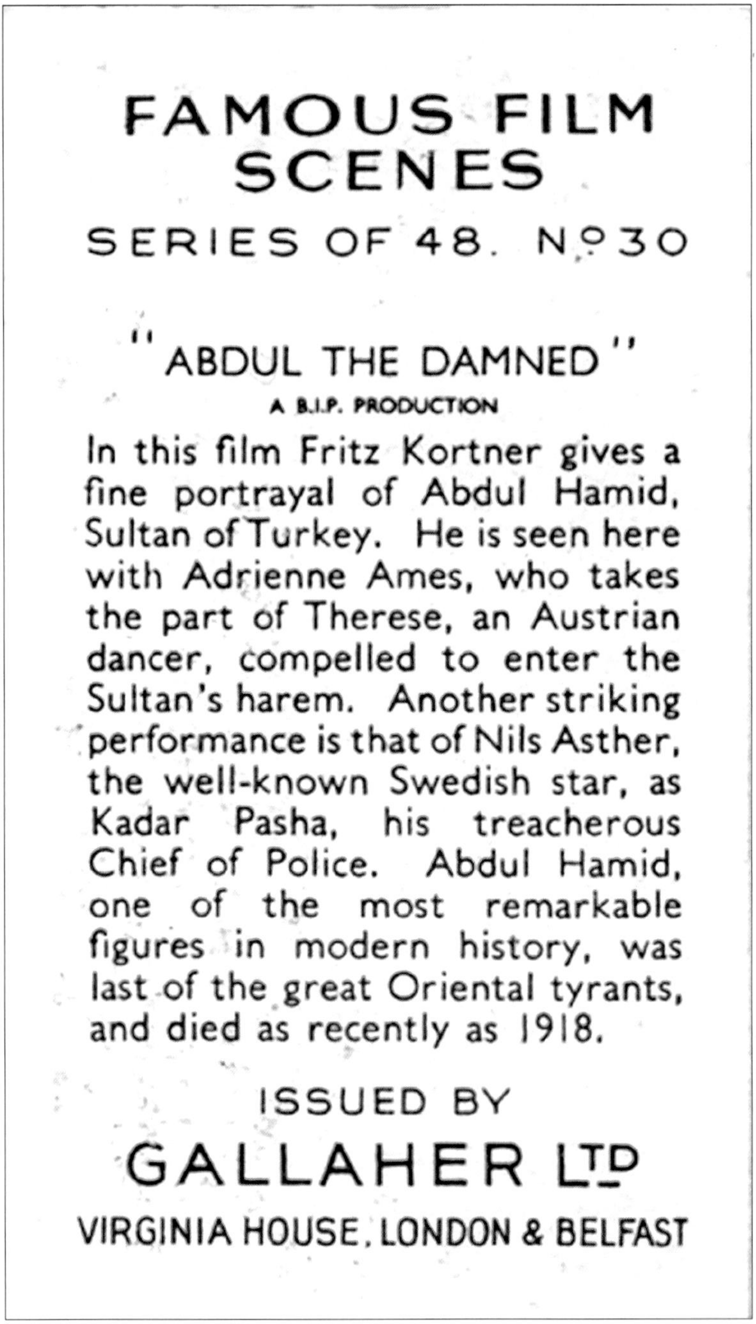

FAMOUS FILM SCENES

SERIES OF 48. N.º 30

"ABDUL THE DAMNED"

A B.I.P. PRODUCTION

In this film Fritz Kortner gives a fine portrayal of Abdul Hamid, Sultan of Turkey. He is seen here with Adrienne Ames, who takes the part of Therese, an Austrian dancer, compelled to enter the Sultan's harem. Another striking performance is that of Nils Asther, the well-known Swedish star, as Kadar Pasha, his treacherous Chief of Police. Abdul Hamid, one of the most remarkable figures in modern history, was last of the great Oriental tyrants, and died as recently as 1918.

ISSUED BY

GALLAHER LTD

VIRGINIA HOUSE, LONDON & BELFAST

The reverse of thr Abdul the Damned cigarette card.
(Author's collection)

Robert in a studio photograph, *c.* 1936.
(Author's collection)

Rose Perfect, alongside whom Robert starred at Blackpool, 1936.
(Author's collection)

A studio photograph of Robert by J. Capstick FRPS, Blackpool,
c. 1936. (Author's collection)

Robert, Sylvia Cecil and the cast of *Gaiety Whirl*, Ayr, 1937.
(University of Glasgow Library collection)

Poster for *On With The Show*, 1936.
(Author's collection)

Programme for *On With The Show*, 1936.
(Author's collection)

Tessie O'Shea, who starred at Blackpool with Robert in 1938.
(Author's collection)

Sheet music for 'Tears In My Heart', published in 1937.
(Author's collection)

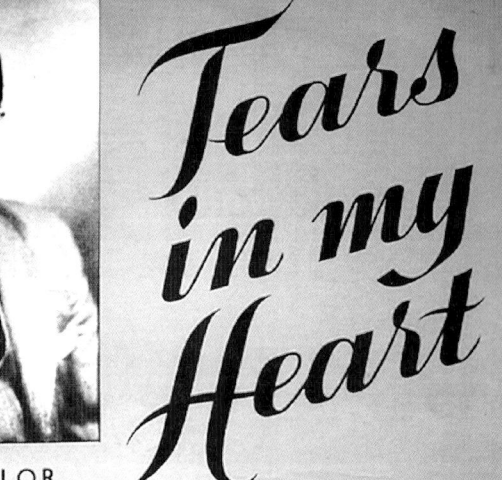

Sheet music for 'When Granny Wore Her Crinoline', published in 1938.
(Author's collection)

Press release, 1938.
(*Gramophone* magazine)

Advertisement: Offers Invited,
1938.
(*Gramophone* magazine)

Robert, 1938: a photograph by French, 21 Harrington Road, Kensington. (Author's collection)

Naylor family grave, Luddenden cemetery.
(Bob Naylor)

Peggy Desmond, who worked with Robert in 1938.
(Author's collection)

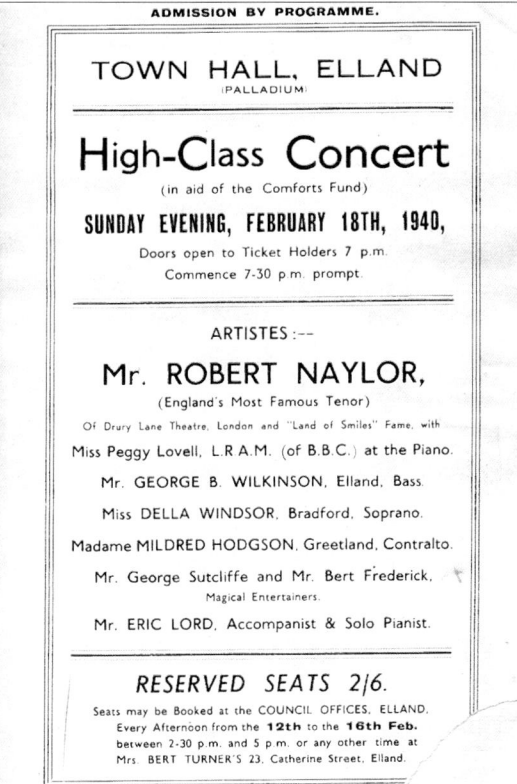

Programme for a concert in
Elland, 1940.
(Author's collection)

ADMISSION BY PROGRAMME.

TOWN HALL, ELLAND
(PALLADIUM)

High-Class Concert
(in aid of the Comforts Fund)

SUNDAY EVENING, FEBRUARY 18TH, 1940,
Doors open to Ticket Holders 7 p.m.
Commence 7-30 p.m. prompt.

ARTISTES :--

Mr. ROBERT NAYLOR,
(England's Most Famous Tenor)

Of Drury Lane Theatre, London and "Land of Smiles" Fame, with

Miss Peggy Lovell, L.R.A.M. (of B.B.C.) at the Piano.

Mr. GEORGE B. WILKINSON, Elland, Bass.

Miss DELLA WINDSOR, Bradford, Soprano.

Madame MILDRED HODGSON, Greetland, Contralto.

Mr. George Sutcliffe and Mr. Bert Frederick,
Magical Entertainers.

Mr. ERIC LORD, Accompanist & Solo Pianist.

RESERVED SEATS 2/6.

Seats may be Booked at the COUNCIL OFFICES, ELLAND,
Every Afternoon from the **12th** to the **16th Feb.**
between 2-30 p.m. and 5 p.m. or any other time at
Mrs. BERT TURNER'S 23, Catherine Street, Elland.

Robert at a dinner party, *c.* 1941.
(Greaves photographers)

NEW VICTORIA

GRAND CONCERT, Sunday, Nov.22

(IN AID OF NAVAL CHARITIES)

DOORS OPEN 2.15 p.m   COMMENCE 3.00 p.m.

Robert Naylor - Wilfred Pickles

(by courtesy of the B.B.C.)

CLEM COULSON; JOHNSON, STEEL & DORIS; HENRY GROUDSON
The following B.B.C. Personalities will repeat their Broadcast
Performance:-
**DOROTHY ADAMS GILL, JACK MARKHAM & BERT RHODES, ALEC HOWIESON
& VAL GREEN**
RICHARD NORTH (by courtesy of the B.B.C.), and

THE BAND OF THE DUKE OF WELLINGTON'S REGIMENT,

Including the
RHYTHMIC COMBINATION OF THE HAVERCAKE HURRICANES.
**Front Stalls 3/6, Circle 3/6, Back Stalls 2/6, Balcony 1/6
TICKETS NOW ON SALE.**

Concert at the New Victoria, Bradford.
(*Telegraph & Argus*, Bradford)

THE GOOD
OLD DAYS
*Old-Time Music-Hall
from the City Varieties
Music-Hall in Leeds*
(by arrangement with Harry Joseph)
WITH
Ken Wilson ★ Granger Brothers ★ Julia Bretton
Stanley Watson and Diane
James Young with Jack Hudson and Marie Cunningham
Morris and Cowley
The Robert Naylor Valentine Girls
CHAIRMAN, ROBIN HUNTER
Musical Director, Alyn Ainsworth
Produced by Barney Colehan
at 8.30 this evening

BBC TV's *The Good Old Days*, featuring the Robert Naylor Valentine
Girls, 1956. (*Radio Times*)

Jean Hindmarsh, soprano with D'Oyly Carte and originally one
of the Valentine Girls.
(D'Oyly Carte Opera Company)

ROBERT NAYLOR
Teacher of Voice Production and Singing

Pupils have gained the following successes
at the 1954 Harrogate Musical Festival :—
Two First Prizes · Three Second Prizes

For Terms apply :
2 RADLYN COURT
PARK AVENUE
HARROGATE
Phone 2998

Studios :
HARROGATE
SKIPTON
BRADFORD
(Only a few vacancies)

Business card for Robert
Naylor, Teacher of Voice
Production and Singing.
(Harrogate Operatic Society)

Robert, *c.* 1960. (Author's collection)

Robert and Dorothy, his second wife, *c.* 1960.
(Author's collection)

Robert, *c.* 1966.
(Author's collection)

Label of Metropole test pressing, 1926.
(Maurice Robson)

Parlophone test pressing, 1932 .
(Maurice Robson)

Piccadilly Records advertisement, 1931. (*Gramophone* magazine)

Parlophone Farewell Party: private pressing, 1933. (Author's collection)

CRYSTALATE'S LATEST ACHIEVEMENT!

REX
THE KING OF RECORDS

A FULL SIZE 10″
RECORD FOR
.. on Sale 7th September

A new Record by the makers of the famous Broadcast and Imperial Records — and the most sensational value ever offered to the Public.

On "Rex" you can enjoy all the latest Song and Dance Hits, or Novelty Records by first-class British and American Artistes and Bands, perfectly recorded, at the amazingly low price of One Shilling.

BY THE MAKERS OF

AND

BROADCAST
'TWELVE'

IMPERIAL

CRYSTALATE 60 CITY ROAD LONDON E.C.1

Rex Records advertisement, 1933.
(*Gramophone* magazine)

Rex records advertisement featuring Robert Naylor. (*Gramophone* magazine)

Eclipse record label by 'Derek Powell', 1934. (Author's collection)

Robert and Cecilia in costume.
(Author's collection)

CHAPTER SEVEN
The War Years 1939–1945

o it was that in 1940 Robert returned home to Yorkshire, 'with a view', as one local paper so eloquently put it, 'to rendering voluntary service in any public effort of importance which might be made for the prosecution of the war and the services of the men in the armed forces.'[172] Upon making this decision, Robert got in touch with an old friend, the Mayor of Dewsbury, Councillor Harold France, and asked him whether there was any useful occupation he could fulfil. It was not his intention, it seems, to accept any monetary engagements for singing for the duration. In the absence of his son, Captain J.C. France, who was engaged in the worsted department of Messrs James France and Co. Ltd, the mayor offered Robert his son's position in the business.[173] Robert, having had practical experience in a managerial capacity with Patons & Baldwins before he entered the singing profession, readily accepted the position. In fact, Robert went to live with Harold at his home at Westfields, Mirfield, much to the delight of the whole family. The mayor informed the newspaper reporter that 'Mr Naylor had not lost his sense of business and is fulfilling his important position in the most capable manner possible.'

Westfields is an imposing Victorian villa with a portico entrance. Inside, a mosaic tiled floor leads to a central staircase with a blue stained-glass window in the roof. The house was situated in landscaped gardens and had an orchard. Today it is occupied by Kirklees Social Services, and modern functional extensions have been added to increase office accommodation.

Although Robert went to live at Westfields, his son Michael and his nanny, Miss Over, continued to live at Robert's house in Wembley, London. What Robert's plans were for his son at this point is not clear. What does seem clear is that his stay with the France family could only be temporary. Perhaps he intended to get himself settled into a place of his own before sending for his son. Whatever his intentions were, events were to overtake him.

On the night of 13 September 1940 Wembley was bombed by the Luftwaffe, and Robert's house was damaged. It wasn't alone; between September 1940 and May 1941 London was bombed for fifty-seven nights in a row: 9,000 bombs fell on Wembley, killing 149 people and damaging over half the houses in the borough.[174] Miss Over and Michael were evacuated to live with Robert's mother, Sarah, at Montana, Burnley Road, Luddenden Foot, Yorkshire. Apparently Miss Over found living in the Calder Valley not to her liking, and returned to London at some point during the war, declaring she would rather be bombed than live a moment longer at Luddenden Foot.

With the nanny's departure, Sarah felt herself unable to cope alone with her grandson. As a result, Michael was privately fostered by his Uncle James and Auntie Florence, who lived nearby on Warley Wood Lane in Luddenden Foot. It may be that Michael couldn't be accommodated with his father at Westfields, but it rather appears that Robert was reluctant to care for his son. Sadly the fostering arrangements only served to further alienate Michael from his father.

On Sunday 11 February 1940 Robert performed at the Empire Theatre, Dewsbury, to raise money for the Dewsbury & District General Infirmary and the Comforts for the Troops Fund. The comfort funds were organised in towns and villages throughout the country as fund-raising efforts that sent parcels (usually containing cigarettes and chocolate) and family news to those serving far from home in the Armed Forces, so that troops could keep in touch with their home area and even receive goodwill messages from family and friends.

A reviewer of the Dewsbury concert wrote: 'One of the

outstanding features was the magnificent singing of Mr Naylor who was in remarkable fine form. He held the rapt attention of the vast audience who applauded him with demonstrative fervour. Mr Naylor gave generously of his brilliant talents and enhanced his great reputation. He had the most sympathetic accompanist in Miss Peggy Lovell, the popular BBC recording star. Mr Naylor's further public appearances in this district, where he intends to pursue his voluntary efforts for war charities, will be anticipated with a great deal of pleasure.'[175] The function was under the patronage of Harold France, in his role as Mayor of Dewsbury. He paid a glowing tribute to Robert, who had been largely responsible for the concert's organisation and presentation, describing him as a 'great man' with a personality. Also on the bill were the Yorkshire comedian Albert Modley; Miss Phyllis Ward, a local vocalist and successful amateur operatic performer; the Eight Girls, a song and dance troupe; Betty Beanland, character vocalist of the BBC; Bert Lyndon, Blackpool's favourite light comedian; Levante, the famous illusionist; Gladys Turnstill, a contralto from London; and Bert and Bern, comedy violinists.

A further concert followed within days. Billed as a 'High Class Concert in aid of the Comforts Fund', this was held at the Town Hall, Elland, on the evening of 18 February, a Sunday. It starred 'Mr Robert Naylor (England's Most Famous Tenor) of Drury Lane Theatre, London and *Land of Smiles* fame, with Miss Peggy Lovell, LRAM (of BBC) at the piano'. During the first half of the concert Robert presented *A Fantasy of Song*, which was the title he had used on his variety tours before the war for a medley of popular songs. In the second half he performed 'Patiently Smiling' from *The Land of Smiles* and 'A Dream Of Paradise', music by Hamilton Gray and words by Claude Lyttleton – a song dating from around 1875. The concert also included a number of local singers – Mr George Wilkinson, bass, from Elland; Miss Della Windsor, soprano, from Bradford; and Madame Mildred Hodgson, contralto, from Greetland, Halifax.

Then without warning, on Tuesday 20 February, Councillor Harold France died suddenly at his home. Although he had not been in good health, this had not prevented him from carrying out his business and municipal duties, and his death was not only a great shock to his family and wide circle of friends but also to the town and district, where he was a generous benefactor and was greatly respected by hundreds of people. Despite the loss of Harold, his patron and friend, Robert continued to live with the France family until his second marriage, two years later.

In May 1940 *The Stage* reported that, 'Chas E. Cole arranged a programme for members of a bombing squadron in the North on May 19th. Contributors included Robert Naylor who was accompanied by Peggy Lovell.'[176] No further details about this concert are known. This is the only recorded instance I can find of Robert entertaining the troops.

In addition to the comforts funds there were also the Spitfire funds, which were common across British towns from the outset of the Second World War. Based on a much older tradition of presenting warriors with weapons and armour, the idea of donating aircraft and tanks was promoted by Lord Beaverbrook. Individuals, organisations or towns could present the cost of an airframe; this was set at £5,000 for a Spitfire, although the real cost was closer to £12,000 – still remarkably cheap compared with today's £1 billion fighter jets. Aircraft were to bear the name of the donor on the fuselage. Many towns and organisations went to great lengths to raise the money required.

On Sunday 14 October there was a concert in Leeds in aid of the local Spitfire Fund. Twenty acts took to the stage at the 2,500-seat Paramount Theatre on the Headrow in a programme that lasted over four hours. Robert was among the star attractions, which also included the Ivy Benson All-Girl Band. The orchestra, made up of musicians from the former Leeds Empire Theatre Orchestra, was under the direction of Charles E. Smith. Other artists appearing included comedian Allen Modley, brother of Albert; Leeds-born ukulele player Stanley King; the Four Aces, four boys and a guitar; Jack Lawton, organist; Tom Henry, vocalist from Henry Hall's Dance Band; Morton Fraser and his harmonica; Jack Gordon and Sid Bryan, 'a song, a piano and a surprise'; Bebe Norma, 'xylophone personality'; Marion Dawson, comedienne; and comics Duggie Wakefield and Dick Henderson, father of Dickie. It was reported that a sizeable sum was raised by the event.[177]

The Bradford Sub-Committee of the Newspaper Vendors' Benevolent and Provident Institution held an all star concert at the New Victoria Cinema, Bradford, starting at 2.30pm on Sunday 10

November. Robert was second on the bill, which was headlined by the BBC organist Sandy MacPherson. Also on the programme were Mary O'Hara, soprano; James Wilkinson, bass-baritone; and the comedian Fred Gwyn, who acted as compere. The accompanist was Mr Norman Constantine. The Bradford *Telegraph & Argus* reported that 'Robert Naylor (tenor) with Peggy Lovell at the piano, delighted the audience.' The concert raised £70 towards the Newspaper Vendors' Fund.

On Sunday 24 November, at 3pm, Robert was in a further concert in Bradford, this time at the Ritz Cinema on Broadway, in aid of the Special Constables Benevolent Fund. Robert starred alongside the jazz trumpeter Nat Gonella, who became a household name in the decades following his emergence as a star in the 1930s. Also on stage were the comedian Harry Hemsley; Robert's old associate, the pianist Patricia Rossborough, billed as the 'Queen of Syncopation'; the singer/actress Stella Moya; and the harmonica player Morton Fraser. Other names on the bill were H. Park Shackleton, Norma Dawn, the Pioneer Corps Band, Inspector Coulson, the Bradford City Police Band (by kind permission of the Chief Constable) and the Alhambra Orchestra. The newly built and luxurious 2,037-seat Ritz had been accorded a civic opening eighteen months earlier on 8 May 1939.

On 18 January 1941 the BBC's Programme For Forces broadcast a forty-five minute programme that featured Robert singing with the BBC Salon Orchestra, conducted by Leslie Bridgewater. Bridgewater is a prime example of a light music man whose career was largely made by the BBC, for whom he worked for many years; he was often heard on the radio. In addition he wrote incidental music for a number of films, composed light concert suites, conducted the BBC Salon Orchestra from 1939 to 1942 and formed the Leslie Bridgewater Quintet (piano, played by him, and strings).

A 'Grand Concert' was held at the Elite Cinema in Bradford at 2.00pm on Sunday 2 March. It was in aid of the Northern Command Comforts Fund and starred Robert, described as 'England's leading tenor'. The Elite Cinema was at the top of Toller Lane. Having undergone extensive refurbishment some years earlier, it could accommodate 1,200 patrons. When the cinema re-opened it was billed as Bradford's latest and most up-to-date, with luxurious seating and beautiful lighting effects. Throughout the 1930s the Elite made good use of its large stage in presenting a range of cine-variety programmes. Films were accompanied by the Elite Symphony Orchestra, with Norman E. Rouse as musical director. The grand concert also included Howard Rogers, D'Albert, Mavis, Olive Carr, the Police Vocal Union and Norman Pearson and His Band.

In June *The Land of Smiles* made a return visit to the Alhambra Theatre, Bradford. Richard Tauber had first taken the show there in November 1939. This time Tauber was with Robert's one-time partner Josie Fearon. It is possible that Robert met the two stars while the show was in town. If so, it must have seemed strange that he, who had deputised for Tauber at Drury Lane and starred at the Alhambra Theatre with Josie Fearon, was now working as a textile manager.

It was now almost three years since Cecilia's untimely death. Back in the West Riding, and once again near to his family, Robert began seeing a lot of his uncle's widow, Dorothy Naylor. They were both alone, and must have found solace in each other's company during the dark days of the war. She and her son John were now living at 20 Emm Lane, Heaton, Bradford, a house owned by the Midland Bank, which used its cellars as a storage facility. Because Dorothy was Robert's aunt, their growing relationship was inevitably frowned upon by some relatives. However, despite the lack of family approval, on Sunday 14 September 1941 the couple was married quietly at St Barnabas's Church, Ashwell Road, Heaton, Bradford. Robert was aged forty-two and Dorothy was thirty-six. The local paper briefly reported on the wedding: 'Known as the "English Tauber" of musical comedy, Mr Robert Naylor the noted tenor was married at St Barnabas Church yesterday. The service was conducted by Canon R. Whincup, with a few friends in attendance.'[178] No mention was made of family being present, and certainly neither Robert's mother nor his brother were at the ceremony to offer their blessings. The witnesses were Harold Watson, Dorothy's father, and Arthur Smith, a business friend of Robert's. Robert gave his occupation as textile manager. The couple went to live at 20 Emm Lane.

Before his father's second marriage Michael Naylor was still being looked after by his uncle and aunt, who were both fond of the boy; he was apparently happy living with them. Although they wanted to adopt him, his father had other plans. After his marriage to Dorothy he brought Michael to live with them at Emm Lane in Bradford. In 1942, when Michael was aged about ten, Robert sent him as a boarder to Woodhouse Grove School, Apperley Bridge, Bradford. The school, whose motto is '*Bone et Fidelis*' (Good and Faithful), was originally founded in 1890 as an all boys boarding preparatory institution for the sons of Methodist ministers. Over the years the school expanded its intake to include all those from families willing to pay the tuition fees. When he left the school in 1948, like his father Michael initially worked in the textile industry.

Throughout the war years Robert continued to work for James France & Co. Ltd. The wool trade was still flourishing and the city was still prosperous. There was a camaraderie among the merchants and manufacturers, who met at the Bradford Club in Piece Hall Yard. This aimed to provide most of the comforts of a private residence for gentlemen of the town, providing business lunches and a newsroom with low armchairs, newspapers and periodicals. Many of the town's businessmen were involved in charity organisations, such as the Bradford Lions, the Rotary Club or the Masons.

The Connaught Rooms on Manningham Lane, Bradford, at one time housed up to thirty Masonic lodges. During the years that Robert was involved in the textile industry he was an active Freemason. He may have been initiated into the fraternity on the recommendation of Harold France, who was a prominent figure in the movement – being a past Great Standard Bearer in Great Priory and a member of the Fearnley Preceptory of Knights Templar in Dewsbury. However, Robert's links with the Masons may have stretched back to his days in London, when he was an active member of the Concert Artistes Association.

On 16 November 1941 Robert was a guest, along with pianist Charlie Kunz, on the BBC radio show *The Happidrome*, which ran from 1941 to 1947. Harry Korris, Cecil Fredericks and Robbie Vincent were the stars; the Happidrome was a fictitious theatre at which they worked. Fredericks played Ramsbottom, with Vincent as Enoch, and Korris as Mr Lovejoy, the theatre manager. Each week's guests were supposed to be performing at the theatre. Some months earlier, on 6 August, fellow Calderdale tenor Walter Widdop had been a guest on the same show.

The following year, on Friday 1 May 1942, the ladies of Huddersfield Women's Luncheon Club held a meeting at Whiteley's Café, Westgate, Huddersfield, and were entertained by a talk given by 'the celebrated Yorkshire tenor, Robert Naylor'. The title of his address was 'Twenty Years Of Song', and it was interspersed with songs from the shows in which he had appeared. He also sang a few choruses of popular songs such as 'Blue Heaven', from *The Desert Song,* and 'Song of the Vagabonds' from *The Vagabond King.* The press reported that 'Mr Naylor had appeared with the Sadler's Wells Opera Company when they were in Huddersfield a few months ago, and had a part in *Madam Butterfly.* He has been associated with this company for a good many years, and is singing with them at the present time.[179] When he is not fulfilling engagements, Mr Naylor and his pianist Miss Peggy Lovell, spend a lot of time touring camps and entertaining the troops.' The President, Mrs T. Smalles, thanked him for his 'interesting and enjoyable' address and recital, and also expressed thanks to Miss Lovell. 'The recital was concluded by the singing of 'You Are My Heart's Delight', which Mr Naylor has sung 4,000 times.'[180]

Later in the year Robert starred alongside Wilfred Pickles in another charity concert held at the New Victoria in Bradford on the afternoon of Sunday 22 November. The New Victoria, with its twin octagonal towers, has dominated the city centre of Bradford since it was opened in 1930. In those days afternoon teas were served in the circle café/tea lounge; there was also a huge restaurant, flanked by square pillars supporting ornate lights, which was first used to provide a celebration lunch on the opening day and soon became the up-to-the-minute place to dine. Later known as the Gaumont and then the Odeon Film Centre, it finally closed its doors in 2000, and despite the sterling efforts of the Bradford Odeon Rescue Group it still faces the threat of demolition.

Like Robert, Pickles came from Calderdale, having been born in 1904 at Conway Street off Hopwood Lane, Halifax. He was a founder member of the Halifax Thespians, and became a newsreader for the BBC in 1941, where his conversational style and friendly northern accent made him an instant hit with radio listeners. After the war his radio programme *Have A Go* had a regular audience of 20 million, and became a national institution. In addition to Robert and Pickles, the bill included Clem Coulson, Johnson Steel & Doris, Henry Groudson, Dorothy Adams Gill, Jack Markham and Bert Rhodes, Alec Howieson, Val Green and Richard North. The concert also featured the Band of the Duke of Wellington's Regiment.

On 24 April 1944 Robert was heard again on the radio in a programme broadcast on the BBC Home Service. He performed with Sylvia Welling, and the accompaniment was provided by Reginald Foort on organ. Miss Welling was no stranger to broadcasting, having appeared in the radio production of *Wild Violets*[181] in February 1937 with Webster Booth. In 1942 she played Prince Charming in *Cinderella* at Streatham Hill Theatre, London. Reginald Foort was one of the most famous theatre organists of all time. Born in Daventry, he made his radio début as a pianist on 15 January 1923 and as an organist on 12 May 1926 in a relay from the New Gallery cinema in London. This was the first of a long series of cinema organ recitals he made. Foort was the BBC's resident organist from 1936 to 1939, before Sandy MacPherson succeeded him.

Around this time John Naylor, Robert's stepson, recalls going with Robert one day to the Exchange railway station in Bradford to meet someone. At the station they bumped into the famous tenor Walter Widdop, and John was introduced to him; John remembers him as being a very nice chap. He recalls how the two tenors chatted amiably for a few minutes on the station platform, clearly knowing each other well. This was during the war years and Walter was living at Bower's Hall, Barkisland, after his London home had been bombed.[182] Throughout the Second World War Widdop brought pleasure to thousands of servicemen during tours of South Africa and Canada, and did an ENSA (Entertainments National Service Association) tour of the Middle East. By contrast Robert's contribution to the war effort, while every bit as valid, was on a much more modest scale.

Robert was heard on the Home Service on 17 April 1945, alongside Sandy MacPherson on organ and the Celtic Singers. Hal Roderick (Sandy) MacPherson was born in Ontario and began his career playing in Loews theatres in Canada and America. He was brought over to London for the opening of the new Empire Theatre in Leicester Square, which had installed a four manual twenty rank

Wurlitzer organ. He was to stay on as organist there for the next ten years. His signature tune was 'Happy Days Are Here Again' (from *Chasing Rainbows,* 1929) by Jack Yellen and Milton Ager. During the 1930s he wrote a regular column for the magazine *Cinema Organ Herald.* When war was declared in 1939 normal BBC broadcasts were initially suspended, and the only music broadcast was by the organist Sandy MacPherson, who could be heard playing for up to twelve hours a day, until listeners protested. It has been said, perhaps a little unfairly, that it was the over-exposure of MacPherson at this time that killed off the theatre organ.

On 29 September 1945 Robert was heard on the BBC's new Light Programme, which had been launched two months earlier. The Director General of the corporation, W.J. Haley, had announced on the cover of the *Radio Times* that it was to be for the 'civilian listener'. There can be no doubt that the war changed the sound of BBC radio dramatically, the Light Programme style being very much based on the informal American style of the Forces Programme. The new station offered general entertainment, with a plethora of shows that had not been heard before the war on the old National Programme. Robert's broadcast was a half-hour slot with Sylvia Welling, accompanied by Reginald Foort on organ. It is likely this was a repeat of a broadcast heard on the Home Service the previous year.

As the summer of 1945 drew to a close, the families of men and women who were still away on military service awaited their demobilisation and safe return home. By now air-raid drills and blackouts had become things of the past. Life was slowly beginning to return to normal, although the rationing of essential goods and food didn't end completely until 1954. Under the leadership of Clement Attlee, the new Labour government began some of the greatest changes in Britain's long history – nothing less than a reconstruction of the nation. For those in work this was a period of improving standards of living, and for most families there was once again money available for entertainment and leisure.

CHAPTER EIGHT
Later Years 1946-1968

*O*nce the war was over, Robert resumed his full-time musical career; it is likely that this had always been his intention. In 1945 he was once again being represented by Ibbs and Tillett, the concert agents who had acted for him before the war. John Tillett, in a letter dated 10 September 1945, gave a list of singers available for a planned concert. Robert is included, and his fee is given as 25 guineas, the same as Walter Widdop's. Robert is still listed in the agency's Artistes' Brochure as late as 1951-2.[183]

However, re-marriage and his changed circumstances meant that Robert no longer performed professionally; his new wife may not have wanted him to work in London. Instead he became a teacher of voice production and singing in Bradford. By now he and Dorothy had moved to live at 18 North Park Road, Heaton, one of the large stone-built villas facing Lister Park. To begin with Robert gave lessons at home.

In the summer of 1946 Robert made two further radio broadcasts. The first was on 4 July at 5.30pm, when Robert performed on the BBC Light Programme alongside Janet Davis, soprano, accompanied by Frederick Bayco on organ. The programme, entitled *I'll Play You,* was introduced by Sandy MacPherson. Frederick Bayco was the resident organist at London's Dominion Theatre in the 1930s. In 1949 he was among the guest organists to play at the New Victoria Theatre in Bradford. The *Telegraph & Argus* reported:

> Those people who listened to last night's radio feature, *I'll Play You* introduced by Sandy MacPherson, must surely have been moved by the lovely rich tenor voice of Mr Robert Naylor. The broadcast came from the Theatre Royal, Halifax, and it was pleasing to hear Mr Naylor in such grand form singing in his native town. Mr Naylor now lives in Bradford, and many organisations in the city and outside have reason to thank him for his services. No worthy cause is turned down by him and he has delighted thousands upon thousands of West Riding people during his frequent appearances at charity concerts. He is a great artist with a great heart.[184]

Robert's second broadcast that summer was on 20 August 1946, again on the BBC Light Programme, in a thirty-minute broadcast with Reginald Foort on organ. This programme was his final radio broadcast as a performer.

The same year Robert starred in the Bradford Amateur Operatic & Dramatic Society's production of *The Vagabond King* at the Alhambra Theatre. The 1925 operetta by Rudolf Friml, book and lyrics by Brian Hooker and W.H. Post, tells a highly romanticised tale concerning the fifteenth-century poet François Villon. The show opened on Monday 11 November for one week, and received a glowing review in the press:

> For well over three hours last night, comfortably seated in the packed Alhambra Theatre, Bradford, I lived and marvelled at that lovable rogue Francois Villon, and fully enjoyed every minute . . . Robert Naylor as Francois Villon commands attention throughout his magnificent performance. I

have often enjoyed his tenor voice on concert and radio, but never better than in last night's production. Mr Naylor is an instant success with his superb acting and singing, and there could be no more convincing 'Vagabond King'. He has a strenuous part, into which he puts his whole life and soul to earn full marks for an outstanding and colourful performance.[185]

Robert's principal activity, however, was as a music teacher. Soon he opened a studio in Bradford, in a rented room above Bradford's diocesan offices, at Church House on North Parade; he also gave lessons at a studio in Skipton. The pianist Norman Constantine often accompanied the students. He was a professional musician who was well known in Bradford, having played with the Savoy Symphony Orchestra that provided the music at the Savoy Cinema and Café in Darley Street. Later, along with Harold Gee and Margaret Mountain, Norman formed the Palm Court Trio, which played at Collinson's Café on Tyrell Street for many years after the war. He also performed at the lunch hour recitals, which were a regular feature at Bradford Mechanics Institute during this time. After he had finished playing at Collinson's for the day, Norman made his way up Darley Street to Church House, in order to play for Robert.

Students remember Robert as being well-mannered and well-spoken. He always wore a suit and often sported a bow tie or a cravat. He had a typical smoker's cough and sometimes sounded wheezy. He often sucked sweets, especially Vocalzone lozenges which he recommended to his students.[186] During the 1950s he typically charged his students 5 guineas for ten half-hour lessons.

One successful student was the boy soprano Christopher Robin. Christopher came from Baildon, Shipley, where he sang in the local church choir. He later transferred to Bradford Cathedral, where, under the guidance of Dr Charles Hooper and his deputy Kathleen Rhodes, his talent blossomed. Christopher had lessons with Robert in Bradford and entered various music festivals during the late '40s and early '50s, and won a number of festival competitions in 1952. One of these, The Huddersfield Boys' Open

Event, featured the song 'Tell Me, Lovely Shepherd' by William Boyce, in an arrangement by Elizabeth Poston. A recording was made of this later that same year at a local studio, with the sound cut directly into a metal disk in one take. The session benefited from the piano accompaniment of Norman Constantine. This song is currently available on a CD entitled *The Better Land, Volume Six, Great Boy Sopranos, Recorded 1912-1970.*[187]

In 1953 Robert, Dorothy, John and Michael moved to live in Harrogate, at Flat 2, Radlyn Court, 20 Park Avenue. This was an old school building (Trinity College, later Radlyn School) that had been converted into flats; it has now been demolished, and on the site is a new apartment block called Radlyn Oval. Some time after moving to Harrogate Michael left home and went to work for Rothmans, the tobacco company, in Rhodesia, and Robert lost all contact with his son. Michael married twice and had a number of children, but sadly Robert never met either of his daughters-in-law or any of his grandchildren.

The following year Robert was persuaded to come out of retirement by Councillor Ernest Robinson, chairman of the Harrogate Operatic Players. The society was to stage a production of *The Land of Smiles*, and Robert agreed to resurrect the role that had made him famous twenty-two years earlier. The show opened at the Royal Hall on Monday 15 March for a week, with a much heftier Robert playing Prince Sou-Chong. Several members of the cast paid tribute to the work Robert put into the amateur show, services he gave freely. The local newspaper review noted, 'Though a little unsteady in the pianissimo lower range, he showed himself to be still master of the ringing operatic tenor that won him the name of "the English Tauber".'[188]

The *Harrogate Advertiser* took pains to outline the plot of the operetta:

> The theme is an old one: East and West should stay apart, although each has obvious attractions to the other. The Countess Lisa[189] won by Prince Sou Chong from the courts of Vienna to Shangtung, is happy with him until Chinese law ordains his polygamy. His acceptance of concubines is purely formal –

he shares her western views on marriage –
but the idea so affronts Lisa as to close her
days for him. The end is the Prince's
renunciation of his rights over her. Mr
Naylor then has to project the character of a
noble man heart-rent by love and the
demands of his civilisation. In this he
succeeds splendidly, while it is a joy to hear
his tenor voice lifting above and no doubt
encouraging the chorus in its fine work.[190]

The town's other paper was equally lavish in its praise for this
'sparkling show':

Another important point in this altogether
excellent production by Charles Ross is that
for its main player one of the early and true
inventors of the title of Sou-Chong, Robert
Naylor, the Yorkshire tenor, has given his
services this week to play once more the
part he made famous in the Drury Lane
production when he succeeded Richard
Tauber, at the third performance. Naturally,
his interpretation is outstanding. He has a
magnificent tenor without a hint of strain
about it, a sure sign of a man who now
teaches rather than performs, a voice
superbly trained and admirably used. And
his stage movements and acting are a lesson
for everyone taking part this week. Perhaps
the simplest tribute to Robert Naylor's
performance is to say that he expressly
avoids emphasising the contrasts there must
be between his experience and that of the
other players. If this remains to some extent
a one-man show, it is because Lehár and his
collaborators made it so.[191]

Robert's connection with local opera societies didn't end there. In 1955 he took over the management of the Bradford Opera Group. Two years earlier an advertisement had appeared in the local press, requesting people interested in opera to contact G. Delni at an address in Manningham. Six people attended the first meeting at the home of Guido Delni, late principal baritone of La Scala, Milan, and from this small beginning the Bradford Opera Group was born.[192] It made its public début at the Civic Theatre, situated on Chapel Street, Little Germany, in an evening of miscellaneous operatic items.

The first full production was of Mozart's *Impresario*, which was staged at the Co-operative Hall, Southgate, the setting for most of the early productions. The opera is short, and is a burlesque of an audition held by a theatre director, with two sopranos and a tenor as principal parts. The plot features jealousies, rivalries, tantrums, falsity and humour. In the early days the group's productions were staged with piano accompaniment; later there was a small orchestra, made up of local musicians. To begin with soloists were drawn from within the group, but later they came from all over Yorkshire. In 1966 the group moved its productions to the Princes Ballroom at the Midland Hotel, before finally taking up residence in the new Central Library Theatre. The group celebrated its silver jubilee with a production of Verdi's *A Masked Ball*.[193]

When Guido Delni moved to Nottingham Robert took over the running of the group. During his tenure he used the group's annual productions as an outlet for his talented students, providing them with an opportunity to perform on stage before an audience.

During 1954 Robert was invited by the BBC producer Alick Hayes to train a group of nine girls as a singing nonet for sound and television broadcasting. Alick Hayes produced the radio series *Just William* from 1945 to 1956; he was instrumental in bringing the Oxford–Cambridge Boat Race to television; and he wrote a single episode of *Coronation Street* in 1961. He was also a notable actor. The girls that Hayes and Robert chose from auditions were known as the Robert Naylor Valentine Girls, and came from Leeds, Harrogate, Aireborough and Batley. They made a number of short broadcasts for a variety of networks at the BBC studios in Leeds, under the title *Musical At Home*. Largely devoted to Edwardian music, their first programme was broadcast on Saturday 23 October 1954 on the Northern Ireland Home Service, and a further two programmes in the series were broadcast by the station also on Saturday evenings, 6 and 20 November. Then just before Christmas, on 23 December, the Robert Naylor Valentine Girls were featured in a programme entitled *Birthday Book No. 7,* broadcast on the North of England Home Service. In the New Year the Northern Ireland Home Service resumed its run of the girls' *Musical At Home* programmes, with broadcasts on 12 and 26 February and 12 and 26 March. Six more *Musical At Home* programmes featuring the Robert Naylor Valentine Girls were heard weekly on the North of England Home Service, commencing on Thursday 8 December.

On Monday 14 December the Robert Naylor Valentine Girls were heard in a programme called *Nineteenth Century Drawing Room.* The programme, broadcast on the Home Service at 8.45pm, included such old favourites as 'Alice Where Art Thou?', written in about 1880 by Joseph Ascher (music) and Wellington Guernsey (lyrics) – the tune was used in the introduction to the BBC TV series *Open All Hours*; and 'In The Twi-Twi-Twilight', with music by Herman E. Darewski and lyrics by Charles Wilmott. It was Herman Darewski (1883–1947) and His Band that drew dance crowds to the Bridlington Spa each summer throughout the 1920s and '30s.

An unidentified newspaper review of the broadcast noted:

> It is pleasant once more to record an instance of entertainment in the North Region. Robert Naylor's Valentine Girls, heard on Monday night, was planned to give an opportunity for a number of talented 'solo singers' who had passed auditions but for whom there seemed little likelihood of a microphone appearance. The setting of a musical at home in a nineteenth-century drawing room gave opportunity for some beautiful madrigal singing and for the kind of musical comedy ensemble rarely heard these days. The programme was helped too by the simplicity of its presentation – and by the expert accompaniments of Mr Bert Halliday.[194]

On Wednesday 4 January 1956 the Robert Naylor Valentine Girls made their only television appearance, when they appeared on BBC TV's *The Good Old Days,* an old-time music hall concert broadcast from the City Varieties Theatre, Leeds. This hugely popular television programme ran for thirty years, first being broadcast on 20 July 1953. Initially the show was broadcast irregularly because the BBC was already running a show called *Music Hall.* The City Varieties Theatre provided a fitting period venue, with velvet drapes and galleried upper floor with boxes. The 'Good Old Days' image was completed by an audience in Victorian/Edwardian costume and title credits in appropriate period lettering.

The Good Old Days was produced by Barney Colehan, who was born in Calverley, near Leeds. He first gained prominence in 1946 as the BBC radio producer of *Have A Go,* with Wilfred Pickles, and was awarded an MBE in 1981. Robert's stepson John remembers Barney Colehan visiting the family home in Harrogate. This may have been around the time that the Robert Naylor Valentine Girls were invited to appear on his TV programme; however, it is possible the Colehans knew the Naylors socially.

Reviewing the *Good Old Days* broadcast, a Yorkshire Post reporter noted, 'Another hit with the audience were the Robert Naylor Valentine Girls, a group of young ladies with pleasant voices, who have been enjoying a great deal of success recently.'[195]

During August 1956 the Robert Naylor Valentine Girls were heard for the last time, when the BBC Light Programme broadcast five *Musical At Home* programmes each Thursday evening that month. It is possible that these were repeats of programmes first heard on the Home Service earlier in the year.

With the Valentine Girls, Robert had made his final foray into show business. For the next decade he concentrated on teaching his pupils at his home in Harrogate. He was singularly successful as a teacher, and a number of his students went on to appear on the professional stage. One was Pat Lambert, from Harrogate, who had appeared with Robert in the Harrogate Operatic Society production of *The Land of Smiles.* She went on to do four seasons with the Fol-de-Rols, the famous touring song and laughter show founded by George Royle at the Floral Hall, Scarborough, in 1911 and taken over in 1919 by Greatrex Newman (1892–1984), a prolific writer of songs and sketches. It was Newman who made the Fols a national institution, with companies in Eastbourne, Hastings, Llandudno and Sandown. In 1960 the company had the honour of being included in the Royal Variety Show. Pat Lambert made her London début in pantomime, starring opposite Charlie Drake and Edmund Hockridge in *The Sleeping Beauty* at the London Palladium 1958–9. In 1961 she was in the West End production of *The Music Man* with Van Johnson and Dennis Waterman. Pat had also been one of Robert Naylor's Valentine Girls.

Another of the Valentine Girls was Jean Hindmarsh, who was born in Leeds in 1932 and attended the city's Lawnswood High School for Girls. She later studied at the Royal College of Music in Manchester. After a successful audition she joined the D'Oyly Carte Opera Company in March 1956 as principal soprano, appearing as Mabel in *The Pirates of Penzance*, Princess Ida in *Princess Ida*, Elsie Maynard in *The Yeoman of the Guard* and Gianetta in *The Gondoliers*. Although she officially left the company in 1960 she returned for several guest engagements between 1961 and 1969. Jean can be heard on four D'Oyly Carte recordings: as Yum-Yum in *The Mikado* (1957), Mabel in *Pirates* (1957), both recorded at the Kingsway Hall for Decca; and as Josephine in *HMS Pinafore* (1960) and Rose Maybud in *Ruddigore* (1962), both recorded at Walthamstow Town Hall for Decca.[196]

Miss Peggy Roberts was yet another Valentine Girl, and while she did not become a professional singer, she gave sixty years' dedicated service to the Harrogate Operatic Players, appearing in many of their annual productions. She served on the committee for forty-two years, fourteen of them as Chairman. At the time of writing she is the society's president. In July 2007 Peggy turned eighty, and the society paid tribute to her in their newsletter under the heading 'Our Valentine Girl'.

On Friday 20 April 1956 Robert's mother, Sarah, who had been ailing for some time, died from heart trouble; she was eighty-one years old. She was buried alongside her husband in the Naylor family grave at St Mary's Church, Luddenden. In her later years she had spent most weekends with her eldest son James and his wife Florence, who had previously looked after Robert's son Michael. Yet apparently it was Robert, because of his stage success, who was always his mother's blue-eyed boy, something that must have rankled with James and Florence.

The Stage, in their edition of 6 December 1956, reported that 'Robert Naylor has discovered a pupil destined for great things. He is Robert Darnborough of Bingley.' Darnborough, then about sixteen years old, studied with Robert Naylor in 1956–7. During that time he won prizes at a number of local music festivals, including the festival at Blackpool in November 1956. He then went to study at the Opera School based at Morley College in London for three years. His potential grand opera career was abruptly ended when he suffered throat damage in a motorcycle accident on his way to the Edinburgh Festival, but he recovered sufficiently to undertake light opera work and in 1960 he appeared at the Theatre Royal, Drury Lane, in *My Fair Lady,* with Ann Rogers and Alec Clunes. He appeared again at Drury Lane in *Camelot,* with Laurence Harvey, in 1964. Darnborough recalled: 'Robert Naylor was a lovely man. He was warm-hearted and couldn't do enough for me. I used to go to his studio on North Parade, Bradford, and I had extra lessons at his home in Harrogate. He still had a wonderful voice and could still hit those high Cs. He was a marvellous teacher and he was really like a father to me at that time.'[197] Dissatisfied with having to accept West End musicals rather than grand opera, Robert Darnborough resigned from his professional stage career and trained as a school teacher. He continued to perform in an amateur capacity for many years afterwards, often accompanied by the local virtuoso pianist John Briggs.

In 1958 Robert moved house for the last time, to Corner Close, 21 Langcliffe Avenue, off Leeds Road, Harrogate. The property is a large detached villa commanding a corner position. From here he continued to give singing lessons. His stepson confided that, when not engaged with his students, Robert took a lively interest in horse racing; he enjoyed having a flutter, and regularly placed bets over the telephone, not always with great success.[198] Robert followed the fortunes of Bradford (Park Avenue) AFC, and sometimes attended a home match to watch them play. The football ground was adjacent to Park Avenue Cricket Ground, where he also occasionally went to watch Yorkshire CCC play in the county championships.

Another student was David Taylor, who was nineteen years old when he started lessons; he remembers Robert Naylor 'with great affection'. He too had lessons at Robert's studio in Church House.

The room they used was 'quite large and had lots of resonance', he recalled. David also played rugby league for Keighley, and Robert took great interest in his student's exploits on the pitch. Owing to work commitments and his marriage, David gave up lessons for a while, but resumed a few years later when Robert had moved to Harrogate. He remembers:

> His health was none too good by that time. A lady by the name of Mary was the accompanist then.[199] Even late in life he still possessed a remarkable and powerful tenor voice. As a teacher he used the classic Italian *bel canto* method with much use of the diaphragm. He used a warm-up song called *Caro Mio Ben*[200] as he reasoned it was a nice easy piece which opened up the voice. He recommended breathing exercises and drinking plenty of water. I remember that he had a great sense of humour. He was a fine teacher and a fine man.[201]

By the 1960s society seemed entirely youth-orientated, with its emphasis on the new and the modern. It was a decade that can best be summed up as a heady mixture of optimism and hedonism. Rock music determined attitudes, clothes and hairstyles, and this evolved into pop art, which embraced just about everything else. It was a period that brought about a social and cultural revolution. One of the catalysts was the recovery of the British economy after the post-war austerity and the end of rationing, which had lasted until 4 July 1954. People flocked to the London theatres to see shows like *Hair*, which featured not only rock music, but also nudity and controversial opinions about the Vietnam War. It was all a far cry from the stage entertainment before and immediately after the war – the world that Robert had known.

For a while, however, Robert continued to accept students. One was a teenage girl called Pauline Wood, who well remembers her lessons:

The year was 1963 when I went to Robert Naylor for voice training. He rented a room at Church House in Bradford. I remember being ushered in by a bald-headed man in a grey suit who turned out to be the pianist. Mr Naylor was thick-set and of medium build. He was well-spoken and smartly dressed. He concentrated on improving my breathing. I noticed a difference after six months. He told me to get Nigroids for my vocal chords. He sucked sweets nearly the whole time I was there. They were little black sweets and I got some from the chemists.[202] They certainly opened up my vocal cords. He was a great teacher.'[203]

Quite often Robert took his more able students to a local recording studio, so they might hear themselves singing. This studio was run by Jack Thistlethwaite and was called Excel Services. Originally at 42A Otley Road, Shipley, it later moved to 49 Bradford Road, Saltaire, Shipley. The premises were equipped with an isolation booth – a small soundproofed room that kept out external sounds and kept in the internal sounds. For a fee one could make a record and have it pressed. Originally the company produced 10in 78rpm shellac discs, and later on 7in 45rpm and 12in 33⅓rpm vinyl records. It seems that Robert may have made some private recordings here as teaching aids for his students. Jack Thistlethwaite was a somewhat shy and retiring man, who has never received the praise he deserved. He was a gifted audio specialist and invented the early walkie-talkie phones used by Bradford Police.

In his later years Robert put on considerable weight and became increasingly inactive. His stepson recalled, 'He felt constantly tired, and would often stay in bed all morning. But he came to life when he was teaching. It was what gave his life meaning. I think his greatest contribution was as a teacher of voice, he really was a very good teacher.'

Robert's final years were dogged by ill-health. Like many of his generation, he had been a life-long cigarette smoker and this did not help. On Friday 19 January 1968 he died at his home at Langcliffe

Avenue; the family doctor, Dr G.M. Tyler, certified the cause of death as congestive cardiac failure. Robert's funeral service was held the following Tuesday at 11.00am at St Mark's Church, Harrogate, before a private cremation at Stonewall Cemetery. At St Mark's Church the Rev J. Sandwith led the service. In addition to the small group of family members, representatives from the Harrogate Operatic Players and the Leeds Thespians Operatic Society were also in attendance. Among the many floral tributes was a large bouquet from the singer Harry Secombe, who early in his career had received help from Robert. Michael, never close to his father, did not attend.

The *Yorkshire Post* had half a column headed 'Death At 68 Of Famous Tenor', and the Bradford *Telegraph & Argus* reported most fittingly on the 'Death of the English Tauber'. There were also obituaries in the *Harrogate Advertiser* and the *Halifax Courier*. In London on Wednesday 24 January the General Committee of the Concert Artistes Association met and stood in silence to his memory.[204] His passing went unreported in the national press.

After Robert's death his widow Dorothy went to live with her sister in Lightcliffe, near Halifax. She then moved to live with her son, the Rev. John Naylor, first at West Woodburn, near Hexham, where John had his parish, and then to Husborne Crawley, Bedfordshire, when John took over the incumbency of St James's Church there in 1972. She died on 26 October 1974, in hospital at Aylesbury, Buckinghamshire. Robert's son Michael was found dead in his flat in Portsmouth in January 1994.

Many details about Robert Naylor's career remain uncertain. During his residence in London between 1922 and 1939 I have every reason to believe that he was working constantly. Many of his singing engagements would have been at private social functions of the kind I have mentioned. Now, seventy or more years later, it is almost impossible to track down every one of these events.

The same is true of the period between 1939 and 1945, when Robert had returned to live in the West Riding and was holding down a full-time job in the textile industry. He accepted hundreds of singing engagements, for which he was not paid; for the most part these were fund-raising concerts given to support the war effort and organised by various welfare charities. But there were other engagements too. For instance, I am certain he performed regularly for the troops at various military camps. He also gave freely of his time to support the activities of many Rotary clubs, Lions clubs and Masonic lodges, as well as at other private functions. Few of these engagements would have been publicly advertised, and as a result the full extent of his voluntary work throughout the war years can only be guessed at.

From those pieces of the puzzle that I have been able to find, I have tried to create a picture, if not quite a full-length portrait, of Robert Naylor's life and career. In the inter-war years it was far less common than it is today for a young man to pursue a professional stage career. It took courage to move to London, and he must have faced some initial parental resistance. However, supported by Cecilia, he showed a determination to succeed. What Robert discovered, of course, is what hundreds have discovered before and since – that fame is fickle, and the world of show business can be brutal and unfair. Adulation does not always go to those with the greatest talent, something that was as true then as it is today.

In the years since the last war Robert, like so many of the names in this book, has been almost entirely forgotten. Yet in his day Robert's singing brought pleasure to thousands of people, via his stage appearances, broadcasts and gramophone recordings. His numerous recordings were all originally released on 10in 78 rpm discs and were never re-issued on vinyl, in either long player (LP) or extended player (EP) format. Fortunately twenty of his recordings are held for posterity in the British Sound Archive of the British Library.

That Robert was gifted with a fine voice goes without saying, and it seems that his fine voice never deserted him. The old proverb says that 'those who can, do, and those who can't teach' – but assuredly Robert could do, and did, most successfully for many years, while later in life he chose to devote himself entirely to his students, and was regarded as one of the foremost teachers and voice specialists in the North of England. This is perhaps where, in the end, he found his greatest rewards.

Footnotes

1   *I'll Sing You A Thousand Love Songs: The Denny Dennis Story*, Mike Carey (Pinnacle Printing, Derby, 1992).

2   'Shepherd House', Tom Sutcliffe, *Halifax Antiquarian Transactions* (1926). NB Two Lister clocks are displayed at the Shibden Hall Museum, Halifax.

3   Tales of the Hill People, *Halifax Courier*, 25 July 2003.

4   Ibid.

5   Taken from the history of the school written by Thomas Cox, who was headmaster in the late nineteenth century. In 1985 the school was merged with another to form Crossley Heath Grammar School. The original Heath School is a listed building now used by Calderdale Education.

6   *Complete Handbook of Voice Training*, Richard Anderson (Parker Publishing Company, West Nyack, NY, 1979).

7   For a detailed history see *Music Making in the West Riding of Yorkshire: the exploration of a unique musical phenomenon*, ed. Adrian Smith (R.H. Wood, Huddersfield, 2000).

8   A Golden Voice From The Past', *Halifax Courier*, 25 November 1966.

9   The British National Opera Company emerged from the collapse of the Beecham Opera Company in December 1920. The BNOC lasted from 1922 to 1929.

10 'Singing All The Way', *Halifax Evening Courier*, 18 January 1968.

11   Maurice Robson's sleeve notes to *Walter Widdop: Songs and Arias,* 1992, Voices from the Past, audio cassette no. WW100

12   Another local singer to join the Beecham Company was the contralto Edna Thornton. She was born at Low Moor in Bradford in 1875. She also performed at Covent Garden and was especially admired for her Wagnerian roles. She sang in the world premier of Holst's *The Perfect Fool* in 1923, and was a mainstay of English operatic life in the first thirty years of the last century. She died in Worthing in 1964.

13   The mill was badly damaged by a fire in 1925. Later called Riding Hall Mills, the building was demolished in 1980. See *Pennine Mill Trail,* compiled by Ken Powell (Save Britain's Heritage, London, 1981).

14   *Sostenuto* is an Italian term which means 'sustained', where notes are held for longer than their notated value.

15   Copies of the Music Festival certificates and adjudicator's remarks are in the author's private collection.

16   The British Federation of Musical Competition Festivals, 48 Devonshire Street, London WC1.

17   *Amateur Operatics: A Social & Cultural History,* John Lowerson (Manchester University Press, 2005)

18   This may possibly have been a professional name. 'Le Vallon' is the title of a song by the French composer Charles Gounod.

19   This incident was recounted to music historian Maurice Robson by Mr and Mrs Teal when he interviewed them at their home in the 1960s.

20   This particular medal is in the author's collection. The silver medals were loaned to the author by Mrs B. Feavers.

21   The Wharfedale Competitive Music Festival was still active in the 1930s, when the Honorary Secretary was Mr T. Ackroyd, Hon. RCM, ARCM, of 46 Leeds Road, Harrogate.

22   *Todmorden Advertiser,* 21 January 1921.

23   Ibid.

24   Quoting Henry Mills, secretary (in the programme for the Empress Theatre, Brixton, London, 15 October 1922). The offices of the National Sunday League were at 221 High Holborn, London WC2.

25   *These Tremendous Years 1919-1938* (Daily Express Publication, 1938).

26   *After The Ball*, Ian Whitcomb (Allen Lane, London, 1972).

27   *Music in the Twenties*, Ronald Pearsall (David & Charles, London, 1976).

28   Peter Cliffe, 'Robert Naylor', *The Historic Record*, July 1996.

29   *The History of Broadcasting in the United Kingdom. Vol.3. The Great Age of Wireless*, Asa Briggs (Oxford University Press, 1995).

30   *But - What Do You Do in the Winter? 100 Years of the Concert Artistes' Association*, Larry Parker (CAA, London, 1996).

31   *The Stage*, 13 January 1927.

32   *The Stage*, 27 January 1927.

33   The Federation of British Music Industries used to be at 117-23 Great Portland Street, London W1.

34   'Martha Revived', *The Stage*, 1 December 1927.

35   *The Stage*, 1 March 1928.

36   *The Stage*, 29 March 1928.

37   *The Jazz Singer* (1927) made by Warner Bros and starring Al Jolson, wasn't released in Britain until 27 September 1928.

38   *Ibbs & Tillett: The Rise and Fall of a Musical Empire*, Christopher Firfield (Ashgate Publishing, 2005).

39   *The Times*, 23 November 1928.

40   Joseph Holbrooke (1878-1958) was an English composer of some note in his day, but is now almost entirely forgotten.

41   *The Stage*, 9 May 1929.

42   *The Times*, 16 July 1929.

43   *The Times*, 29 July 1929.

44   *Sweethearts of Song: A Personal Memoir of Anne Ziegler and Webster Booth*, Jean Collen (Lulu, 2006).

45   Music by Ivor Novello, lyrics by Donovan Parsons.

46   Stephen Constantine, *Social Conditions in Britain 1918-1939* (1983).

47   *The Stage*, 13 February 1930. Miss Gladys Knight was an English concert singer.

48   The episode is recounted in *Duet* by Anne Ziegler and Webster Booth (Stanley Paul, London, 1951).

49   *The Oxford Companion of Popular Music*, Peter Gammond
      (Oxford University Press, 1991).

50   *All You Need Is Love – The Story of Popular Music* by Tony
      Palmer (Weidenfeld & Nicolson and Chappell & Co. Ltd,
      London, 1976).

51   From: 'Islington: Social and cultural activities', A History of
      the County of Middlesex: Volume 8: Islington and Stoke
      Newington parishes (1985), pp. 45-51.

52   *The Gramophone*, May 1930.

53   Piccadilly 5043.

54   Piccadilly 5067.

55   *Glasgow Herald*, 8 September 1930.

56   Lea Seidl, soprano (1895–1987).

57   *The Times*, 10 September 1930.

58   Parlophone R790.

59   Parlophone R 792.

60   Parlophone R816.

61   *George Scott Wood*, Barry McCanna (Memory Lane,
      September 2004).

62   *The Gramophone*, June 1924.

63   www.emiarchivetrust.org.

64   *Liebestraum* is German for love dream, or dreams of love.

65   In writing this chapter I am indebted to the memoirs of
      Walter McQueen-Pope who was press representative at Drury
      Lane from 1931 for twenty-one years: *Fortunes Favourite:
      The Life & Times of Franz Lehár*, Walter McQueen-Pope
      (Hutchinson, 1953).

66   Ibid.

67   *Operetta: A Theatrical History*, Richard Traubner
      (Routledge, 2003).

68   *The Oxford Companion to Popular Music*, Peter Gammond
      (Oxford University Press, 1991).

69   *The Times*, 9 May 1931.

70   'New Light Opera By Franz Lehár', *Yorkshire Post*, 9 May
      1931.

71   'Local Tenor's Ordeal', *Halifax Daily Courier & Guardian*, 13
      May 1931.

72   A copy of the telegram, sent from Southampton Street Post Office, The Strand, WC2, and dated 12 May 1931, is in the author's private collection.

73   Halifax Daily Courier & Guardian, 14 May 1931.

74   *The Times*, 27 May 1931.

75   *Punch*, 27 May 1931.

76   'Tenor's Triumph', *Halifax Daily Courier & Guardian*, 15 June 1931.

77   *Halifax Daily Courier & Guardian*, 20 June 1931.

78   Halifax Daily Courier & Guardian, 20 June 1931.

79   Fortunes Favourite, op. cit.

80   *Telegraph & Argus*, Bradford, 2 March 1954.

81   Parlophone 939.

82   Parlophone 940.

83   Edith Day and Geoffrey Gwyther, 'If You're In Love You'll Waltz' c/w 'Rio Rita', Columbia DX55, recorded 10 April 1930.

84   Parlophone R1028.

85   Parlophone R1040.

86   *The Times*, 13 August 1931

87   *Abbey Road*, Brian Southall, Peter Vince and Allan Rouse (Patrick Stevens Ltd, Cambridge, 1985)

88   Parlophone R1060.

89   Parlophone R1121.

90   *The Times*, 19 January 1932.

91   *Siffleur*: a whistler. This is a largely forgotten art – but whistling can be musical. Many performers in musical hall and on the variety stage were professional whistlers, the most famous of whom was Ronnie Ronalde.

92   Parlophone R1133.

93   Parlophone R1151.

94   *The Times*, 1 March 1932.

95   Parlophone R1200.

96   Parlophone R1235.

97   *The Gramophone*, June 1932.

98   Parlophone R1305.

99   *Oxford Companion to Popular Music*, Peter Gammond (Oxford University Press, 1991).

100 *Popular Music of the Twenties*, Ronald Pearsall (David & Charles, London, 1976).

101 Parlophone 1318.

102 *The Singing Bourgeois: Songs of the Victorian Drawing Room and Parlour*, 2nd edition, Derek B. Scott (Ashgate Publishing, Aldershot, 2001).

103 *The Gramophone*, November 1932.

104 'Stage Talk', *Telegraph & Argus*, Bradford, Thursday 14 September 1933.

105 Parlophone R1401.

106 *The Times*, Saturday 25 February 1933.

107 Parlophone R1470.

108 See National Sunday League concert on page 17.

109 Shelf Hall was an Italianate mansion with a large columned portico, standing in 27 acres of park land. Samuel Watkinson died just before the Second World War and the house was used by the army to house Italian prisoners of war. The house was demolished in the 1950s, and the grounds now form Shelf Hall Park.

110 Quoted in *A History and Guide to the Parish of St Paul's Church* (Church History Group publication, 1992).

111 Undated report, *Time* magazine.

112 *The Stage*, 13 July 1933.

113 Still standing, the building is now a Pentecostal church.

114 For a full account of the era of theatre organs see: The Mighty Organ, Geoffrey Wyatt, 1974, Oxford University Press, Oxford.

115 The Cinematography Films Act 1927 meant the British cinemas had to show a quota of British made films. A flood of British films hit the screens following the introduction of the act, culminating in over 190 films being produced in the year of 1936.

116 'Aberdeen Reopening 1933' by Jim Pratt, *Call Boy* (winter 1988).

117 *The Stage*, 24 August 1933.

118 'Stage Talk', *Telegraph & Argus*, Bradford, Thursday 14 September 1933.

119 Parlophone R1583.

120 *The Gramophone*, September 1933.

121   *The History of Broadcasting in the United Kingdom. Vol 2. The Golden Age of Wireless*, Asa Briggs (Oxford University Press, 1995)

122   Parlophone R1622.

123   *The Gramophone*, November 1933.

124   Quoted from *The Etude*, a US magazine devoted to music (February 1911; now in the public domain).

125   Parlophone R1706.

126   Sometimes called May H. Morgan.

127   Imperial-Broadcast 4001.

128   *'Let's Face the Music and Dance': The Golden Age of Popular Song*, Benny Green (Pavilion Books, London, 1989).

129   A video of the 78rpm record being played made a surprise appearance on the internet web-site YouTube in January 2008 http://www.youtube.com

130   See 'Gay Vienna' – Myth and Reality, Henry Schnitzler, *Journal of the History of Ideas, Jan 1954.* University of Pennsylvania Press.

131   Imperial-Broadcast 4002

132   *Jack Doyle: The Gorgeous Gael*, Desmond Lyman (The Lilliput Press, 2007).

133   'Come to Lovely Largs', *Scottish Daily Record and Mail* (Friday 1 June 1934).

134   At the time of writing this can be viewed at: www.britishpathe.com.

135   The American Society of Composers Arrangers and Publishers.

136   Imperial-Broadcast 4016.

137   Imperial-Broadcast 4006.

138   Imperial-Broadcast 4030.

139   *The Gramophone*, December 1934.

140   Further information about Eclipse 806 can be found in the discography at the end of the book.

141   The Columbia Gramophone Co. Ltd, the Parlophone Co. Ltd and the Vocalion Gramophone Co. Ltd all had offices at this time in Clerkenwell, London.

142   Rex 8344: 'Merry Widow Waltz Song' (orchestra only), 'Vilia' (Anona), 'You'll Find Me At Maxims' (Robert and chorus), 'Girls, Girls, Girls' (Robert and chorus), 'Valse

Duet' (Robert and Anona), 'Merry Widow Waltz
Song' (reprised by Anona and Robert with chorus).

143 Rex 8344 and Rex 8345.
144 *The Gramophone*, January 1935.
145 Rex 8377.
146 *The Times*, Friday 1 March 1935.
147 Rex 8449.
148 *Film Weekly*, 20 September 1935.
149 *The Times*, 2 March 1935.
150 Rex 8388.
151 *The Gramophone*, April 1935.
152 Rex 8529.
153 *The Gramophone*, July 1935.
154 Rex 8538.
155 A copy of the letter from Sir Landon Ronald is in the author's private collection.
156 A copy of the programme for the evening is in the author's private collection.
157 *And The Bands Played On – An informal history of British Dance Bands*, Sid Colin (Elm Tree Books, London, 1977).
158 Rex 8677.
159 *The Gramophone*, February 1936.
160 Rex 8720.
161 *The Gramophone*, March 1936.
162 *Scottish Showbusiness: Music Hall, Variety & Pantomime*, Frank Bruce (NMS Publishing, Edinburgh, 2000).
163 The Gaiety Theatre held its last show on Saturday 31 January 2009. South Ayrshire Council has taken a number of steps to protect and preserve the unique building until a decision is taken about its future.
164 *The Stage*, 21 July 1938.
165 Copyright 1936, music by Horatio Nicholls (Lawrence Wright), words by Edward Lockton.
166 Al Bowlly recorded the song on 1 July 1938 with Felix Mendelssohn and his Orchestra. The record was released on Decca F-6727.
167 *Glasgow Evening Times*, 1 November 1938.
168 *Halifax Courier*, 2 January 1939.
169 *The Stage*, 17 August 1939.

170 *And The Bands Played On – An informal history of British Dance Bands*, Sid Colin (Elm Tree Books, London, 1977)

171 The Rev. John Watson Naylor in discussions with the author in 1994.

172 *Batley Reporter*, 17 February 1940.

173 James France & Co. Ltd (woollen and worsted yarn spinners for rugs, carpets, blankets, knitting and hosiery), Albert Mills, Savile Town, Dewsbury.

174 www.brent-heritage.co.uk.

175 *Batley Reporter*, 17 February 1940.

176 *The Stage*, 30 May 1940.

177 The theatre first opened in 1932 as the Paramount Theatre, built for and operated by Paramount Pictures Ltd. It was renamed the Odeon in April 1940 and finally closed in 2001.

178 'Wedding Of Famous Tenor Vocalist', *Telegraph & Argus*, Monday 15 September 1941.

179 During the war Robert guested with the Sadler's Wells Operatic Company. The company left the capital when their theatre was requisitioned for war use; it later sustained bomb damage. They relocated to the Victoria Theatre in Burnley, but during these years they were essentially a touring company dedicated towards raising war-time spirits in provincial towns.

180 *Huddersfield Examiner*, Saturday 2 May 1942.

181 *Wild Violets*, a musical comedy operetta by Bruno Hardt-Warden, with music by Robert Stolz. It was adapted for broadcasting from the English version by Holt Marvell, Hassard Short, Desmond Carter and Reginald Purdell, and was produced by Martyn C. Webster.

182 Still standing, Bowers Hall is now a polo club.

183 *Ibbs & Tillett: The Rise and Fall of a Musical Empire*, Christopher Firfield (Ashgate Publishing, 2005)

184 *Telegraph & Argus*, Friday 5 July 1946.

185 'Bradford Amateurs' Triumph', *Telegraph & Argus*, Tuesday 12 November 1946.

186 Vocalzone lozenges were first created for Enrico Caruso, the renowned Italian tenor, in the early twentieth century. The creator was a chemist in Carmarthen, a small town in south-west Wales. They are still available today.

187   Amphion PHI CD 220 – Amphion Recordings, Norton Lodge, 109 Beverley Road, Norton-on-Derwent, Malton, North Yorkshire,YO17 9PH.

188   *Telegraph & Argus*, Tuesday 16 March 1954.

189   Played by the talented Pat Lambert: see page 145.

190   *Harrogate Advertiser*, 16 March 1954.

191   *Harrogate Herald*, 17 March 1954.

192   *Bradford Pictorial*, November 1964.

193   *Telegraph & Argus*, 20 February 1980.

194   A copy of this unidentified and undated press cutting is in the author's collection.

195   'Edwardian Music Hall Revived at City Varieties', *Yorkshire Post*, c. January 1956.

196   See *Who Was Who in the D'Oyly Carte Opera Company 1875–1983* by David Stone at http://math.boisestate.edu/GaS/whowaswho/index.htm.

197   Robert Darnborough in conversation with the author, September 2008.

198   From the author's conversations with the Rev. John Naylor.

199   Mary Hobkinson.

200   *Caro Mio Ben* (Come Once Again), attributed to Giuseppe Giordano (1751–98).

201   David Taylor in conversation with the author, August 2009.

202   Nigroids are small liquorice and menthol flavoured sweets invented by Ferris and Co. Ltd, Manufacturing Chemists, Bristol. They were marketed as being 'invaluable for singers'.

203   Pauline Wood in a letter to the author.

204   *The Stage*, 1 February 1968.

Discography

compiled by Arthur Badrock and Bob Naylor;
revised by Daniel O'Hara

DUOPHONE RECORDS
Made, probably, at 15–19 Cavendish Place, London W1

20 September 1928, accompanied by S. Pole, piano
DB45-1 Sigh No More Ladies (Aiken)
unissued/rejected

The only other recordings made on this day, according to the company's matrix file, were DB41 to DB44 by the Duophone Military Band conducted by Charles Leggett. This solitary title by Robert Naylor may have been in the nature of a trial recording for him. If satisfactory it would have been issued in the short-lived D500 series, but it was not; two titles by the tenor Parry Jones were. There is a slight possibility that a rejected test might turn up. Several such tests surfaced in a Norfolk auction room a few years ago, but not DB45.

PICCADILLY RECORDS
Made at Highbury Athenaeum, 96a Highbury New Park, London N5
Piccadilly Records were manufactured by the Metropole Company, and the plain matrix number in the wax denotes take -1 (shown here for clarity as, for example, 1677--).

February–March 1929, with piano
1677--
'For You Alone' (Henry Gheel)
Piccadilly 5021, Octacros 456

1678--
'The Star' (Rogers)

c. **May 1930, with orchestra**
3564--
'Sigh No More, Ladies' (Aiken)
Piccadilly 908, 5043, Octacros 470

3565-2 'Until' (Teschemacher, Sanderson)
A double-sided test coupling 3564-- and 3564-2 is extant.

c. **August 1930, with orchestra**
3779--
'I Attempt From Love's Sickness To Fly' (Purcell, arr. F. Adlington)
Piccadilly 5067, Octacros 483

3780-2
'The English Rose' (from *Merrie England*, Edward German)

PARLOPHONE RECORDS
Made at 72a Carlton Hill, London NW8, with orchestra conducted by George Scott-Wood unless otherwise indicated

17 September 1930, with piano
Frederica (Harry S. Pepper – Franz Lehár)

WE3623-1
I Live For Your Love
Parlophone R790

WE3624-1
O Maiden, My Maiden
---

c. 15 October 1930, with orchestra
Frederica (Harry S. Pepper – Franz Lehár)

WE3711-2
Wayside Rose
Parlophone R792

WE3712-2
Wonderful, So Wonderful
---

c. 19 November 1930, with orchestra
Private Lives (Noel Coward)

WE3792-2
Someday I'll Find You
Parlophone R816

WE3793-1
The World Is Waiting For The Sunrise (Lockhart, Seitz)
---

17 May 1931, with orchestra
The Land of Smiles (Harry Graham – Franz Lehár)

WE4079-2
Beneath The Window Of My Love
Parlophone R940

WE4080-2
You Are My Heart's Delight
Parlophone R939

WE4081-1
Patiently Smiling

WE4082-2
A Cup Of Tea With You (with Olive Groves, soprano)
Parlophone R940

c. **29 August 1931, with orchestra**
Waltzes from Vienna (Desmond Carter – Johann Strauss II)

WE4249-2
Love Will Find You (with Dorothy Bennett, sop.)
Parlophone R1028

WE4250-2
While You Love Me (with Dorothy Bennett, sop.)

---

c. **12 September 1931, with orchestra**
WE4260-1
Love Everlasting (Castling, Friml)
Parlophone R1060

WE4261-2

A Southern Song (Dean, Freeman, Ronald)

Victoria and her Hussar (Harry Graham – Paul Abraham)

WE4262-2

Goodnight (with Dorothy Bennett, sop.)

Parlophone R1040

WE4263-2

Pardon, Madame (with Dorothy Bennett)

---

19 December 1931, with orchestra

WE4335-3

The Song Of Songs (Lucas, Moya)

Parlophone R1133

Note: Takes one and two were recorded at an earlier session (date unknown), but rejected. It is possible Robert Naylor also made other recordings on that and the present session.

20 December 1931, with orchestra

The Desert Song (Oscar Hammerstein II – Sigmund Romberg)

WE4404-1

The Desert Song (with Edith Day, sop.)

Parlophone R1121, Parlo F437

Rose Marie (Otto Harbach, Oscar Hammerstein II – Rudolf Friml)

WE4405-2

Indian Love Call (with Edith Day, sop.)

WE4406-1
For You Alone (O'Reilly, H. Geehl)
Parlophone R1133

22 January 1932, with orchestra
Goodnight, Vienna (Marvell – Posford)

WE4421-3
Goodnight, Vienna
Parlophone R1151

WE4422-1
Dear Little Waltz

March 1932, with orchestra
The Desert Song (Oscar Hammerstein II – Sigmund Romberg)

WE4490-2
One Alone (with Edith Day, sop.)
Parlophone R1200

The Land of Smiles [Harry Graham – Franz Lehár]

WE4491-2
Love, What Has Given You This Magic Power (with Edith Day, sop.)

WE4492-1
Gipsy Moon (Borganoff – Eyton)
Parlophone R1235

WE4493-2
I Want Your Heart (Desmond Carter, Haydn Wood)

Note: A double-sided test coupling E4492-1 and E4492-2 is extant.

10 September 1932, with orchestra
WE4744-2
In The Garden Of Tomorrow (Graff, Deppen)
Parlophone R1305

WE4745-1
Somewhere A Voice Is Calling (Newman, A. F. Tate)
Parlophone R1318

WE4746-1
You Loving Me (Stanley, Brodzky)
Parlophone R1305

Frasquita (Reginald Arkel – Franz Lehár)

WE4747-1
Serenade (Farewell, my love, farewell)
Parlophone R1318

Late November, 1932, probably made at Abbey Road Studios, London NW8
THE DAILY MAIL MYSTERY RECORD, various artists

OB4509-1
Side 1 includes Robert Naylor
RO 100

Note: The label states: 'Stars from Columbia, His Master's Voice, Parlophone, Regal and Zonophone. £1,950 in prizes for correct or most correct lists of Artists. Closing date 14 January 1933.' On this record Robert Naylor sings six bars of *You Are My Heart's*

Delight, which originally were thought to be a dub from Parlophone R939. However, the accompanying piano behind Naylor moving seamlessly into Billy Mayerl's piano solo suggested otherwise. Now Bob Naylor has confirmed that Robert Naylor travelled to London especially to make this recording, and it is therefore likely that Billy Mayerl was his accompanist.

10 December 1932, with orchestra
WE4885-1
Ave Maria (Weatherly, Mascagni)
Parlophone R1412

WE4886-1
You, Just You (Carter, Stolz)
rejected

WE4887-1
Ich Liebe Dich, My Dear (Jack Hart, Tom Blight)
Parlophone R1401

WE4888-1
The Great Awakening (Johnstone, Kramer)
Parlophone R1412

20 December 1932, with orchestra
Wild Violets (Desmond Carter – Robert Stolz)

WE4886-2
You, Just You
Parlophone R1401

March 1933, with chorus and orchestra of the London Hippodrome, cond. Samuel Rogers (probably recorded at the London Hippodrome)

The One Girl (Clifford Grey/Herbert Sargent/Melville Gideon – Frank Eyton)

WE5001-2
I'll Tell The Stars I Love (lyric: Grey)
Parlophone R1470

WE5002-1
Dreams (The Night I Made You Mine – lyric: Gideon)
---

8 June 1933, with piano accompaniment by Horatio Dayn
WE6100-1
She That I Love (Maurice Besly)
Parlophone R1583

WE6101-2
Bless This House (Helen Taylor, May Brahe)
---

21 September 1933, with instrumental accompaniment [a trio]
WE6183-1
Love Is Mine (Teschemacher, Gartner)
Parlophone R1622

WE6184-1
I Know A Lovely Garden (G. d'Hardelot)

Probably 21 September 1933
THE FAREWELL RECORD recorded at 72a Carlton Hill, NW8
Various artists including Robert Naylor [un-numbered sample/ unpublished]

Note: On this recording Robert Naylor, pianist Patricia Rossborough, comedian Ronald Frankau, and other Parlophone artists, entertain staff at the Parlophone Farewell Party prior to relinquishing the studio. Robert Naylor sings *Vesti La Giubba* from *Pagliacci* by Leoncavallo accompanied by an orchestra led by George Scott Wood.

11 November 1933, with orchestra conducted by George Scott-Wood
CE6288-1
Two Little Words (Helen Taylor, May Brahe)
Parlophone R1706

CE6290-1
I Still Love Mary (H. Ramsay, B. Sievier)

IMPERIAL BROADCAST RECORDS
Made at 165 Broadhurst Gardens, London NW6

c. 22 February 1934, with orchestra
Bitter Sweet (Noel Coward)

6562-2
I'll See You Again (with Sylvia Cecil, sop.)
Imperial Broadcast 4002

The Dubarry (Carl Millocker)

6563-1-2
I Give My Heart (with Sylvia Cecil, sop.)

Bitter Sweet (Noel Coward)

6564-1
I'll Follow My Secret Heart
Imperial Broadcast 4001

Waltzes from Vienna (Kennedy – Fritz Rotter)

6565-2
Gay Vienna

Note: Matrices 6566 and 6567 are by the tenor, Tom Burke.

22/23 February 1934, with orchestra
Prince Charming (Max Kester – Ray Noble)

6568-2
Love Is A Song (with Sylvia Cecil, sop.)
Imperial Broadcast 4006

6569-2
Near And Yet So Far (with Sylvia Cecil, sop.)
---
c. **March 1934, with orchestra**
The Student Prince (Sigmund Romberg)

6572-2
Serenade (with Sylvia Cecil, sop.)
Imperial Broadcast 4016
Rose Marie (Rudolf Friml)

6573-1
Rose Marie (with Sylvia Cecil, sop.)

Blossom Time (G.H. Clutsam – Schubert)

6578-2
Thine Is My Heart
Imperial Broadcast 4030

6579-1
Once There Lived A Lady Fair

A double-sided test coupling 6578-1 and 6578-2 is extant.

ECLIPSE RECORDS
Made at 165 Broadhurst Gardens, London NW6

Late September 1934
Robert Naylor as DEREK POWELL

2147-2
My Song For You (Eyton, Spoliansky)
Eclipse 806 (8-inch disc)

2148--
The Isle Of Dreams (Fenhow, McCully)

Some years ago vocal recordings expert Alan Williams identified the singer as Robert Naylor. It has not been possible to confirm with the Eclipse recording file as it was only completed up to matrix 2136. The highest issued matrix traced is 2551 but there is no company documentation relating to these last 400 odd masters. Arthur Badrock has compiled a matrix file from 2137 from records seen, but this therefore has no details of any rejected or unissued recordings, nor recording dates. He suggests the dates given in the recording file up to matrix 2136 do not always ring true as recording dates, suspecting they are often the dates when the masters were received at the factory. No other issues labelled Derek Powell are known.

REX RECORDS
Made at 165 Broadhurst Gardens, London NW6

April 1934, with orchestra
F800-2
Everybody's Songs Pt 1
Rex 8388

F801-2
Everybody's Songs Pt 2

Robert Naylor appears with Sylvia Cecil, sop., and Foster Richardson, bass-bar.

c. **late-November 1934**
with chorus and orchestra, and Anona Wynn, soprano

The Merry Widow (Franz Lehár)
F1046--
Gems from *The Merry Widow,* Pt 1
Rex 8344

F1047--
Gems from *The Merry Widow,* Pt 2
---

with orchestra (same session)

Blossom Time (GH Clutsam – Franz Schubert)

F1048--
Vocal Gems from *Blossom Time,* Pt 1
Rex 8345

F1049--
Vocal Gems from *Blossom Time,* Pt 2
---

c. mid-December 1934
F1089--
One Night Of Love (Kahn, Schertzinger)
Rex 8377

F1090-2
Tell Me To-Night (Eyton, Spoliansky)

A double-sided test coupling F1090-- and F1090-2 is extant.

c. March 1935, with orchestra
My Heart is Calling (Robert Stolz)

F1202--
My Heart Is Always Calling You (lyric by Harry S. Pepper)
Rex 8449

F1203--
You, Me And Love (lyric by Tommie Connor)

Mid-April 1935, with orchestra
F1278--
Love Was A Song (Dunn, Spoliansky)
Rex 8529

F1279-2
For Love Alone (Sievier, Thayer)
---

c. June 1935, with orchestra
Glamorous Night (Christopher Hassall – Ivor Novello)

F1376-2
Glamorous Night
Rex 8538

F1377-2
Shine Through My Dreams
---

c. November 1935, with orchestra
As featured in the Richard Tauber film *Heart's Desire*

F1628--
Vienna, City Of My Dreams (Edward Lockton – Rudolf Sieczynski)
Rex 8677

F1629--
My World Is Gold because you love me (Clifford Gray – Richard Tauber)
---

c. January 1936, with the band of HM Irish Guards, vocal quartet and organ
F1704--
Here's A Health unto Our New King (Edward Lockton – Horatio Nicholls)
Rex 8720
Robert Naylor is not present on the reverse.

This discography was compiled by Arthur Badrock, who sadly passed away in June 2009. He was an eminent discographer, record collector and researcher who, in addition to writing books, had numerous articles published. His knowledge of the history of the UK record industry will be greatly missed.

In compiling this discography we would like to acknowledge valuable contributions from John Watson, Frank Andrews, Maurice Robson, and Alan Williams.

Robert's recordings are now out of copyright and selections of them are available on non-commercial compact discs from the author. Please contact b.naylor291@btinternet.com for details.

Filmography

For Love of You, British Pathé, 12 November 1934.

Abdul The Damned (1935), British International Pictures, 109 minutes, directed by Karl Grune, in which Robert makes an all too brief appearance, is available at present on DVD from VCi Video. The full cast is as follows:

Abdul Hamid II Kislar, His Double Fritz Kortner
Kadar Pasha Nils Asther
Ali, the Grand Eunuch Esmé Percy
Talak Pasha John Stuart
Therese Adrienne Ames
Hassan Bey Walter Rilla
Hilmi Pasha Charles Carson
Abbas Alfred Woods
Omar Patric Knowles
Young Turk Conspirator Eric Portman

Doctor Clifford Heatherly
General of the Bodyguards Henry Longhurst
English Lady Annie Esmond
Chief Inquisitor H. Saxon Snell
Officer of the Firing Squad George Zucco
Opera Singer Robert Naylor
Young Turk Singer Warren Jenkins
Malik, a Spy Henry Paterson
Modiste Charlotte Francis

Let's Go Gay, British Pathé, 26 March 1936.

Bibliography

Anderson, Richard, *Complete Handbook of Voice Training* (Parker Publishing Company, West Nyack, NY, 1979)

Anonymous, *These Tremendous Years 1919-1938* (*Daily Express*, 1938)

Baker, T.F.T., 'Islington: Social and cultural activities', *A History of the County of Middlesex:* Volume 8: *Islington and Stoke Newington parishes* (1985)

Briggs, Asa, *The History of Broadcasting in the United Kingdom*, Vol. 3: *The Great Age of Wireless* (Oxford University Press, 1995)

Bruce, Frank, *Scottish Showbusiness: Music Hall, Variety and Pantomime* (NMS Publishing, Edinburgh, 2000)

Carey, Mike, *I'll Sing You A Thousand Love Songs: The Denny Dennis Story* (Pinnacle Printing, Derby, 1992)

Church History Group, *A History and Guide to the Parish of St Paul, Buttershaw, in the Diocese of Bradford* (1992)

Cliffe, Peter, 'Robert Naylor', *The Historical Record* (185 The Wheel, Ecclesfield, Sheffield S35 9ZA, July 1996)

Colin, Sid, *And The Bands Played On - An informal history of British Dance Bands* (Elm Tree Books, London, 1977)

Collen, Jean, *Sweethearts of Song: A Personal Memoir of Anne Ziegler and Webster Booth* (Lulu, 2006)

187

Constantine, Stephen, *Social Conditions in Britain 1918-1939* (Methuen, London, 1983)

Cox, Thomas, *A Popular History of the Grammar School of Queen Elizabeth at Heath near Halifax* (F. King Printers, Exchange Buildings, Northgate, Halifax, 1879)

Firfield, Christopher, Ibbs & Tillett: *The Rise and Fall of a Musical Empire* (Ashgate Publishing, 2005)

Gammond, Peter, *The Oxford Companion of Popular Music* (Oxford University Press, 1991)

Green, Benny, *Let's Face the Music and Dance: The Golden Age of Popular Song* (Pavilion Books, London, 1989)

Hartington Jones, James, *The German Attack on Scarborough* (Quoin Publishing, Huddersfield, 1989)

Heywood, Freda and Malcolm, *Todmorden Hippodrome: 100 Years of Theatre 1908-2008* (Upper Calder Valley Publications, 2007)

Jouni, Koskimäki, *Happiness is . . . a Good Transcription: Reconsidering the Beatles Sheet Music Publications* (University of Jyväskylä, Finland, 2006)

London Weekly Diary of Social Events (The London Diary Publications Ltd, 56 Bloomsbury Street London, WC1, August 1931)

Lowerson, John, *Amateur Operatics: A Social & Cultural History* (Manchester University Press, 2005)

Lyman, Desmond, *Jack Doyle: The Gorgeous Gael* (The Lilliput Press, 2007)

MacQueen-Pope, Walter, *Fortune's Favourite: The Life and Times of Franz Lehár* (Hutchinson, 1953)

McCanna, Barry, 'George Scott-Wood', *Memory Lane* (PO Box 1939, Leigh-on-Sea, Essex, SS9 3UH)

Neave, David and Susan (eds), *The Spa, Bridlington* (East Riding of Yorkshire Council, 2008)

Palmer, Tony, *All You Need Is Love – The Story of Popular Music* (Weidenfeld & Nicolson and Chappell & Co. Ltd, London, 1976)

Parker, John, *Who's Who in the Theatre*, 10th edition (Pitman, London, 1947)

Parker, Larry, *But – What Do You Do in the Winter? 100 Years of the Concert Artistes' Association* (CAA, London, 1996)

Pearsall, Ronald, *Music in the Twenties* (David & Charles, London, 1976)

Platt, Jim, 'Aberdeen Re-Opening', *Call Boy Magazine* (The British Music Hall Society, 6 New River Crescent, Palmers Green, London, N13 5RF, winter 1988)

Powell, Ken, *Pennine Mill Trail* (Save Britain's Heritage, London, 1981)

Ronald, Landon, *Who's Who in Music* (Shaw Publishing, London, 1937)

Schnitzler, Henry, 'Gay Vienna – Myth and Reality', *Journal of the History of Ideas* (University of Pennsylvania Press, January 1954)

Scott, Derek B., *The Singing Bourgeois: Songs of the Victorian Drawing Room and Parlour*, 2nd edition (Ashgate Publishing, Aldershot, Hampshire, 2001)

Smith, Adrian (editor), *Music Making in the West Riding of Yorkshire: the exploration of a unique musical phenomenon* (R.H. Wood, Huddersfield, 2000).

Sutcliffe, Tom, 'Shepherd's House', *Halifax Antiquarian Transactions* (1926)

Tauber, Diane Napier, *Richard Tauber* (Art & Educational Publishers Ltd, London, 1949)

Traubner, Richard, *Operetta: A Theatrical History* (Routledge, 2003)

Turnbull, Michael T.R.B., *Joseph Hislop: Gran Tenore* (Scholar Press, 1992)

Whitcomb, Ian, *After The Ball* (Allen Lane, London, 1972)

Wyatt, Geoffrey, *At The Mighty Organ* (Oxford Illustrated Press, 1974)

Ziegler, Anne and Booth, Webster, *Duet* (Stanley Paul, London, 1951)

Articles, Interviews, Liner Notes

I am particularly grateful to the archives of the following national publications: *The Times* newspaper, London; *The Stage* Newspaper Ltd, London; *The Gramophone* magazine, London, *Punch* magazine, London, *Film Weekly*, London, and *Theatre World*, London.

I am grateful too for the information gained from the press-cuttings of various regional newspapers: *Telegraph & Argus*, Bradford; *Bradford Pictorial (defunct)*; *Halifax Daily Courier & Guardian*, *Huddersfield Examiner*, Yorkshire Post Newspapers Ltd; *Harrogate Advertiser*, *Harrogate Herald (defunct)*; *Batley Reporter*, *Scottish Daily Record*; *Glasgow Evening Times*, *Glasgow Herald*.

Maurice Robson, interview with Mr and Mrs Herbert Teal, Elland, c. 1960
Maurice Robson, *Walter Widdop Songs and Arias*, cassette liner notes, 1992

Websites

www.allmovie.com: information about films
www.brandon-heritage.co.uk: information about Brandon School
www.brent-heritage.co.uk: information about Wembley
www.charm.rhul.ac.uk: the recording of 78rpm records, from the Centre for the History and Analysis of Recorded Music
www.museum.woolworths.co.uk/1930s-music.htm: information on the history of Woolworth's records in Britain

All inaccuracies are, of course, entirely my own.

Index

2LO 20
1920s 19–20
1930s 43
1960s 155

Abbey Road studios 75, 91, 95
Abdul the Damned 111, 112
Abdul Hamid II: 111–12
Aberdeen 20, 26, 89–90, 99
Abraham, Paul 75
Adair, Alan (Basil F. Leakey) 130
Adair Wounded Fund 130
Adelphi Theatre, London 41
Adlington, Fred 72
agents, concert 34
Aitken, W.A. 49
amateur operatics 10, 146, 148, 153
Associated British Pathé 103, 104, 120
Austin, Charles 72
'Ave Maria' 83
Ayr 125

Back In Town 103
Baillie, Isobel 25, 96
Baines, Arthur Clifford (Stainless Stephen) 77
Baker, George 72
Balanchine, George 57
Baldwin and Partners Ltd, J. & J. 8
ballad concerts 21–2
bands 116, 118

Barrfields Pavilion, Largs 101
Bath 130
Bayco, Frederick 145
Baylis, Lilian Mary 21
BBC (British Broadcasting Corporation)
    Empire Service (World Service) 26
    first broadcast 20
    Light Programme 144, 145, 146
    musicians 53
    personnel 93–4
    royal charter 27
    see also broadcasts (radio); radio
BBC Military Band (*formerly* Wireless Military Band) 118
Behn, Aphra 47
Beka (Beka-Grand) 5
Belfast 20, 26
'Beneath The Window of My Love' 71
Bennett, Billy 80
Bennett, Dorothy 74, 75
Besly, Edward Maurice 93
Best, W.T. 32
Birmingham 20, 21, 27, 37
Bitter Sweet 98
Blackpool 5, 31, 98, 120–1, 127, 129
'Bless This House' 93, 95
Blight, Tom 82
Blossom Time 105–6
Blumleim, Alan 55
Blunt, Dr 120

La Bohème (Puccini) 35–6, 37, 38
bombing, London 132, 136
Bon Frères Club 33
Boocock & Sons, W. 2
Boosey, William 81
Booth, Webster 21, 39, 45, 112
Boughton, Rutland 21, 27
Bournemouth 20, 24, 94, 125
Bournemouth Municipal Orchestra
(*later* Bournemouth Symphony
Orchestra) 24, 125
Bradford
bishop 120
cinemas 139–40
football 154
Masons 141
music 5, 56, 138, 139, 145, 146, 147,
150, 154, 156
newspapers 82, 139, 157
schools 141
theatres 90, 103, 142
Widdop 143
work 85, 141
Bradford Amateur Operatic &
Dramatic Society 146
Bradford Choral Society 5
Bradford Opera Group 150
Brahe, May Hannah 93, 95
Brandon Board School 22
Brentford Football Club 86
Bridgewater, Leslie 139
Brindle, Harry 37
Brinsworth House 86
Bristol 130
British Broadcasting Corporation
(previously Company) *see* BBC
British Empire Exhibition 36
British Federation Musical
Competition Festivals 9–10
broadcasts (radio)
1924: 23–4
1925: 25, 26
1926: 26, 27
1928: 31, 33, 36
1929: 37, 39
1930: 46, 47, 52
1931: 58, 72, 73, 74, 76

1932: 77
1933: 87, 93
1934: 97, 99, 103, 105
1935: 114–15
1936: 118, 124
1937: 125, 126
1941: 139, 141
1944: 143
1945: 143, 144
1946: 145
1954: 150, 151
1955: 151
see also BBC; radio
broadcasts (television) 124–5
Bullard, Renee 62, 69
Butt, Sir Alfred 45

CAA (Concert Artistes Association;
now Club for Acts and Actors)
28, 35, 37, 39, 43, 47, 53
Capitol Picture Theatre, London 73
Cardiff 6, 20, 26
Carl Rosa Opera Company 37–8, 39, 87
Carlisle Choral Society 21
Carlton Hill studio 54, 91, 92, 94, 105
Carmen (Bizet) 38
Carroll, Sydney W. 65
cars 52
Cecil, Sylvia 98, 99, 101, 102, 103,
105, 112–13, 125
Cellier, Alfred 47
Central London Choral And
Orchestral Society 23
Chalupiec, Barbara Apolonia (Pola
Negri) 57
Chamberlain, Neville 131
Chelsea Palace Theatre, London 21
choral societies 4
Chough Musical Society 42
churches 10
cine-variety 88, 89, 140
cinemas 33, 48, 95, 139–40
City of London Printer's Musical
Society 36
Clapham, Charlie 74
Clare, Diana (Esther Coleman) 123,
124

192

Clayton, Sarah Elizabeth *see* Naylor, Sarah Elizabeth
Cleveleys 122
Club for Acts and Actors (CAA; *formerly* Concert Artistes Association) 28, 35, 37, 39, 43, 47, 53
Coates, Edith 32
Coe, Walter Percy 22
Colehan, Barney 152
Coleman, Esther (Diana Clare) 123, 124
Coleman Street Ward Club 32
Collinge, Frances 14
Columbia Graphophone Company 53, 56
Comforts for the Troops Fund 136, 137
concert agents 34
Concert Artistes Association (CAA; *now* Club for Acts and Actors) 28, 35, 37, 39, 43, 47, 53
Constantine, Norman 147
Courtneidge, Cicely 41–2
Coward, Noel 97
cricket 34, 37, 39, 154
Croft, Annie 79, 80
Croft, David 80
Crowther, Joseph Hilton 103
Crump, William Bunting 3
Crystalate Record Company 97, 106, 107
'A Cup of Tea With You' 71

Daily Mail Mystery Record 82
Dampier, Claude 99
dance bands 116
Darewski, Herman E. 151
Darnborough, Robert 154
Daventry 26
Davies, Sir Henry Walford 9
Davies, Horatio 105
Dawson, Peter 22, 42
Day, Edith 57–8, 72, 73, 74, 75, 76, 77, 78, 79
De Groot, David 24, 29, 73
Deane, Tessa 73

'Dear Little Waltz' 78
Decca 107
Delni, Guido 150
depression, economic 43
The Desert Song 58, 76, 79, 131, 142
Desmond, Peggy 129
Dewsbury & District General Infirmary 136
d'Hardelot, Guy (Helen Rhodes) 94, 127
Dominion Theatre, London 95
Donnelly, Dorothy 104
Dorothy 47
Doyle, Jack 98–9
D'Oyly Carte Opera Company 153
'Dreams (The Night I Made You Mine)' 84
The Dubarry 98
Duophone label 34
Dwyer, Bill 74

Eastbourne 120
Eclipse label 106
economic depression 43
Edward VIII: 124
Edwardes, Felix 60
Electrical & Musical Industries (EMI) 55, 75, 91, 96
electrical recording 54–5, 106
Elite Cinema, Bradford 139–40
Elvin, Joe 86
EMI 55, 75, 91, 96
Empire Service (World Service) 26
'The English Rose' 50
'The English Tauber' 69, 140, 148, 157
Entertainment Artists Benevolent Fund 86
Everybody's Songs 112–13
Excel Services 156

F.W. Woolworth (stores) 106
A Fantasy of Song 124, 129, 137
Farrar, Cecilia (*née* Elizabeth Alice Farrar; RN's first wife)
  CAA 28
  career 14, 39

courtship 13
death 129
illness 122–3
marriage 16–17, 132
son's birth 78
see also performances (Farrar);
performances (RN and Farrar)
Farrar, Hannah 13
Farrar, Walter 13
Faust (Gounod) 21, 29, 32, 130
Favour, John 3
Fearon, Josie 69, 87, 88, 90, 93, 94,
95, 140
Fields, Gracie 99
films 111
First World War 7
Fol-de-Rols 152–3
Foort, Reginald 143
football 36, 37, 86, 103, 154
'For You Alone' 24, 48, 49, 77
France, Harold 135, 137, 141
Francis, Cyril 54
Frankau, Ronald 92
Frederica (Lehár) 50–2
Freemasons *see* Masons
Friml, Rudolph 44, 76, 104–5, 146

Gaiety Theatre, Ayr 125
Gaiety Theatre, London 84
Gaiety Whirl 125–6
gardening 37
gardens, as song theme 80
'Gay Vienna' 97
Geehl, Henry Ernest 48–9
Gems From Blossom Time 109
Gems from the Merry Widow 108
George V: 120
George VI: 125
German, Edward 22
Gielgud, John 47
'Gipsy Moon' 79
Glamorous Night 114
'Glamorous Night' 114
Glasgow 12, 20, 50, 51, 129
Godfrey, Sir Dan 24
golf 37
The Good Old Days 152

Good-Night Vienna 77–8
'Goodnight' 75
'Goodnight Vienna' 78
Gordon, Harry 99
Graham, Harry 60–61, 75
Gramophone Company (HMV) 31,
56
gramophone records 56, 106
see also sound recordings
gramophone societies 56
gramophones 31, 56
'The Great Awakening' 83
Grey, Clifford 44–5
Grossmith, George 60
Groves, Olive 71–2, 118
Guild of Singers and Players 87
Guildhall School of Music 29–30, 31,
35, 98, 115, 123

Halifax
First World War 7
music 4, 5, 6, 112
newspapers 66, 67, 157
schools 3
theatres 6, 15, 146
wool trade 1
work 2, 5, 6, 8, 10, 112, 113,
142
Halifax Choral Society 4
Hall, Henry 116
Hamilton, W. 12
Hammerstein, Oscar 76
Handley, Tommy 77, 94
The Happidrome 141
Harbach, Otto 76
Harold Wood Music Society 29
Harrogate 148, 152, 153, 154, 157
Harrogate Operatic Players 148, 153
Hart, Jack 82
Hartley, Fred 119
Hastings 28
Hayes, Alick 150
Heart's Desire 119
Heath Grammar School 3
Hebden Bridge 12
'Here's Health Unto Our New King'
119–20

Heritage School and Hospital for Crippled Children 117–18
Highbury Athenaeum 48
Hinchcliffe, Arthur 5, 6
Hindmarsh, Jean 153
Hislop, Joseph 50, 51, 52
The House That Jack Built 41, 42
Houston, Renee 57
Huddersfield Women's Luncheon Club 142
Hulbert, Jack 41
Hyde, Walter 30
Hymans, Kendrick Reginald (Ken 'Snakehips' Johnson) 132

'I Attempt From Love's Sickness to Fly' 50
'I Give You My Heart' 98
'I Know A Lovely Garden' 91, 94
'I Live For Your Love' 52
'I Still Love Mary' 95
'I Want Your Heart' 79
Ibbs, Robert Leigh 34
Ibbs & Tillett 34, 145
'Ich Liebe Dich, My Dear' 82
'I'll Follow My Secret Heart' 97
'I'll See You Again' 98
Imperial-Broadcast label 97, 98, 104, 105
Impresario (Mozart) 150
'In the Garden of Tomorrow' 80
'Indian Love Call' 76
Irene 57
Irving, Ernest 63, 73
'The Isle Of Dreams' 106

J. & J. Baldwin and Partners Ltd 8
James France and Co. Ltd 135, 141
Jenkins, David 53
Johnson, Ken 'Snakehips' (Kendrick Reginald Hymans) 132
Johnstone, Gordon 83

Kelly, S. Kneale 93
Kemp, Harry 102
Kennedy, Jimmy 97

Kiepura, Jan 109, 111, 112
Kingsway Hall, London 31
Klein, Herman 94
Kramer, Arthur Walter 83
Krish, Serge 123
Kürty, Hella 62, 69

Laidler, Francis 103
Lambert, Pat 152, 153
The Land of Smiles (Lehár) 59–69, 140, 148–149
Lane, Lupino (Henry William George Lupino) 83–4
Lane Wilson, Henry James 23
Lanza, Mario 104
Largs 101
Lark, Kingsley 14
laryngitis 95
Lawrence Wright Music Company 81, 121, 128
Le Vallon, Paul 10, 14
Leakey, Basil F. (Alan Adair) 130
Leeds 6, 11, 103, 138, 150, 152
Leggett, Charles 52–3
Lehár, Franz
  Frederica 50
  The Land of Smiles 59, 66–7
  The Merry Widow 59, 61, 108
  'Serenade' 81
  and Steininger 104
  and Tauber 61
Léon, Viktor 108
Let's Go Gay 120
Lewis, Joseph 37, 58
light music *see* popular music
Light Programme 144, 145, 146
'Lights Out' ball 120
Lindstrom group 53
Lister, Thomas 2
Liszt, Franz 57
Lloyd Webber, Andrew 60
London
  1920s: 19–20
  1930s: 43
  bombing 132, 136
  Kingsway Hall 31
  Promenade concerts 25

theatres 21, 41, 60, 73, 78, 84, 95, 126–7, 132
'Tin Pan Alley' 81, 121
London and North Eastern Railway 39
'Love Everlasting' 76
'Love Is A Song' 105
'Love Is Mine' 91, 94
'Love Was A Song' 114
'Love, What Has Given You This Magic Power?' 79
'Love Will Find You' 74
Lovell, Peggy 137, 142
Ludd, Dennis (RN's stage name) 10
Luddenden 2
Luddenden Foot Council School 3
Luddenden Foot United Methodist Chapel 4, 10
Lupino, Henry William George (Lupino Lane) 83–4

MacPherson, Hal Roderick (Sandy) 139, 143–4, 145, 146
Madam Butterfly (Puccini) 32, 38–9, 142
Manchester 6, 10, 14, 20, 26, 38, 87, 153
Mansion House 43
Martha (Flotow) 30
Martin, George 53–4
Marvell, Holt (Eric Maschwitz) 77, 78
Mascagni, Pietro 83
Maschwitz, Eric (Holt Marvell) 77, 78
Maskelyne, Jasper 78
Maskelyne's Theatre, London 78
Masons 29, 141
May, Bobby 102–3
McCormack, John 21, 42, 93, 112
McKinney, Nina Mae 90
McQueen-Pope, W. 62, 64, 68
medals 12
Melba, Nellie 108
Melody Maker 81
Memories from Musical Plays 102
Merrie England (German) 22

The Merry Widow (Lehár) 59, 61, 108–9
The Messiah (Handel) 14
Metropole Records 48
microphones 117
Middlesborough 27
military bands 118
Mirsky, M. 30
Moore, Grace 109
Moss Empires 57
Mrs Sunderland Music Festival 11
Music Hall 105
music hall entertainers 86
music publishers 81
Musical At Home 150–1, 152
musical competition festivals 9–10
musical education 30
musicians, financial affairs 39
My Heart is Calling You 111
'My Heart is Calling You' 111
'My Song For You' 105, 106
'My World Is Gold (Because You Love Me)' 118, 119
Mytholmroyd 13

National Institute for the Blind 23–4
National Sunday League 15–16
Naylor, Anthony Michael (RN's son) 78, 123, 130, 136, 140–1, 148, 157
Naylor, Cecilia (*née* Elizabeth Alice Farrar; RN's first wife) *see* Farrar, Cecilia
Naylor, Dorothy (*née* Watson; RN's second wife) 85, 140, 145, 148, 157
Naylor, James (RN's brother) 1, 2, 8, 17, 136, 153
Naylor, James (RN's uncle) 85
Naylor, James Watkinson 85
Naylor, John (RN's stepson) 85, 132, 143, 157
Naylor, Jonathan 2
Naylor, Martha 2
Naylor, Michael *see* Naylor, Anthony Michael
Naylor, Robert (Bobbie)
    Abdul the Damned 111, 112

accommodation 21, 36, 135, 148, 154
agents 34
birth 1
CAA 28
cars 52
death 156–7
'The English Tauber' 69, 140, 148, 157
film of RN performing 103, 104, 120
financial affairs 39
Guildhall School of Music 29–30, 35
holiday house 122
The Land of Smiles 64–9
laryngitis 95
leaves London stage career 133
marriage to Cecilia Farrar 16–17, 132–3
marriage to Dorothy Naylor 140
music competitions 9, 11–12
recreational interests 37, 154
repertoire 26
Royal Naval Air Service 8–9
school 3
singing, first interest in 4
son's birth 78
stage names (Ludd; Powell) 10, 106
teaching 145, 147, 152, 154
temperament and appearance 2, 90–1, 147
tenor voice 4, 21
textile career 8, 10, 135, 141
as understudy 50, 51, 62
war years 135–44, 157–8
'You Are My Heart's Delight' 64, 65, 69, 71, 82, 90, 142
see also broadcasts (radio); performances (RN and Farrar); singing partners (RN's); sound recordings
Naylor, Robert Sutcliffe (RN's father) 1, 2, 113–14
Naylor, Sarah Elizabeth (*née* Clayton; RN's mother) 1, 2, 16, 136, 153

'Near and Yet So Far' 105
Negri, Pola (Barbara Apolonia Chalupiec) 57
New Brighton 24
New Victoria, Bradford 142
New Victoria Cinema, London 95
Newcastle 20, 26, 89
Newman, Greatrex 152–3
Newman, Robert 25
Newspaper Vendors' Benevolent and Provident Institution 138–9
newsreels 103
Newton, Eileen 81
Nicholls, Horatio (Lawrence Wright) 81, 119, 120, 121, 124, 128
Nielson-Terry, Phyllis 73
Nineteenth Century Drawing Room 151
non-conformist churches 10
Northern Command Comforts Fund 139
Not Forgotten Association 107, 118
A Novel Interpretation of Liebestraum 57
Novello, Ivor 41, 98, 114

'O Maiden, My Maiden' 52
Octacros label 48
O'Donnell, Walton 118
O'Hagan, Kathleen 86
Oil Industries Club 58
Old Vic Opera Company 21, 32, 33, 35, 38, 47
On with the Show 120, 122, 127–8
'Once There Lived A Lady Fair' 105
'One Alone' 79
The One Girl 83, 84
'One Night Of Love' 109
operatics, amateur 10, 146, 148, 153
operettas 46, 61, 108
organists, theatre 89, 143, 144
Ormond, Hugh 95
Orpheus Choir 12
O'Shea, Teresa Mary 127–8
Otello (Verdi) 38
Over, Miss (Naylors' nanny) 78, 123, 136

Pagani's Restaurant 29
Pagliacci 126
Palm Court Trio 147
'Pardon Madame' 75
Parlophone Company Ltd 52, 53–4,
  55
  1931 recordings 71, 74, 76
  1932 recordings 79, 80
  1933 recordings 83, 91, 92, 94,
  95, 105
  Carlton Hill studio 54, 91, 92,
  94, 105
  see also EMI
Pathé (Associated British Pathé) 103,
  104, 120
'Patiently Smiling' 71, 137
Patons & Baldwins 8, 10
Pavilion Theatre, Bournemouth 125
Perfect, Rose 85, 87, 121–2
Perfect Understanding 82
performances (Farrar)
  1920: 13
  1921: 15, 16
  1923: 21, 22–3
  1924: 23, 24
  1925: 24, 25
  1926: 27
  1927: 29
  1928: 32–3
  1930: 43, 53
  1935: 117
  performances (RN and Farrar)
  1921: 15
  1924: 23, 24
  1925: 24, 25
  1926: 27
  1927: 29
  1928: 32
  1930: 43, 53
  1935: 117
  repertoire 50
Performing Rights Society 81
'Phyllis Has Such Charming Graces'
  23
piano accordions 55–6
Piccadilly Hotel Orchestra 24
Piccadilly label 47–8, 49, 50, 77

Pickles, Wilfred 142
The Pied Piper of Hamelin 127
Plymouth 8, 9, 20
Plymouth Competitive Music Festival
  9
Polygram 108
Popplewell, Ben 125
popular music 26, 50, 117
Portman, Eric 112
Posford, George 78
Powell, Derek (RN's stage name) 106
Press Club 129
Preuss, Oscar 53, 54
Priestley, William 4
prizes 35
Promenade concerts 25

radio 20, 26, 27, 116, 117
  see also BBC; broadcasts
Radium Institute and the Mount
  Vernon Hospital for Cancer 131
RAF (Royal Air Force) 9
railways 10–11, 143
Ramsay, Harold Arthur 95–6
recordings *see* sound recordings
records *see* gramophone records;
  sound recordings
Reith, Sir John 27
revues 42
Rex label 107, 108, 109, 111, 112,
  114, 119
Revnell and West 122
Rhodes, Helen (Guy d'Hardelot) 94
Rhondda Music Festival 22–3
Richardson, Foster 24, 113, 123
Rigoletto (Verdi) 33
Rio Rita 74
Riscoe, Arthur 84, 104
RNAS (Royal Naval Air Service) 8–9
Robert Naylor Valentine Girls 150–2,
  153
Roberton, Sir Hugh 12
Roberts, Peggy 153
Robin, Christopher 147–8
Robinson, Stanford 114–15
Rogers, James Hotchkiss 49
Romberg, Sigmund 44, 46, 76, 104,

105
Ronald, Sir Landon (Herbert Russell)
    30–1, 115–16
Rose Marie 44, 76–7, 105
The Rose of Persia 110
Rotter, Fritz 97
Royal Air Force (RAF) 9
Royal Free Hospital 96–97
Royal Naval Air Service (RNAS) 8–9
Russell, Henry 30–1
Russell, Herbert (Sir Landon Ronald)
    30–1, 115–16

Sanderson, Wilfred Ernest 49–50
Sargent, Malcolm 39
Savage Club 37
Scarborough 7
Scharrer, Irene 80
Schertzinger, Victor 109
Scott, Stanley H. 59–61
Scott-Wood, George 55–6
seaside resorts 101
Secombe, Harry 119, 157
Second World War 131, 132, 136
'Serenade' (Lehár) 81–2
'Serenade' (Romberg) 104
'She That I Love' 93
Sheffield 20
Shepherd House Farm 2
'Shine Through My Dreams' 114, 124
'Sigh No More' 49
silver medals 12
singing partners (RN's) 58, 100
    Bennett, Dorothy 74, 75
    Cecil, Sylvia 98, 99, 101, 102, 103,
        105, 112–13, 125
    Coleman, Esther 123, 124
    Croft, Annie 79, 80
    Day, Edith 58, 72, 73, 74, 75, 76, 77,
        78, 79
    Fearon, Josie 87–8, 90, 93, 94, 95
    Groves, Olive 71
    Perfect, Rose 121
    Winn, Anona 108
        see also performances (RN and
        Farrar)
Smith, Judy Lockhart 54

society 19–20, 43, 155
'Someday I'll Find You' 53
'Somewhere A Voice Is Calling' 81,
    82, 113
'The Song Of Songs' 77, 122
Songs from the Shows 72, 75
sound recordings
    1912: 5
    1928: 34
    1930: 47–8, 49, 50, 52
    1931: 53, 71, 74, 76, 115
    1932: 77, 79, 80, 83
    1933: 83, 84, 91, 93, 94
    1934: 97, 98, 104, 106, 108,
        109, 112
    1935: 107, 111, 114
    1936: 118–19
    Abbey Road studios 75, 91, 95
    Carlton Hill studio 54, 91, 92,
        94, 105
    electrical recording 54–5, 106
    Excel Services 156
    Kingsway Hall 31
    Ronald 31
    stage performers 106
    West Hampstead studios 107–8
    see also gramophone records
'A Southern Song' 76, 115
Special Constables Benevolent Fund
    139
Spitfire funds 138
Spoliansky, Mischa 105, 106, 110,
    114
St Anne's-on-Sea 17
St Giles Home for British Lepers 46–
    7
Stage Golfing Society 37
Stainless Stephen (Arthur Clifford
    Baines) 77
'The Star' 49
State Theatre, London 126–7
Stein, Leo 108
Steininger, Franz (Franz Vienna) 104
Stoll, Sir Oswald 57
Stolz, Robert 83, 111
Stone, Christopher Reynolds 94
The Student Prince 104

Suites and Duets 25
Sunderland, Susan 11
Sutcliffe, Fred 5–6
Sutton, Randolph 75, 98
Swanson, Gloria 82
Syncrophone Ltd 48

Tarri, Suzette 53
Tate, Arthur F. 81
Tauber, Richard
    career 21, 62, 69
    and Fearon 69, 140
    films 105, 112, 119
    The Land of Smiles 59, 63, 65,
      66, 69, 140
    and Lehár 61
    recordings 49, 79, 96
Tauberlieder 61
Taylor, David 154–5
Taylor, Helen 93
Teal, Herbert 5, 8, 11
television 124–5, 152
'Tell Me Tonight' 109–10
'Tell The Stars I Love' 84
tenor voices 4
Teschemacher, Edward 50
Thayer, Patrick 114
theatre organists 89, 143, 144
Theatre Royal, London 60
theatres 88
    Ayr 125
    Bournemouth 125
    Bradford 90, 103, 142
    Halifax 6, 15, 146
    London 21, 41, 60, 73, 78, 84,
      95, 126–7, 132
    organists 89, 143, 144
'Thine Is My Heart 105, 106, 109
Thistlethwaite, Jack 156
The Three Musketeers 44, 45–6
Tillett, John 34
'Tin Pan Alley', London 81, 121
Todmorden 13, 14, 15, 16, 129
Torquay 94
Trinder, Tommy 89–90
Trusound Pictorial Records Ltd 92
Turner, Eva 127

'Two Little Words' 95

understudies 50–1
'Until' 49, 50

The Vagabond King 146–7
Valentine Girls *see* Robert Naylor
    Valentine Girls
Variety Artistes' Benevolent Fund 86
variety halls 117
Victoria and her Hussar 75
Vienna, Franz (Franz Steininger) 104
'Vienna, City Of My Dreams' 118,
    119
Vivian, Mona 103
vocal style, change in 117
voice types 21

W. Boocock & Sons 2
Waifs and Strays Society 127
Waltzes from Vienna 74–5
wars 7, 131, 132, 136
Waters, Elsie and Doris 105
Watkinson, Annie 85
Watson, Dorothy *see* Naylor, Dorothy
Watson, Harold Alderson 85
'Wayside Rose' 52
Weatherley, Fred E. 83
Welling, Sylvia 143
Wembley Park, London 36, 136
West *see* Reynell and West
Westfields, Mirfield 135–6
'When Granny Wore Her Crinoline'
    128
'While You Love Me' 74
Widdop, Walter 6–7, 141, 143, 145
Wilbur, Jay 107
Wild Violets 83
Wilkins, Anona Edna (Anona Winn)
    108
Wilkins, Samuel 2
Wilson Brothers Bobbin Company
    Ltd 13
Wilton, Robb 126
Winn, Anona (Anona Edna Wilkins)
    108
wireless *see* radio

Wireless Military Band 24, 118
Wireless Orchestra 24
Wodehouse, Sir Pelham Grenville 44
'Wonderful' 52
Wood, Haydn 79
Wood, Henry 25
Wood, Pauline 155–6
Woodhouse Grove School 141
wool sorters 8
wool trade 1
Woolworth, F.W. (stores) 106
'The World is Waiting For The
     Sunrise' 53
World Service *see* Empire Service
Worshipful Company of Girdlers 32

Wright, Lawrence (Horatio Nicholls)
     81, 119, 120, 121, 124, 128
Wright Music Company *see* Lawrence
     Wright Music Company

The Yeoman of the Guard (Gilbert and
     Sullivan) 15
'You Are My Heart's Delight' 61, 64,
     65, 69, 71, 82, 90, 142
'You, Just You' 82, 83
'You Loving Me' 80
'You Me And Love' 111

Ziegfeld, Florenz, Jr. 83

Publisher's Note